Future

Anterior

Future Anterior
Volume XXII, Numbers 1–2
Summer / Winter 2025

Mari Lending, Alena Rieger, and Simon Mitchell

The Potential of Provenance

Wherever there is a transfer of anything ascribed value, there is provenance: on coffee beans, clothing tags, in the art market, on the construction site. Change requires stability, and provenance, at its most basic and ideal, aims at stabilizing claims of ownership and authorship in anticipation of possible transactions. When objects of all sorts began circulating globally on an unprecedented scale in the eighteenth century, provenance emerged as a concept and as a mechanism to exert control, enable estimation, and create value. Provenance offered a means through which objects could be authenticated, priced, and placed within hierarchies of cultural and economic worth. Art historian Stacey Pierson has aptly shown the power of provenance when recounting the itineraries of a teapot—in fact more than one—which gained value and meaning through being owned by the celebrity lexicographer Samuel Johnson.[1] Even though the connection between the objects in question and their famed owner turned out to be partly invented, Pierson shows how provenance has the power to imbue even mundane objects with meaning and desire. Provenance traditionally records the trajectories of precious and more mobile objects that can otherwise easily be displaced, exchanged, or appropriated. In such cases—not least in the art and antiquities trade and within colonial acquisitions in contexts of empire—the provenance record may also produce politically charged narratives that validate, capitalize on, enable, and disable ownership.

In their seminal collection *Provenance: An Alternate History of Art* (2012), Gail Feigenbaum and Inge Reist expanded the idea of provenance toward broader questions of origin and trajectory.[2] The contributions in this issue of *Future Anterior* continue that expansion into the field of architecture, from the extractive origins of buildings to their sometimes surprising afterlives. Architecture moves, though unlike an artwork, an archaeological artifact, an ethnographic object, or a manuscript, a building's provenance poses a distinct set of challenges. Uwe Fleckner and Mari Lending write in their introduction to *Provenance in Architecture. A Dictionary* that "any cut into time will show architecture performing in all sorts of states between complex origins and uncertain destinations," and explain how "architectural provenance reconsiders core aesthetic concepts such as origins, authorship, attribution, authenticity and authentication, as well as labour and ownership of resources, property and land."[3] In other words, a building's life and potential transformations complicates questions of authorship, value, and fantasies of continuity.

The concerns we raise here are central to discourses of critical preservation: What really happens to a building when it is exchanged? How are buildings recorded, and what kinds of knowledge (or loss of knowledge) does that documentation produce? From our perspective, provenance is not only a way of stabilizing meaning but a means for tracing complications, ruptures, and the multitemporal layers of architectural work. In this special issue on provenance, we scale up and zoom in to investigate how provenance in architecture may provide ways of understanding architectures of the past, present, and future—an endeavor that takes its cue precisely from specific and often overlooked moments of transaction, crises, and temporal collisions, that looks into details that evoke global systems of exchange, and that is able to pin down the many ambiguous in-betweens and mundane clues that make architecture historical.

The research project *Provenance Projected: Architecture Past and Future in the Era of Circularity* transposes provenance from discrete objects to architectural culture at large, while promising to operate beyond the retrospective record of the passage of objects through time. Buildings, unlike artworks, are inhabited, extended, amended. Not even a protected status can freeze them in time. They are unruly and ever-changing entities, deeply implicated in social, legal, environmental, and economic processes. Buildings consist of materials with different life expectancies; their purposes may evolve or become obsolete. Provenance evolves along with the complex lives of architectural phenomena—and beyond the objects themselves, in interpretation and as reception history. The contributions in this issue show that architectural provenance works across multiple temporalities and spatial registers: from the sourcing and extraction of materials, through construction and transportation, to occupation, alteration, maintenance, demolition, reuse, or recirculation. In this expanded frame, provenance can describe origins, but also extends through the ongoing involvements of owners, users, caretakers, institutions, and materials, that continue the work of composing and recomposing the lives and histories of buildings.

Provenance allows us to see buildings, fragments, artifacts, and even landscapes not as static objects with fixed boundaries but as flexible, networked, and coauthored entities with rich social biographies and complex afterlives. As many previous editions of *Future Anterior* have shown, buildings as well as monuments are mutable, movable, and replicable. Using the optics of provenance, we turn to the vast cast of actors involved in the transformation of architecture and the means by which they do so. Buildings are authored not by architects alone but by their owners, custodians, legislators, contractors, material suppliers, inhabitants, and artists, to mention a few. Architectural provenance is not merely a record of reuse or ownership but an account of power, bureaucracy, influence, rupture, and renewal.

If provenance is a lens for seeing architecture as collectively authored and continuously reshaped, it also calls for a rethinking of how architectural histories are constructed and narrated. Provenance is often conceived as a retrospective tool—one that establishes continuity through linear narratives of origin and succession. This is shaped by assumptions of historical progress, in which architectural development is cast as sequential, authoritative, and singular. Such notions of provenance privilege certain events and perspectives while rendering others peripheral. This issue explores how provenance might be reimagined as a forward-bound and creative instrument for change: one that registers where architectures come from and how they are adapted, unsettled, and revalued.

With this collection we bring together scholars, practitioners, artists, and educators who use provenance to look at transfers, misuse, adaptation, and reinvention across geographies and chronologies. Importantly, these essays are not linked by a single topic like material reuse or restitution, but united by a way of seeing: Provenance here becomes a lens, a practice, a historical orientation. By revisiting topics like material procurement, ownership, and authorship, we suggest that provenance is more than a proofing mechanism. It tracks not just what happened but how things are made to matter, what is preserved, overwritten, or forgotten. From a variety of angles, the authors in this issue use provenance to connect extraction points with places of deposit, to stretch across the messy and rich centuries-long histories of buildings, to record the ways in which owners have transformed their property, revisit overlooked events of famous buildings, to question ownerships and authenticity, to assert the importance of custodians, and to track value changes in objects.

Through photographs by Shitamichi Motoyuki taken between 2001 and 2012, Matthew Mullane considers the afterlives of postimperial Japanese architecture and unfolds the ways in which Japan has looked, or not, upon its colonial past. Both the article and the photographs display a sharp eye for the ordinariness of repurposed relics and the critical history they reveal. Instead of monumentalizing each remnant, Mullane shows how architectures of empire and their subtle provenances are folded into everyday life, neither fully remembered nor entirely forgotten.

Gustav Elgin and Alena Rieger both look at historical structures that have been silenced by their famed authors, owners, or guests. Elgin looks at a vernacular house on the North-German coast where Edvard Munch spent time in 1907–8; Rieger at the Maison du Peuple in Brussels, designed by Victor Horta. Both Elgin and Rieger view their subjects through the legal frameworks and cultural processes that redefined them. Elgin places celebrity and signature in parentheses, while turning to centuries of German property law across changing political regimes. In doing so, a spectacularly mundane house and its trajectory of tradition and exception takes the place of the biographical circumstances of a famous resident. Via Roman property law, Rieger looks at the theft of an art nouveau monument demolished in the 1960s and partially stolen in the 1980s. Like Elgin, Rieger describes a history that would have been unknowable without celebrity signatures but that has also been obscured by them. Even though the archives would barely have existed without the author function, these narratives focus on the interference of other actors—in the Horta case, the owners who had the power to destroy the building. Provenance allows both Elgin and Rieger to reorganize and reprioritize evidence, and in doing so, present fragments of a new past.

A recent UNESCO heritage listing makes the starting point for Alfredo Thiermann, Pedro Correa, Ella Neumaier, and Xavier Nueno, who uncover a history behind the official narrative of the Chilehaus, designed by Fritz Höger, commissioned by the industrialist Henry B. Sloman, and completed in 1924. Beyond the heritage value of this monument of brick expressionism, the authors look for its raison d'être by following the money that accumulated in Hamburg, back to the mines of the Atacama Desert, Chile. Through drone photography, the authors capture the scars in the desert left by nitrate extraction, traces that mark the environmental and human costs embedded in the Chilehaus's material and economic history. Provenance here is employed to critique a narrow understanding of heritage and expand the signifying frames of architecture. Along similar lines of extraction, this time of lime, Thomas McQuillan recounts a geology of provenance through the undoing of an entire island. His focus is not a building but one of architecture's source materials. The island of Langøya is a site transformed through extraction. What remains is a simulacrum in the Oslofjord, an island rebuilt from waste, masquerading as restored nature. "An Island, Translated" presents a cast of authors including geologists, botanists, and industrialists who once studied, mapped, and profited from the island. Each brought a distinct relationship that reframed its value and identity.

Nikos Magouliotis considers the role of Kyriakos Pittakis as a custodian whose informal and inventive acts of preservation salvaged numerous antique bits and pieces from across Athens and assembled them into a temporary spolia-wall on the Athenian Acropolis, partly based on photographic evidence produced by Félix Bonfils and published in 1870. This moment of archaeological authorship was a moment of true authority, where Pittakis becomes an author who temporarily paused the movement of fragments of unknown provenience and uncertain destinations. Here provenance lets us see the proximity between preservation and destruction. A different kind of authorship is explored by Flavia Crisciotti, who follows the evolving reception of Carlo Scarpa's tailored Venetian easels made for the display of paintings. When recently offered at auction, these devices became collectable objects of desire. While both the museum and the art market have capitalized on Scarpa's fame and signature, the authorship of these coproduced and skillfully crafted devices became more fully described when the easels appeared as circulating commodities beyond their intended use. In this article, provenance frames issues such as authenticity, seriality, and the singular when these supporting devices are enrolled into cultural canons of value.

Amandine Kastler and Erlend Skjeseth discuss layered, fragmented, and anachronic architecture that does not distill the past but adds to it. Provenance allows them to look at history through the architectural object, as fragmented rather than continuous, while existing buildings become part of the evolving present rather than obsolete and sacred relics of the past. Charlotte Malterre-Barthes describes the provenance of a typical North American house detail to advocate for a revised approach to architecture that confronts its material supply. Provenance, in this context, is a lens for understanding architectural extractivism as it is embedded in the manufacture of ordinary construction details, revealing the supply chains, labor conditions, and ecological harm that make them possible. Continuing the ordinary, Simon Mitchell explores how architectural materials circulate in fragmentary and unfinished trajectories within reuse economies, through an ethnographic study of a reuse warehouse in Oslo. Rather than seeking coherence or completeness, Mitchell centers the incomplete, granular, and often invisible objects that quietly shape the built environment but are rarely included in its histories.

Through an architect intervention, Nicholas Coates and Eskil Buskov Selmer explore how a mid-twentieth-century Scandinavian company positioned itself as a universal solution in postcolonial markets. The trade of Siporex between a small village in Norway and the former capital of the Ivory Coast has left many unexpected imprints on Abidjan.

Finally, we conclude this spectrum of architectural provenance with a photographic series by the artist duo Lake Verea. The series shows the Palacio de Bellas Artes in Mexico City as a constellation of fragments with diverse material and rich cultural provenances. By isolating specific details, including imported marbles from Italy and Tiffany mosaics from the United States, the project presents the building as a layered site of global circulation. The works offers an artistic approach to provenance, treating buildings as assemblages whose parts emerge from the various histories, geographies, and many hands involved in its making.

In a moment of multiple and intersecting crises—ecological, political, and epistemic—we need frameworks that do more than preserve a singular or dominant version of the past. We need tools that activate existing materials and account for their evolving meanings and uses. Together, the articles in this issue build provenance as a way of addressing complex issues. Through history and practice, they look at how provenance can be used to construct and disrupt ownerships, to record and revalorize, and to recast buildings and their associated materials for new and uncertain futures. If Stacey Pierson and Dr. Johnson's teapot taught us about the power of provenance, then this collection also searches for its critical potential. With a shared focus on things as they move in moments of crisis, transfer, and change, this issue presents the contours of different pasts across architectural production. Together, these texts approach provenance not only as documentation but as a method of writing, critique, and projection. As architecture moves, so too does its history.

Biographies

Mari Lending is a professor of architectural history and theory at the Oslo School of Architecture and Design, and the director of the international research project *Provenance Projected: Architecture Past and Future in the Era of Circularity.*

Alena Rieger is a PhD fellow at the Oslo School of Architecture and Design. Her dissertation examines twentieth-century building demolitions and material provenance and is supervised by Mari Lending as part of the international research project *Provenance Projected: Architecture Past and Future in the Era of Circularity.* Rieger's work has been supported by grants and fellowships from the Canadian Centre for Architecture, the Canada Council for the Arts, and the Manitoba Arts Council. She was awarded the J.B.C. Watkins Award in Architecture (2023) and is a recipient of the SSHRC Doctoral Fellowship (2023–27).

Simon Mitchell is a postdoctoral researcher in the international research project *Provenance Projected: Architecture Past and Future in the Era of Circularity* at the Oslo School of Architecture and Design. He holds a PhD in architecture from the University of Manchester, funded by the Arts and Humanities Research Council (2023). Working at the intersection of ethnography, archival theory, and architecture history, his current research focuses on the storage lives of architectural fragments. Originally trained in architecture, Simon has practiced across Europe and in Asia, tutored at the Manchester School of Architecture and the GEC Academy in Beijing, and published on behalf of the Bauhaus Dessau Foundation.

Notes

[1] Stacey Pierson, "The Power of Provenance: Dr Johnson's Teapot and the Materialization of Fame," *Journal for Provenance Research and the History of Collection,* no. 1 (2022): 29–43.

[2] Gail Feigenbaum and Inge Reist, eds., *Provenance: An Alternate History of Art* (Getty Research Institute, 2012).

[3] Uwe Fleckner and Mari Lending, *Provenance in Architecture. A Dictionary* (Hatje Cantz, 2025), 7 and 8.

In This Issue

Postimperial Reuse: The Photography of Shitamichi Motoyuki
Matthew Mullane

The afterlives of imperial and colonial architecture are unpredictable. Surveying the remnants of the former Japanese empire for example, we encounter a wide variety of reuse. In South Korea, a former colonial bank becomes a museum to colonial oppression. In Taiwan, the shattered gates of colonial shrines are reassembled to memorialize the Japanese presence. And in Japan, imperial monuments take on new names to celebrate postwar peace. Sometimes buildings are obliterated from the record or subject to slow, incremental reuse that obscures imperial provenance. Such volatility makes historicization difficult. As evidenced by the relative lack of colonial structures in mainstream histories of Japanese architecture, this volatility also makes difficult history easy to ignore. While architectural historians continue to struggle with the empire's legacy, artists such as Shitamichi Motoyuki have produced important visual supplements. Over the past two decades, Shitamichi has surveyed Japan and its former colonies in search of postimperial reuse. He has discovered inventively reused military architecture in Japan and vestiges of Shinto shrines in the former colonies. He has also performatively reused military architecture in Japan to showcase the ease with which so-called difficult heritage can be transformed. This article argues that his work simultaneously uncovers a lost lineage of Japanese architecture and theorizes the ways that imperial provenance is contested by regional politics and individual memory.

Unfinished Collapse: Provenances of the Am Strom 53 Houses
Gustav Elgin

The provenance of the half-timbered house Am Strom 53 in Warnemünde, Germany, is noteworthy not only for the brief tenancy by Edvard Munch between 1907 and 1908, but because its four-hundred-year-plus itinerary as a property object charts an intricate trajectory through Northern Germany's shifting property regimes: (pre)feudal, Hanseatic, fascist, communist, and neoliberal. Drawing on archival and on-site investigations, the article reconstructs how Am Strom 53 has reproduced, resisted, and short-circuited these changing regimes of ownership for the better part of five centuries. Taking a cue from recent theories of infrastructure as "that which repeats," the article proposes that provenance research gains critical purchase when the legal infrastructures that define property relations break down. This opens apertures onto the patterned repetitions that, at different historical junctures, have sustained and conditioned relationships to buildings as property. In the case of Am Strom 53, one such aperture is opened by the slow, sputtering collapse of the property form known as the *house mark:* an ancient legal symbol that has periodically resurfaced to haunt both the house and the German property system at large.

Usus, Fructus, Abusus
Alena Rieger

When the pieces of Maison du Peuple (Victor Horta, Brussels, 1896–99) disappeared from their precarious storage site in 1983, questions of ownership, provenance, and material value were placed center stage. In the ensuing legal case, the building's dense post-demolition provenance became subject to the scrutiny of the Belgian courts. The case was an inflection point in a long battle to salvage Maison du Peuple: a disaster for the stolen parts but a liberation for those that remained. The demolition of Maison du Peuple had already catapulted the building to international fame, but the theft of it nearly twenty years later aroused a more local outrage. Custodians and owners rushed to take advantage of a surge of interest in the deconstructed art nouveau icon, in a new cultural moment. Through a detailed unraveling of the most dubious ownerships of Maison du Peuple, this article argues that it was precisely during moments of crisis that the reputation of Maison du Peuple was reconfigured and its future stability secured.

Office Work: Architecture and Extraction Between Atacama and Hamburg
Alfredo Thiermann, Pedro Correa, Ella Neumaier, and Xavier Nueno

This paper argues that the memorialization of UNESCO World Heritage sites operates through processes that highlight certain aspects of buildings while obscuring others. In the case of the Chilehaus (1924), one of Germany's most iconic expressionist buildings, the UNESCO nomination makes only a passing reference to its namesake, Chile. This omission silences the historical and material synchronicities that connect—and separate—the rise of intellectual office work in Hamburg with the industrialization of mining in the Atacama Desert. Evidence of this asymmetrical modernity is still readable on the surface of the desert, which, due to its dryness and specific environmental conditions, is one of the most endurable storage devices on this planet. Analyzing the traces stored in the desert allows us to reconstruct a different understanding of the modernity of the Chilehaus; one that links the functional and aesthetic qualities of the building to networks of global extraction, histories of dispossession, and the planetary transformation precipitated by the rise of the fertilizer industry. The paper argues for a different politics of memorialization, one that questions the commemoration of isolated buildings and asks at what scale the history of industrial capitalism is registered.

An Island, Translated: A Geology of Provenances
Thomas McQuillan
"An Island, Translated" examines the geological, industrial, and ecological transitions of Langøya, an island in the Oslofjord, as a paradigm of material provenance in the Anthropocene. Once a site of scientific inquiry and limestone extraction, the island provisioned the expansion of Oslo through cement production until it was decommissioned and became a landfill for toxic waste. Tracing its layered history, this article explores how shifting regimes of ownership, value, and use reframed the island from natural resource to industrial asset, dumping ground, and real estate. Through commodification, material process, and geological time, the island constitutes the collapse of distinction between natural and human histories. Langøya's strata documents its deep time and modern exploitation to reveal a regionalist Anthropocene marker: a monumental plaster cast formed from industrial waste. Provenance is reconceptualized as a dynamic interplay between matter, meaning, and environmental transformation—extending from buildings to landscapes. Here, Langøya is understood as a reciprocal landscape that records the invisible costs of urban development and the uneasy intermingling of ecological restoration with speculative capitalism, revealing the evolving cultural and geological meanings of extraction.

Between Archaeologies: Kyriakos Pittakis and His Wall of Spolia on the Acropolis
Nikos Magouliotis
In 1836, Kyriakos Pittakis became General Ephor (Overseer) of the antiquities of Athens. Compared to his peers, Pittakis lacked academic education, but he was famous for his passion for protecting the antiquities, and for the unorthodox means he adopted to that end. Pittakis buried ancient fragments in water-wells, he nailed and plastered them together in makeshift "tableaus"—all in order to deter looters. When cleaning the Acropolis plateau from centuries' worth of rubble, Pittakis refused to throw anything away: He stacked unclassifiable fragments on top of each other along the perimeter of the plateau, until these formed an imposing wall of spolia which dominated the experience of the site for decades. His aim was

pragmatic—to store these fragments until their historic provenance was determined—but the result of this cumulative process has evident aesthetic aspirations, echoing older practices of vernacular spoliation. This article understands Pittakis as a person who lived and worked between two different archaeologies: the Western epistemology of his fellow archaeologists and of the Greek state, and the indigenous archaeology of the local population who built ancient fragments into the walls of their houses and churches.

Provenance on Display: "Carlo Scarpa (1906–1978), an Easel"
Flavia Crisciotti
In a softly lit room of the Museo Correr in Venice, slender easels elevate Renaissance masterpieces to eye level. The objects in question—art mounting mechanisms designed by architect Carlo Scarpa (1906–1978)—have become Scarpa's most iconic furniture pieces, apotheosis of Italian postwar design, protagonists of recent exhibitions, and sold at auction. Their iconicity has fueled their transformation from design objects into highly desirable art objects. Long embedded in narratives of Scarpa's greatness, the easels' provenance had never been questioned. Now that these tailored, skillfully crafted objects circulate on the art market, however, their provenance as well as their authorship have become critical. Drawing on early sketches, oral histories, and photographs, this article attends to the easels with a degree of attention usually reserved for the paintings they support.

Anachronic Hybrids: Cuts into Architectural Time
Amandine Kastler and Erlend Skjeseth
This article examines how layered architectural histories can be actively engaged through design rather than preserved as static artifacts. It explores how architectural provenance might support a more attentive cultivation of existing buildings and considers how provenance can act as a driver in the formation of larger-scale extensions within historic settings. An anecdote from the polarizing world of the Norwegian *Arkitekturopprøret* prompts an exploration of the palimpsestic character of a theater building in Oslo where accumulated layers, traces, and contradictions from across centuries are not treated as problems to be resolved but as qualities that might be embraced and cultivated in future projects of reuse and transformation. The old building's mercurial character serves, alongside built works by Kastler Skjeseth Architects, to investigate the potential of buildings to evolve over time. The paper looks at how to transform existing structures through surgical interventions that emerge from close encounters with vernacular architecture, and draw on its morphology, materiality, and

public perception. Different in program and condition, these architectures share sensibilities shaped by memory, time, and circumstance—reflecting a broader shift in contemporary European architectural practice toward more situated forms of building.

Details as Evidence: Architectural Extractivism and the Politics of Provenance
Charlotte Malterre-Barthes
This essay argues that architectural details function as revelatory records of the extractive processes underpinning architecture. If viewed from this perspective, details can help us overcome the distance introduced by architectural extractivism. While designers obsess over the aesthetic and technical qualities of details, their material provenance—the conditions of extraction, labor, and legal frameworks that enable their existence—remain conspicuously absent from architectural discourse. Drawing on Langdon Winner's concept that seemingly neutral artifacts encode political meaning, this paper introduces architectural extractivism as a framework for understanding how the exploitation of materials, labor, and cultures shapes our built environment and why and how it could be challenged. Through close examination of a standard North American suburban house roof detail, the essay traces each component—from wooden trusses sourced through violent deforestation practices to galvanized nails manufactured in petrochemical corridors of "Cancer Alley"—to reveal the global networks of extraction and exploitation embedded in ordinary construction.

Partial Provenances: Staging Minor Matters Inside a Reuse Warehouse
Simon Mitchell
What kind of history can be drawn from a plumbing valve, a glass block, or a board of MDF with a spray-painted replica of a well-known artwork? So mundane and ubiquitous in the built environment, these objects are rarely granted the historical attention afforded to more celebrated architectural fragments one might find in a museum or collection. Yet it is precisely in their invisibility that their importance lies. If we cannot find ways to describe, interpret, or narrate ordinary and overlooked components in architecture, how can we build futures that account for what already exists? Drawing on ethnographic observations from an architectural reuse warehouse in Oslo, Ombygg, this essay stages a set of modest and residual objects—materials held in storage and caught between past and future lives. It reflects on the narrative potential of such objects to challenge dominant ways of thinking through

architecture that favors resolution over uncertainty, and origins over destinations. What emerges is a type of provenance embedded in projection—oriented toward fragments with unfinished trajectories, provisional meanings, and shaped through the infrastructures that evaluate, accumulate, store, and recirculate them. Reframed through their speculative futures, these fragments offer a way of seeing architecture as an ongoing composition that is both granular and continually unfolding.

Architect Intervention: Operation Siporex
Nicholas Coates and Eskil Buskov Selmer

Operation Siporex presents the opportunism arising out of industrial architectural components by following the movement of a single material across continents. Siporex, a brand of autoclaved aerated concrete, was a building block developed in Scandinavia that transformed the building industries in postwar Europe before spreading globally. With its revolutionarily lightweight material properties, Siporex was a material that was designed to move from its inception. First comprised as a set of building elements, the company rapidly developed an all-encompassing ecosystem that was hailed as the system that could meet every need and complete constructions in record time. Simultaneously, away from the building site, Siporex made its way into local vocabularies that in turn began defining new contexts. Following the material from a small town in Norway to the former capital of Cote d'Ivoire, this contribution outlines a larger story of negotiations, strategic uses of governmental development aid, and corporate profitability. Siporex, a hidden building block that transformed the city of Abidjan, remains not only a simple building element but as a promise left behind.

Artist Intervention: One to One: Palace of Fine Arts, Mexico City
Lake Verea

One to One / Bellas Artes is a photographic exploration of the Palacio de Bellas Artes in Mexico City, focusing on fragments from its two distinct periods of construction. Originally designed in the early 1900s by Italian architect Adamo Boari in the art nouveau style and completed in 1934 by Mexican architect Nicolás Mariscal in an art deco style, the building embodies Mexico's complex journey from dictatorship through revolution to modern nationhood. This project reimagines the Palace not as a monolith but as a living entity composed of cracks, dust, materials, and design elements sourced globally. By isolating architectural fragments and reproducing them at a 1:1 scale, Lake Verea invites viewers into an intimate, slowed-down encounter with the monument—one that questions provenance, perception, scale, and historical context. Lake Verea act as conceptual archaeologists, tracing the provenance of materials and the inspiration behind the designs. Through close-up imagery and poetic interpretation, One to One reveals the tension between monumentality and fragility, offering a new visual and emotional reading of a national symbol. This body of work resists linear history, proposing instead a cross-cutting notion of time and space through the silent language of form, surface, and memory.

Figure 1. Nakamura Yoshihei and Anton Feller, Gunsan Modern Architecture Hall. Former Bank of Joseon Gunsan Branch. Photo: Lawinc82. Public domain.

Matthew Mullane

Postimperial Reuse

The Photography of Shitamichi Motoyuki

Where is the architectural history of the Japanese colonial empire? In 2018, three different answers were given by a museum, a tourism council, and an artist. In April of that year, Tokyo's leading venue for contemporary art, the Mori Art Museum, opened an exhibition entitled *Japan in Architecture: Genealogies of Its Transformation.*[1] It offered a sweeping survey of the country's architectural output from prehistory to today using models, photographs, drawings, and even full-scale reconstructions. The exhibition's genealogical conceit reflects a curious disciplinary preoccupation with lineage and inheritance. Many histories of Japanese architecture written in the country feature exhaustive family trees that explain history as a sequence of professional pedigree. Such histories ensure that the provenance of so-called "Japanese architecture" is kept in Japan despite its global dimensions. Indeed, the family tree on display at the Mori Art Museum extended deep into the past but was conspicuously pruned to match the outline of the country's contemporary borders. Even though "Japan" also included colonial holdings in East and Southeast Asia for fifty years, no examples of buildings built in these territories were shown. The absence reflects a gap in the collective national memory, but more specific to architecture, it also suggests that colonialism is inconsequential to the development of modern architecture. This is of course far from the truth. Just as in the United States, Great Britain, the Netherlands, Belgium, and elsewhere, the material opportunities provided by empire fueled the engine of modern architecture's development in Japan.

Meanwhile, in September 2018 the small South Korean port city of Gunsan gathered to celebrate the "Gunsan Time Travel Festival," an annual three-day event dedicated to educating the public about the Japanese colonial occupation through stories of oppression, resilience, and resistance. Events included street parades, concerts, and a variety of guided tours designed as a form of "time travel" back to the 1930s.[2] The city's anomalous collection of well-preserved colonial architecture was a key part of the festivities. Elsewhere in South Korea, most colonial architecture has been destroyed or unceremoniously absorbed into the country's conurbations. Ironically, thanks to Gunsan's quick economic decline after occupation, much of the city's colonial architecture survived the Korean War and later urban development. Preserved structures

Future Anterior
Volume XXII, Numbers 1–2
Summer / Winter 2025

include the European revivalist Customs House, the Dongguksa Sōtō Zen Buddhist temple, the streamline modern Joseon Food Corporation building, and several villas once owned by wealthy Japanese officials and businessmen featuring combinations of Korean, Japanese, and Western stylings. The centerpiece of the collection is the Gunsan Modern Architecture Hall, a converted colonial bank whose exterior Secessionist style and interior curatorial conceit explicitly connect "modern" and "colonial" architecture (Figure 1). As an ensemble, the existing buildings are part of a large-scale urban regeneration project that leverages the city's colonial heritage as a tourist attraction.[3] Gunsan's revitalization is a curious example of "dark tourism" where the "deaths, disasters, and atrocities" of the colonial era are not only memorialized but sold as an immersive experience.[4] If colonial architecture is forgotten at the Mori Art Museum, in Gunsan it is used as stage dressing for a living museum that simulates colonialism for a generation that most likely knows Japan as a pop culture powerhouse, not an occupying force.

A week after the party in Gunsan died down, the Paris contemporary art gallery KADIST hung a photograph in their street-facing window showing a group of elderly men sitting on a piece of concrete (Figure 2).[5] The image might not stop a passerby in their tracks, but it deserves a closer look. The place is Taichung, Taiwan, and the men's ad hoc bench is in fact a toppled Shinto shrine gate, or *torii,* built by the Japanese colonial government to front the 1912 Taichu Shrine. Shitamichi Motoyuki took the photo in 2006 during his tour of the former Japanese colonial empire in search of surviving concrete torii gates and their myriad reuses.[6] Though casually used as a bench, the careful landscaping suggests that its placement is not accidental. In fact, the original torii had been broken and scattered around the city for decades until the local government collected the fragments and repositioned them on the ground in 2000. Curious about this purposeful reconstruction of ruins, Shitamichi asked a pseudonymous local, "Mrs. W," why so many remnants of colonial architecture still exist in Taiwan, even after a 1972 government measure to remove all traces of the colonial period.[7] Mrs. W responded that the torii do not necessarily represent Japanese oppression, but instead Taiwan's "Japanese period," just one of the many turbulent changes that Taiwan has experienced during the twentieth century.[8] The answer echoes what historian Leo T. S. Ching has called the "Taiwan difference," a postcolonial attitude of acceptance and reconciliation made by intergenerational experience, not state-mandated apology.[9] To Mrs. W, the torii represent historical experiences that should be neither suppressed nor celebrated. They are simply monuments to the continuity of a life lived.

Figure 2. Shitamichi Motoyuki, *torii Taichung, Taiwan,* 2006–12. Courtesy of the artist.

Imperial Continuity

These three vignettes evidence the mutability of colonial architectural history in Japan and its former empire. It is a fugitive historical category, a merchandised tourist destination, and an object whose integration with its surroundings is so seamless that we only notice it when it is turned into an image. The history of colonial architecture is mutable because colonial architecture itself is subject to profound, and sometimes violent, acts of transformation. In postcolonial situations, the provenance of colonial architecture is constantly redefined in a cycle of suppression, celebration, and acceptance to match changing political headwinds. For some, the provenance of troubled architecture is no matter. The architecture critic Martin Pawley sardonically represents this position when he writes that buildings "do not care. They have no feelings. . . . So what if Adolf Hitler's command bunker in the former East Prussia becomes a Polish nightclub?"[10] And so what if a colonial torii becomes a bench? Sure, the object itself does not care, but people do. In fact, in the postcolony, people care so much that they will gladly demolish a colonial building to ensure that its haunted politics never have the chance to be reanimated. Case in point is the 1926 Government-General Building in Seoul, the Japanese colonial headquarters that was demolished between 1995 and 1996 amid a wave of nationalist concern that the "evil spirits" of Japan's former rule still exerted influence over the country.[11] Such destruction follows Frantz Fanon's argument that a city is only truly decolonized after "demolishing the colonist's sector."[12] Architecture's relative permanence carries with it contestation over what its continuity means, who determines its power, and how it can be either revitalized or suppressed.

The material continuity of not only colonial architecture but also imperial and militaristic architecture challenges a common telling of modern Japanese history as two exclusive halves: wartime and postwar. The flash of the atomic bombs, the repatriation of millions of colonial subjects, and the desanctification of the emperor in 1945 have been strategically used by Japanese and American actors as a historical bulwark to stop lines of continuity and causality from being drawn between a militaristic empire and a peaceful global trade partner.[13] According to historian Carol Gluck, the rapid US-backed rehabilitation of its former enemy meant that "Japan lost its empire without becoming post-imperial."[14] As a field, Japanese architectural history was slow to inspect its own postimperial condition and "the spectre of entanglements with and comparisons to other empires."[15] Though Japanese language scholarship on colonial architectural history has grown significantly over the past two decades, official recognition is scarce.[16] For example, the state-sponsored National Archives of Modern Architecture (*Kokuritsu kingendai kenchiku shiryōkan*) has exhibited drawings and photographs related to domestic wartime memorials (*chūreitō*), but not colonial structures.[17] Domestic imperial architecture and overseas colonial architecture remain historiographically separated despite their obvious ideological union, and the simple fact that both were often designed by the same architects.[18]

The colonial aporia in modern Japanese architectural history is part of a wider "imperial amnesia" that has dogged the country since the end of World War II.[19] Forgetting was made even easier thanks to decades of bombing, fires, urban growth, and political upheaval that erased or submerged much of Japan's colonial footprint. In fact, the destruction of colonial architecture began even before the empire's collapse. For example, in Singapore, the Japanese military dismantled and burned the island's major colonial shrine, the Syonan Jinja, out of fear that the incoming British forces would desecrate the sacred grounds.[20] Today, a graveyard-like collection of concrete posts are scattered in an inaccessible swamp that only the bravest fans of "dark tourism" on the island dare access. In South Korea, surviving remnants such as the so-called "enemy houses" of Japanese settlers can be difficult to identify in the country's dense cities.[21] Historian Janet Poole has collected stories from people who live with and within these buildings to reveal that their use is not determined by either "pro-demolitionist" or "pro-conservationist" viewpoints, but instead by a "quieter kind of overcoming in the uneasy remaining of the colonial past and present."[22] In Taiwan, following a Kuomintang-led campaign of destruction, Japanese colonial structures have been more recently reused and rebuilt to serve the politics of a "Taiwan-centric" nationalist history project.[23] New shrines and memorials are often detached from the violent specificities of Japanese colonialism in order to celebrate a "multicultural" Taiwanese history that is independent from Chinese control.[24] Meanwhile in Japan, architectural evidence of the empire's former colonial project is often hiding in the open, extant but detached from its original meaning. The towering 1940 *hakkō ichiu* (unify the world under one roof) monument dedicated to the future "Greater East Asia Co-Prosperity Sphere" remains intact, but as the "Tower of Peace."[25] And hundreds of war memorials still dot the country in a plethora of transformed guises, but according to historian Barak Kushner, they more often prompt remembrance of "domestic concerns" than a "holistic consideration of Japan as an empire."[26] These examples in Japan show that "imperial amnesia" is not a passive act of forgetting due to old age. Architectural transformations can be used to hide imperial provenance, prompting an amnesia that is more akin to purposefully striking oneself in the head to forget something too embarrassing or politically inconvenient.

Chancing upon an imperial remnant, our first inclination is to photograph it. Imperial architecture was after all made to be photographed. Like other modern empires, Japan used photography as both "an instrument of nation building and a means of imperial subjugation."[27] And architecture was the most common subject. Photographs of new imperial and colonial buildings appeared in newspapers, photobooks, and on millions of postcards made to convince people that the empire was a "coherent political, historical, linguistic, and cultural space."[28] Photographers were also dispatched throughout Asia to document traditional architecture that proved cultural continuity between Japan and its colonies, as well as ruins that demonstrated the need for Japan's guardianship.[29] In an imperial context, architecture is a potent photographic subject whose presumed permanence stands in for the constancy and predictability of the empire. As one example, imperial shrine societies published photobooks that included examples of both old shrines on the mainland and new shrines in the colonies in a single narrative sequence to emphasize the continuity of rule.[30] Just as photography through the "imperial shutter" determines "what is suppressed and made irrelevant," such architectural photographs assert imperial continuity as the denial of change.[31] But as we've seen, imperial architecture does change, and often in radical and unpredictable ways. Is there then a way of documenting imperial remnants today that does not simply reify their original violence or cynically try to "settle scores of the past"?[32]

Figure 3. Shitamichi Motoyuki, *The Shape of War,* 2001–5. Courtesy of the artist.

Photographing Transformations

In another photograph by Shitamichi, we find ourselves on a narrow path between two houses (Figure 3). In the background is a mysterious curved structure whose roofline is reminiscent of salt storage domes, but it fits so seamlessly with the scenery that it could well be a distant mountain. Upon closer inspection, the gray form is hollowed out with space for storing, or maybe even hiding, something. The structure is in fact a low-profile concrete hangar with exactly enough room inside to park a small military aircraft. Many such hangars were built throughout Japan and its colonies during World War II to secret aircraft away from American bombers. The photograph is part of *The Shape of War* (*Sensō no katachi*) (2001–5), a portfolio of photographs documenting former military structures throughout Japan that have been quietly integrated into everyday life.[33] The series features several other hangars squeezed into unremarkable rural and suburban neighborhoods. What unites them is their continued invisibility. In a previous life they were camouflaged with greenery to hide precious aircraft from aerial surveillance, and today they successfully escape the attention of preservation crews and heritage councils. Their continued secrecy is perhaps due to their prosaic reuse. One exceptional hangar discovered by Shitamichi has been transformed into a storage facility fitted with metal doors that were handcrafted to meet the silhouette of the aircraft that once hid inside. Such meticulous retrofitting exhibits a kind of vernacular adaptive reuse totally divorced from the sanctifying impulses of heritage policy. The owners of these spaces seem to have the same attitude as Martin Pawley: So what if my garage was once a secret hangar?

And so what if zoo animals live in a cage once occupied by an artillery cannon? Shitamichi has a typological eye and in addition to hangars, he has also discovered a wide range of former artillery emplacements. They include barely noticeable circles of concrete in parking lots, generic plinths in the middle of public parks, and even a zoo enclosure. In a photograph of the latter, we see a group of people standing around a circular monkey cage (Figure 4). It is only with an architectural line drawing exhibited on the wall next to the photograph that we understand the structure's unlikely transformation. What was once an open perimeter for a rotating artillery weapon is now a cage separating monkeys and human onlookers. The transition from an architecture of war to an architecture of leisure is striking, but of course not unprecedented. In Germany, people can enjoy the greenery of Berlin's Tempelhof Field or have dinner atop a former flak tower in Hamburg. However, unlike these German examples that are publicly acknowledged as monuments to historical memory, Shitamichi documents structures whose imperial provenance has been obscured by generations of change. This is not to suggest that Germany's reuse of wartime heritage is somehow more enlightened than Japan's. Scholars have critiqued this comparison for decades.[34] Instead, Shitamichi's photographs of reused colonial and military architecture offer a compelling material representation of what anthropologist Ann Laura Stoler calls "imperial duress," the lingering effects of empire that continue into the present through occluded and transformed conceptual frameworks.[35] The continuity of wartime institutions, ideas, and ideologies may not be as obvious as a monument; they could very well be hiding in new shapes.

Finding lost imperial architecture is no simple matter. Shitamichi's work begins in his archive of historical photographs, namely period postcards depicting imperial architecture in its former ideal state. The next step is going out into the world to practice what he simply calls "fieldwork." The term is both more historically and practically complex than it seems. In 2014, Shitamichi formed the Traveling Research Laboratory with sound artist mamoru and graphic designer Masataka Maruyama as a platform for theorizing fieldwork as artistic research. The group organized road trips across Japan to perform fieldwork related to their respective practices, interview fellow artists, and, most importantly, reflect on the nature of fieldwork itself in recorded discussions and small

Figure 4. Shitamichi Motoyuki, *The Shape of War*, 2001–5. Courtesy of the artist.

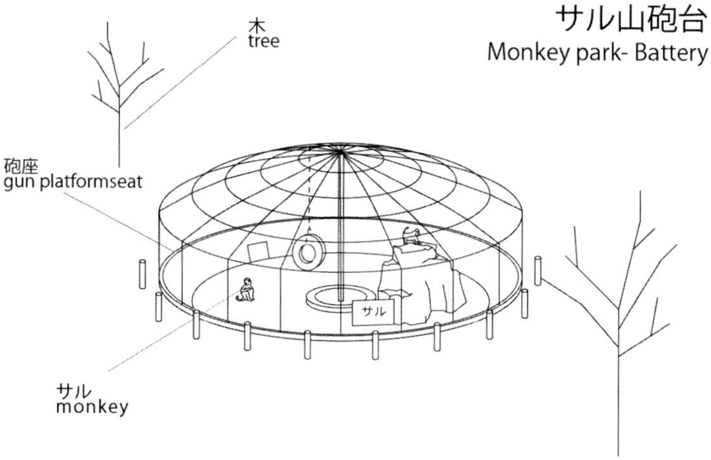

conferences.[36] A touchstone of their conversations was the pioneering work of Miyamoto Tsuneichi and Matusuura Takeshirō, two scholars and fieldworkers whose research was deeply shaped by the Japanese empire. Miyamoto was compelled to scour rural communities for much of the twentieth century after seeing folkways threatened by the homogenizing effects of governmental centralization.[37] Matsuura traveled extensively throughout Hokkaido in the mid-nineteenth century researching the Ainu people, work that was later used by the empire to bolster the island's colonial integration.[38] The historical enmeshment of fieldwork and empire includes architecture as well. In the early twentieth century, historians such as Itō Chūta and Sekino Tadashi traveled throughout China and Korea to draw and photograph architectural similarities that proved the legitimacy of Japanese colonial expansion as cultural reclamation.[39] Like the wartime ruins he documents, the very method that Shitamichi uses originates in empire. However, this blighted source does not mean that it should be forsaken, only that it too has the capacity for transformation.

From 2006 to 2012, Shitamichi expanded his fieldwork to Japan's former colonies for a project entitled *torii.* He traveled to Saipan, South Korea, Taiwan, China, and Russia in search of concrete torii that have survived decades of urban development, natural decay, and turbulent postcolonial politics.[40] Despite the time and distance separating the photographs, they all follow a simple compositional rule: The torii, or what used to be a torii, occupies the center of the image with equal attention granted to its environment. Shitamichi's strategy of hunting by building type is reminiscent of photographers such as Bernhard and Hilla Becher, but unlike the duo's obsessively tight focus on the architectural object, Shitamichi includes the surroundings to hint at the torii's generational transformations. In Saipan, we see a torii in the distance whose white paint and perpendicular form blends into a cemetery's field of crucifixes. In New Taipei City, Taiwan, a torii sits at the top of a staircase carved into a verdant hillside, suggesting that the shrine it once fronted has long been destroyed and the grounds reclaimed by plant life. And in Changchun, China, a torii stands flush with a row of buildings on a busy street, blending into its urban environment as an entryway to a parking lot. The prosaic existence of these torii is radically different from their former use. After settler colonialists first built shrines to claim territory, the government instituted an expansive campaign of overseas shrine building to announce their control and mold people into ideal imperial subjects through coerced worship and cultural assimilation.[41] What is now a lonely piece of concrete on the side of the road was once a sacred portal to ground graced by the disembodied presence of the emperor. With this original function long since erased, the torii are now indexical monuments to urban, architectural, and political change. The story of postcolonial transformation is not necessarily communicated by the gate itself, but rather the myriad ways that it has been reused and adapted to new environments.

Performing Transformation

Once you discover an architectural remnant of war or colonialism, then what? Do you ring the nearest heritage council, or describe it in your field notebook and move along? Perhaps you tag it with graffiti to show your disgust or place a solemn flower in remembrance. Beginning in 2004, Shitamichi began using the sites he discovered as places to party. The first iteration of his seven-part *Re-Fort Project,* entitled *Party Occupying the*

Ruins of War (*Sensō haikyo senryō pātī*), was hosted at a former military weapons testing facility in Chiba and involved friends simply chatting, drinking, and listening to music in an empty concrete bunker. Six other iterations of the *Re-Fort Project* have occurred throughout the country. Each event uses imperial heritage as a stage for group activities that blend play and remembrance without falling too deeply into either irreverence or solemnity. For example, *Re-Fort Project 5,* entitled *When the Sun Vanishes, We Light Fireworks* saw Shitamichi and his friends hire a pyrotechnician to launch fireworks from an abandoned artillery emplacement overlooking a bay in Shimonoseki. With assistance from the Maemichi Art Center, the group organized a two-day public event that included group walks, discussions, beer drinking, and a one-minute-long fireworks show on the morning of July 22, 2009, during a solar eclipse.[42] The performance spectacularized the curious relationship between imperial remains, their environment, and our wavering attention spans that so easily lapse into forgetfulness. Onlookers' eyes were drawn to the cosmic dance of the eclipse and the fireworks flickering in the darkness above the bay, not the hidden concrete platform they were launched from. Nonetheless, that small piece of concrete hiding in the darkness was momentarily transformed from a brush-covered ruin into a stage. And once the sun returned to the sky, the emplacement returned to its previously hidden state, performing the potential of all imperial ruins to move in and out of historical focus.

People live with the wreckage of empire, be it in "enemy houses" or concrete hangars. In *Re-Fort Project 4,* entitled *Our Seven-Day War,* Shitamichi and his friends decided to do the same and camp in an abandoned concrete turret for a week (Figure 5). Several architects joined the experiment, including Ichinose Aya, Toki Ayano, Higuchi Takahiko, and Hama Sadashi, to extend the livable space of the turret with a raised platform constructed from wooden joinery. With this addition, the turret was momentarily transformed into an ad hoc beach house complete with a fabric canopy and views of the sea. The contrast between vacation-worthy scenery and decrepit concrete ruins recalls the work of another postwar architecture sleuth, Paul Virilio, who famously documented abandoned Nazi bunkers on the beaches of France for his book *Bunker Archaeology.* Virilio called them "concrete altars built to face the void of the ocean" and was struck by the fact that these behemoths continued to silently exist with little acknowledgment from surrounding communities.[43] An altar is ceremonial, not to be profaned by everyday activities, and Virilio's study—though critical—left them touched only by his camera. Shitamichi on the other hand uses military ruins as playgrounds. And where Virilio saw the nuclear paranoia of his age embedded in these military "survival

Figure 5. Shitamichi Motoyuki, *Re-Fort Project 4: Our Seven-Day War*, 2007. Courtesy of the artist.

machines," Shitamichi's performances revel in the potential of architectural transformation, even if only for a week.[44]

Monkeys living in an old artillery emplacement, elderly men sitting on a once sacred gate, and parties in an abandoned bunker. There is something slyly humorous about Shitamichi's photographs and performances that disrupts the serious air of imperial history and heritage. His tongue-in-cheek attitude is clearly influenced by "street observation studies" (*rojō kansatsugaku*), a long-standing practice of photographing the bizarre, mundane, and bizarrely mundane in Japanese cities. Street observation was formalized in the 1980s by the artist Akasegawa Genpei and architectural historian Fujimori Terunobu as a platform to find and document strange urban artifacts that serve no discernible purpose.[45] Examples include stairways that lead nowhere, doors that no longer open, and unreachable handrails. All these "properties" (*bukken*), as street observers called them, had a specific function that had been lost or recontextualized by natural disaster, wartime destruction, and postwar development.[46] With a group of other like-minded "architecture detectives" (*kenchiku tantei*), the duo documented and disseminated their fieldwork findings using satirical forms of bureaucratic media, including expressionless photographs, formalized paperwork, and self-serious symposia.[47] Though of course funny, street observation studies was also propelled by a critique of profit-driven urban development and the expectation of maximum spatial efficiency. Akasegawa explained that "capitalism does not tolerate such uneconomical practices" and yet, against all odds, pieces of useless architecture persist.[48] In the words of historian Jordan Sand, street observation became popular because it "reaffirmed that the individual consumer could be more than a passive beneficiary (or victim) of capitalism."[49] Shitamichi's photographs of and performances with imperial remnants likewise highlight the absurdity of architectural persistence while reminding us that heritage and remembrance is not only a top-down affair. Like a staircase climbing to a nonexistent door, shrine gates and bunkers similarly remain intact, and their use—no matter how ridiculous—is up to us.

Inspired by the strong (and still very much alive) tradition of street observation studies in Japan, Shitamichi initiated a collaborative workshop series entitled *Invisible Landscape* (*Mienai fūkei*) in 2010.[50] Now totaling more than a dozen events in Japan and Taiwan, the project invites children and adults to participate in a collective street observation study, but without the aid of a camera. Instead of wandering about taking snapshots, participants are asked to meet in a specific location and carve a route through the city by creating a "word map" (*kotoba no chizu*) that describes what they see (Figure 6). Participants cannot of course document everything, so they must instead make short descriptions of things that catch their attention and connect them into a logical sequence. The resulting word maps are then used as instructions by other participants who then effectively "see" the city through another person's interests and movement. It might seem odd for a photographer to abandon their camera, but the goal of the exercise is to highlight our reliance on photography to document the built environment without self-reflexivity. The group format of the exercise also extends the duration of documentation, meaning that a person who uses a participant's word map later may find the described object in a totally different state. In a video documenting a 2017 iteration of the project, Shitamichi explains that the first goal of *Invisible Landscape* is to encourage awareness of the dynamism of cities and that "some landmarks on the 'map of words' may have moved or disappeared at any time."[51]

Though not explicitly focused on finding imperial remains, *Invisible Landscape* diagnoses the multiplicity of postimperial architectural history. Like the minor urban details discovered and described by Shitamichi's street observers, postimperial architectural history is made up of countless physical objects hiding in plain sight. Their meaning, however, cannot be fixed by a photograph. Instead, the meaning of still-existing imperial architecture is continuously redefined through the negotiation of subjective experience, either with something as simple as

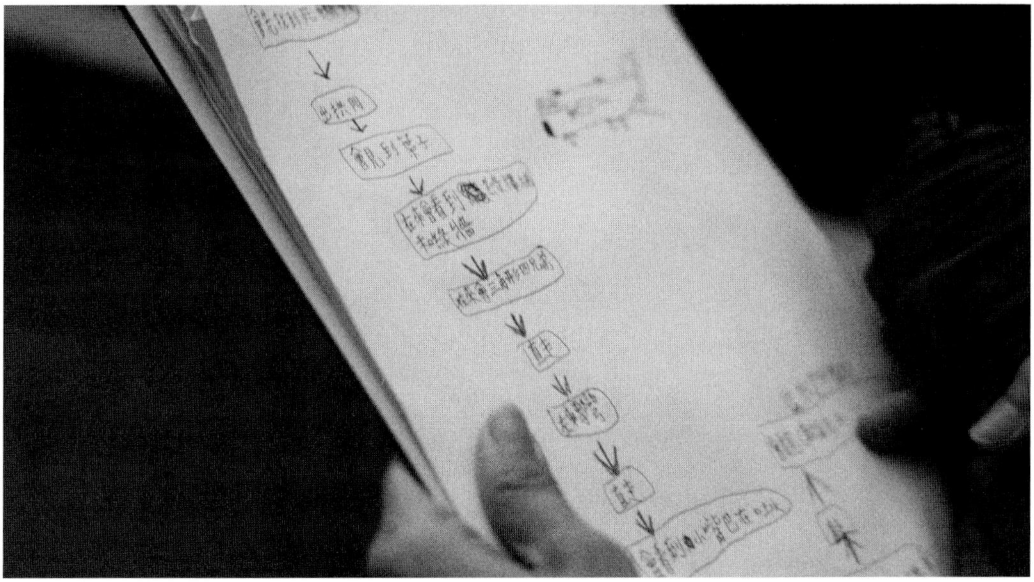

Figure 6. Shitamichi Motoyuki, *Invisible Landscape,* organized in Keelung City, Taiwan, 2024. Courtesy of the artist.

a word map or as complicated as politics. The three scenes described at the beginning of the article evidence that post-imperial architectural history is hardly unified by shared imperial provenance. Shitamichi's photographs of the environments surrounding reused shrines and bunkers capture this heterogeneous reality of adaptation while his performances actively create new opportunities for transformation. Most importantly, Shitamichi's work shows that postimperial reuse is more than just rearranging stones; it is also a creative and self-critical reuse of imperial architecture's media, methods, and concepts.

Biography
Matthew Mullane is an assistant professor of the History and Theory of Architecture at Radboud University in Nijmegen, NL. After receiving his PhD from Princeton University, he was a postdoc at Harvard University, and Tokyo College, The University of Tokyo. His book, *World Observation: Empire, Architecture, and the Global Archive of Itō Chūta* (2025), offers an alternative origin for global architecture history in nineteenth-century Japan. His writing has appeared in *Architectural Theory Review, The Journal of Architecture, Clara, AA Files, Log, gta papers, Public Domain Review,* and elsewhere.

Notes

[1] The exhibition organized objects according to nine transhistorical themes. For a fuller description of each, see Mori Art Museum, *Kenchiku no Nihon ten: sono idenshi no motarasu mono* (Japan in Architecture: Genealogies of its Transformation) (Mori Art Museum, 2018).

[2] For a full list of activities and descriptions of the annual festival themes going back to 2013, see Gunsan Time Travel Festival, last modified February 14, 2025, https://festival.gunsan.go.kr/.

[3] Hyun Kyung Lee, "Beyond 'Imagined' Nostalgia: Gunsan's Heritagization of Japanese Colonial Architecture in South Korea," *International Journal of Asian Studies* 20, no. 1 (2021): 95–96.

[4] Malcolm Foley and John Lennon, "Editorial: Heart of Darkness," *International Journal of Heritage Studies* 2, no. 4 (1996): 195. For more on dark tourism in Japan, see Ide Akira, *Dāku tsūrizumu—kanashimi no kioku wo meguru tabi* (Dark Tourism: A Trip Through Regretful Memories) (Gentōsha, 2018).

[5] See *KADIST,* "Moving Stones," https://kadist.org/program/moving-stones/. Accessed February 27, 2025.

[6] The photograph is part of a larger project entitled *torii* and was shown at the Mori Art Museum in a 2015 exhibition entitled *MAM Collection 01: Two Asian Maps—*

Ozawa Tsuyoshi and Shitamichi Motoyuki. The exhibition was held in an auxiliary space, not the main exhibition halls used for the aforementioned *Japan in Architecture* show.

7 Yoshihisa Amae, "Pro-colonial or Postcolonial? Appropriation of Japanese Colonial Heritage in Present-day Taiwan," *Journal of Current Chinese Affairs* 40, no. 1 (2011): 28–29.

8 Shitamichi Motoyuki, *torii* (Michi Laboratory, 2013), 62.

9 Leo T. S. Ching, *Anti-Japan: The Politics of Sentiment in Postcolonial East Asia* (Duke University Press, 2019), 116–31.

10 Martin Pawley, *Terminal Architecture* (Reaktion Books, 1998), 111.

11 Jong-Heon Jin, "Demolishing Colony: The Demolition of the Old Government-General Building in Chosŏn," in *Sitings: Critical Approaches to Korean Geography*, ed. Timothy R. Tangherlini and Sallie Yea (University of Hawai'i Press, 2008), 54.

12 Frantz Fanon, *The Wretched of the Earth* [1961], trans. Richard Philcox (Grove Press, 2004), 6.

13 Using Allied ships, about six million ethnic Japanese people were transported back to the mainland, and one million ethnically non-Japanese to their respective countries. See Lori Watt, *When Empire Comes Home: Repatriation and Reintegration in Postwar Japan* (Harvard University Asia Center, 2009). For more on the strategic memorialization of the nuclear attacks on Japan as a barrier to colonial memory, see Lisa Yoneyama, *Hiroshima Traces: Space, Time, and the Dialectics of Memory* (University of California Press, 1999).

14 Carol Gluck, "Modernity in Common: Japan and World History," in *Internationalizing Japan Studies: Dialogues, Interactions, Dynamics* (Tokyo University of Foreign Studies, 2017), 33–34.

15 Jordan Sand, "Subaltern Imperialists: The New Historiography of the Japanese Empire," *Past and Present*, no. 255 (Nov. 2014): 274.

16 For a recent book that explicitly joins colonial and modern architecture, see *Telling the Modern History of the Architecture of the Japanese Empire: Past, Present, Future* (*Dainippon teikokuki no kenchikubutsu ga kataru kindaishi: kako genzai mirai*), ed. Kamizuru Hisahiko (Bensei shuppan, 2022). For a fuller list of English and Japanese sources on the topic, see Matthew Mullane, "Architecture of Japan—Meiji Period," *Oxford Bibliographies*, last updated July 24, 2024, https://www.oxfordbibliographies.com/display/document/obo-9780190922467/obo-9780190922467-0100.xml.

17 In late 2023, the archive celebrated its tenth anniversary with a sweeping exhibition entitled *Japanese Modern Architects* (*Nihon no kingendai kenchikukatachi*). The exhibition included wartime memorials, but no colonial works. See the exhibition catalog *Japanese Modern Architects* (*Nihon no kingendai kenchikukatachi*) (Agency for Cultural Affairs, 2022).

18 Just as one example, the famous architect Tatsuno Kingo is celebrated in Japan for designs such as the 1914 Tokyo Station, but he also exerted a huge influence on colonial architecture in Korea. For more, see Tristan R. Grunow, "Paving Power: Western Urban Planning and Imperial Space from the Streets of Meiji Tokyo to Colonial Seoul," *Journal of Urban History* 42, no. 3 (2016): 506–56.

19 Yukiko Koga, *Inheritance of Loss: China, Japan, and the Responsibility of Redemption After Empire* (University of Chicago Press, 2016), 74.

20 Kevin Blackburn and Edmund Lim, "The Japanese War Memorials of Singapore: Monuments of Commemoration and Symbols of Japanese Imperial Ideology," *South East Asia Research* 7, no. 3 (Nov. 1999): 334–35.

21 Janet Poole, "The Remains of Colonial History," in *Spaces of Possibility: In, Between, and Beyond Korea and Japan*, ed. Clark W. Sorensen and Andrea Gevurtz Arai (University of Washington Press, 2016), 22–23.

22 Poole, "The Remains," 40. The terms "pro-demolitionist" and "pro-conservationist" shaped the public debate over the demolition of the Japanese General Government Building between 1995 and 1996. For more, see Hyun Kyung Lee, *'Difficult Heritage' in Nation Building: South Korea and Post-Conflict Japanese Colonial Occupation Architecture* (Palgrave Macmillan, 2019), 159–209.

23 Amae, "Pro-colonial or Postcolonial?," 28–29.

24 Amae, 35.

25 For more on the monument and its use in wartime celebrations, see Kenneth J. Ruoff, *Imperial Japan at Its Zenith: The Wartime Celebration of the Empire's 2,600th Anniversary* (Cornell University Press, 2014).

26 Barak Kushner, "Heroes, Victims and the Quest for Peace: War Monuments and the Contradiction of Japan's Post-Imperial Commemoration," in *Sites of Imperial Memory: Commemorating Colonial Rule in the Nineteenth and Twentieth Centuries*, ed. Dominik Geppert and Frank Muller (Manchester University Press, 2015), 72.

27 Helen J. S. Lee, "Binding Perceptions: Images of Korea in Colonial Documentary Photography," *The Review of Korean Studies* 22, no. 1 (June 2019): 234.

[28] Kate McDonald, *Placing Empire: Travel and the Social Imagination in Imperial Japan* (University of California Press, 2017), xiv.
[29] For more on colonial preservation and photography in Korea, see Hyung Il Pai, *Heritage Management in Korea and Japan: The Politics of Antiquity and Identity* (University of Washington Press, 2013), 134–41.
[30] See Kōkoku Keishin Kai, *Photographs of Japan's Most Famous Shrines* (*Zenkoku yūmei jinja oshashin chō*) (Kōkoku keishin kai, 1922).
[31] Ariella Aïsha Azoulay, *Potential History: Unlearning Imperialism* (Verso Books, 2019), 2.
[32] Ann Laura Stoler, "Introduction: 'The Rot Remains': From Ruins to Ruination," in *Imperial Debris: On Ruins and Ruination,* ed. Ann Laura Stoler (Duke University Press, 2014), 29.
[33] The full portfolio is reproduced in Shitamichi Motoyuki, *Shitamichi Motoyuki sakuhinshū* (Collected Works of Shitamichi Motoyuki) (Tokyo Arts and Space, 2021).
[34] See Sebastian Conrad, *The Quest for the Lost Nation: Writing History in Japan and Germany in the American Century* (University of California Press, 2010).
[35] Ann Laura Stoler, *Duress: Imperial Durabilities in Our Times* (Duke University Press, 2016), 8–10.
[36] See Traveling Research Laboratory, last updated December 16, 2021, https://www.travelingresearchlaboratory.com/.
[37] For more on Miyamoto's use of photography in the field, see Michio Hayashi, "The Uncultured in the Photography of Miyamoto Tsuneichi: Its Historical Complexity and Affective Dimension," in *Japanese Art—Transcultural Perspectives,* ed. Melanie Trede, Mio Wakita, and Christine M. E. Guth (Brill, 2024), 148–75.
[38] On the relationship between Matsuura's fieldwork and the colonization of Hokkaido, see Katsuya Hirano, "Settler Colonialism, Ecology, and Expropriation of Ainu Mosir: A Transnational Perspective," in *Migrant Ecologies: Environmental Histories of the Pacific World,* ed. James Beattie, Ryan Tucker Jones, and Edward Dallam Melillo (University of Hawai'i Press), 135–53.
[39] See Matthew Mullane, *World Observation: Empire, Architecture, and the Global Archive of Itō Chūta* (University of Pittsburgh Press, 2025); and Hyung Il Pai, "Resurrecting the Ruins of Japan's Mythical Homelands: Colonial Archaeological Surveys in the Korean Peninsula and Heritage Tourism," in *Handbook of Postcolonial Archaeology,* ed. Jane Lydon and Uzma Z. Rizvi (Routledge, 2010), 93–112.
[40] The architectural historian Nishizawa Yasuhiko has similarly employed fieldwork to better understand the scope of Japanese colonial architecture. See Nishizawa Yasuhiko, *Nihon shokuminchi kenchiku kikō: Manshū, Chōsen, Taiwan wo aruku* (Colonial Architecture Travelogue: Walking Around Manchuria, Korea, and Taiwan) (Yoshikawa kōbunkan, 2011).
[41] The process of overseas shrine building took decades and evolved over time. For a concise description of its phases, see Nakajima Michio, "Shinto Deities That Crossed the Sea: Japan's 'Oversea Shrines,' 1868 to 1945," *Japanese Journal of Religious Studies* 37, no. 1 (2010): 36–40.
[42] A poster and description of the two-day activity can be found on the Maemichi Art Center blog. See Maemichi Art Center Archive, last updated January 2, 2012, https://maemachi.exblog.jp/11458364/. A DVD documentary was also produced by the Maemichi Art Center. See *Re-Fort Project 5,* DVD (Maemichi Art Center, 2012).
[43] Paul Virilio, *Bunker Archeology* [1975], trans. George Collins (Princeton Architectural Press, 1994), 12.
[44] Virilio, *Bunker Archeology,* 39.
[45] For more on Akasegawa's early experiments in street observation, see Akasegawa Genpei, *Hyperart: Thomasson,* trans. Matt Fargo (Kaya Press, 2010). For an example of Fujimori's own methods of architectural fieldwork, see Fujimori Terunobu, *Kenchiku tantei no bōken: Tōkyō hen* (The Adventures of the Architecture Detective: Tokyo Volume) (Chikuma shobō, 1986).
[46] Akasegawa Genpei, *Hyperart Thomasson* (*Chōgeijutsu Tomason*) (Chikuma shobō, 1987), 26.
[47] For examples, see Akasegawa Genpei, Fujimori Terunobu, and Minami Shinpō, *Introduction to Street Observation Studies* (*Rojō kansatsugaku nyūmon*) (Chikuma shobō, 1986).
[48] Akasegawa, *Hyperart Thomasson,* 14.
[49] Jordan Sand, *Tokyo Vernacular: Common Spaces, Local Histories, Found Objects* (University of California Press, 2014), 105.
[50] Shitamichi's work has been included in exhibitions surveying contemporary art and street observation. See *An Expressive History of Streets and Observation: Modernology Now* (*Rojō to kansatsu wo meguru hyōgenshi: Kōgengaku no 'genzai'*), ed. Hiroshima City Museum of Contemporary Art (Film Art Inc., 2013).
[51] "見えない風景 Walk with your eyes." YouTube, uploaded by Shitamichi Motoyuki, October 25, 2017, https://www.youtube.com/watch?v=HMcTtPd66iU.

Figure 1. Katharina Wiedwald, Palimpsest of the house Am Strom 53, 2024. Rendition of the layered facades: Fachwerk, veranda and Dutch gable, exhibition space and studio. Courtesy of Katharina Wiedwald.

Gustav Elgin

Unfinished Collapse

Provenances of the Am Strom 53 Houses

The house Am Strom 53 dovetails with a line of half-timbered buildings that run along the Warnow River in Warnemünde, a quaint seaside resort some twelve kilometers north of Rostock. It is structured like a palimpsest and consists of (1) a Fachwerk-style building, erected sometime before 1544; overlaid by (2) a Dutch gable and a wood-and-glass veranda, built to accommodate seaside tourists in the 1850s; both transformed into (3) the Edvard-Munch-Haus (EMH), an exhibition space doubling as a studio for artists-in-residence that opened in 1998 (named after painter Edvard Munch, who spent eighteen months in the house's veranda)[1] (Figure 1).

While researching the house's complex history in Rostock's city archives for the exhibition *Poetics of Property* at the EMH, the earliest trace my cocurators Katharina Wiedwald, Jenny Trømborg, and I were able to locate was a 1544 cadastral map—the first known of the area—in which the plot occupied by the house today is already marked as developed. Our imprecise dating of the first of the three strata is, in other words, excused by the fact that the building predates the oldest surviving housing maps of Warnemünde. Archaeometrical techniques would have proven equally unhelpful. More than four hundred fifty years of gradual modifications have seen its materials replaced many times over, most recently when the building was renovated and repurposed into the Edvard-Munch-Haus. At the time, only parts of the facade, the veranda, and a small section of the beamwork were preserved. In sum, the building today has no discernible origin or *arche*.[2] It eclipses Mecklenburg's archives and has long since eclipsed itself materially—a free-floating vector with no fixed beginning or end.

Such objects pose all sorts of problems for histories preoccupied with origins, originals, first causes, and the like.[3] Michel de Certeau described them as "archeo-logical," compulsively obsessed with authenticity and the Freudian *Urvater*.[4] Surely, then, a house that resists origin must also run counter to a historiographical practice concerned with provenance, at least if the term is understood in its modern sense as the tracing of an item's chain of custody to an Ur-proprietor for purposes of authentication. But it is in light of more recent architectural reappraisals of the term that particularly apocryphal buildings, those with uncertain, meandering, and interrupted

Future Anterior
Volume XXII, Numbers 1–2
Summer / Winter 2025

provenances, have begun to register as things of interest.[5] The lens has here been adjusted in such a way that one focuses less on a building's singular origin than on its displacements, including but not limited to its transfers between proprietors, its reproduction across various media, its scripts for bodily movement, the transport routes of its materials, its gradual transformations through weathering and daily repair, to the more abrupt shocks of renovation and restoration. If buildings then sometimes occur to us as reasonably stable or self-contained, this new provenance optic dispels the illusion by revealing a high-resolution picture of the myriad processes that have them uninterruptedly and surreptitiously *repeat* themselves.

The movement of repetition is surreptitious precisely because it is continuous; the constancy of repetition sustains the illusion of stability and self-sufficiency. Only when the repetitions momentarily stop, at the grain boundaries between working and nonworking systems (these are the loopholes through which a provenance optic may insert itself), do the infrastructures that subtend them become visible: "When you turn on the faucet and water does not flow, the entire water system leaps into the cognitive field."[6] Put differently: If smoothly operating systems are silent types, then broken, halting ones are loquacious. By this measure, the house Am Strom 53, and its layered slow-motion collapses,[7] makes for an exceptionally gossipy building.[8]

The House Formerly Known as X̄

The house Am Strom 53 is several different houses. In fact, Am Strom 53 is only one of its more recent designations. Its oldest known referent is a rune-like symbol that a standard keyboard cannot produce: X̄, a so-called *Hausmarke* or house mark. By the time this rune-like symbol appears at the bottom-left of a 1586 legal complaint that the houses' past owners levied against the Hanseatic city of Rostock, it is in the final stages of a very gradual process of obsolescence (Figure 2).

House marks were typically carved onto boundary markers or the beam above a building's front door, denoting at once the proper name of the house and its residing family. Provisionally, one could think of the mark as a mash-up of surname and address (though, as we will see, the comparison to these present-day phenomena underestimates the historical specificity of this particular semantic jointure). Besides signatures on documents or the marking of boundaries, among its routine uses was the designation of ownership, carved also into the mobile belongings of the family that the mark signified.[9] At a time when the village's population consisted exclusively of fishing families, that was incredibly useful if, say, a rowboat had been unmoored

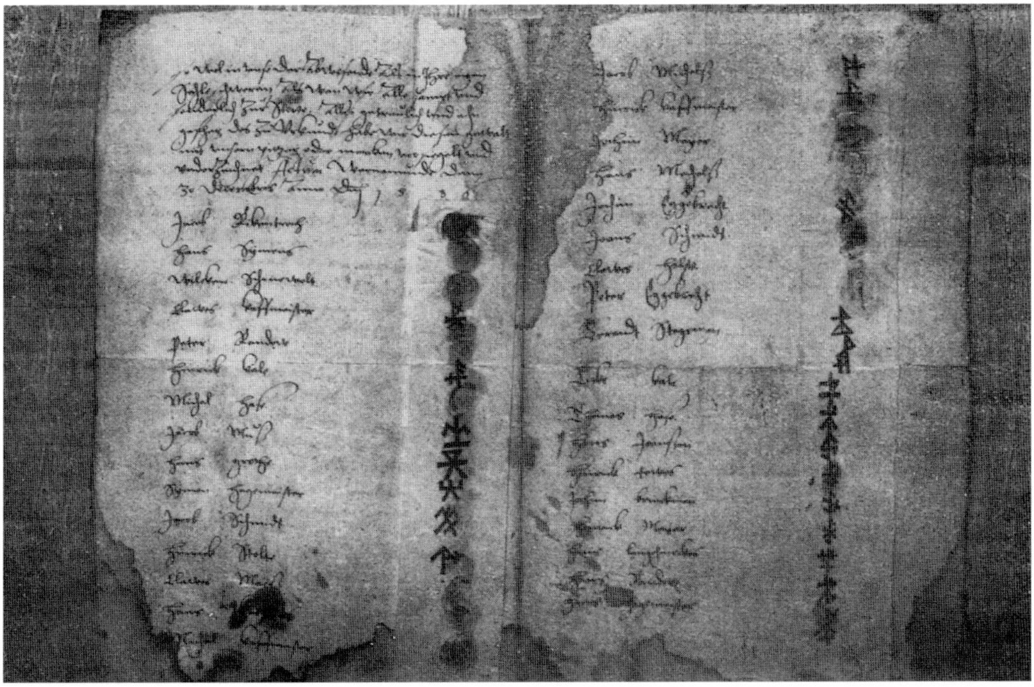

Figure 2. Process Vollmacht with house marks, 1586. The last page shows signatures of thirty-three residents of Warnemünde, with house marks added in ink and embossed seals. The house mark of the house later called Am Strom 53 appears fourth from the bottom on the left side of the document. Courtesy of Landesarchiv Schwerin.

by a storm surge and drifted down the Warnow to Rostock. The mark would allow boats and fishing equipment to be identified and traced back to their proper place, that is, the house they signified: the *Sitz,* or ancestral seat of a family, and the source of the legitimacy of the property claim. House marks were scripts that programmed and called for the repetition of actions: the tracing, return, and, hence, the affirmation of property.

The Non-synchronicity of the House Mark

Folk historian Friedrich Barnewitz, author of what is colloquially known as the *Warnemünder Bibel,* the most comprehensive local history of the village to date, argued in 1925 that this property regime, de jure, at one point had likely granted families allodial title to their houses and plots, implying absolute ownership with no overlord.[10] The house mark would therefore have functioned as an emblem demarcating a microscopic, sovereign territory, passed along patrilineal lines from father to eldest son across generations. With this idea in mind, we return to the contents of the 1586 legal complaint. In it, thirty-three Warnemünder families argue in front of the Hofgericht of Güstrow for the repeal of a trade ban that the city of Rostock had imposed upon the village in 1582.[11] The appeal was untenable. Rostock's powerful commercial guild, the Schiffergesellschaft, was not particularly keen to afford commercial autonomy to a transit village that had, since Rostock had purchased it from the local duke in 1323, given the city's merchants control over one of the central access points to the Baltic Sea. If it is unsurprising that the complaint never made it out of medieval Mecklenburg's labyrinthine court system, then, it should strike one as odd, given what we have claimed about the apparent extent of allodial autonomy, that such a complaint was made at all. Why would families whose sovereignty was allodial, that is, absolute, require the permission of a city council to exercise trading rights?

Now, while the regime characterized by the house mark in the sixteenth century was still formally in place in Warnemünde, it had long since been superseded and captured by Rostock's Hanseatic law, the so-called *Lübsches Recht,* ratified by the Mecklenburg's prince Henry Borwin in 1218. The house mark as it registers as a signature on the 1586 court document, then, is a vestigial remnant of some old Germanic legal code haunting the newer, municipal legal form that the written legal document itself represents.[12] For while *Lübsches Recht* and Rostock's court system had superseded primogenital allod, the house mark continued to dictate a program of action: social customs that remained very much operative. All of this makes the complaint a fairly elegant and self-contained example of what Ernst Bloch called a non-synchronicity: the asymmetrical and hesitant relationship between urban and rural areas in Germany—a territorially uneven modernization process in which old and new cultural forms coexisted in complex unions that complicate the determinism of linear models of historical progress.[13]

Repetitions

The house mark's resilience has in large part to do with how it, and the customary form of allod, maintained themselves in floor plans. Now, like other sixteenth-century Warnemünder houses, ⩱ was constructed according to a standardized and literally straight-forward schema.[14] To maximize the number of buildings that could present a facade toward the Warnow, plots were narrow and tightly juxtaposed. Side aisles, otherwise typical of Mecklenburg farmers' houses, had to be omitted, leaving space only for a slender central hall called the *Diele* that lead into what, in Low German, was called the *voerstuv* (front room) and the *achterstuv* (back room), continuing further into the *olendeel* (retirement quarters, literally "old section" or "old part") at the rear.

This thin, elongated, tract-like building cross-sectioned the lives of the Warnemünder into a tripartite tableau. While voerstuv and achterstuv were inhabited and used by heirs and their families (father, mother, and children), the olendeel housed elders once the firstborn son had taken over the fishing business. The generational journey of a Warnemünder firstborn son thus followed a simple script: birth in the voerstuv, and death in the achterstuv.[15]

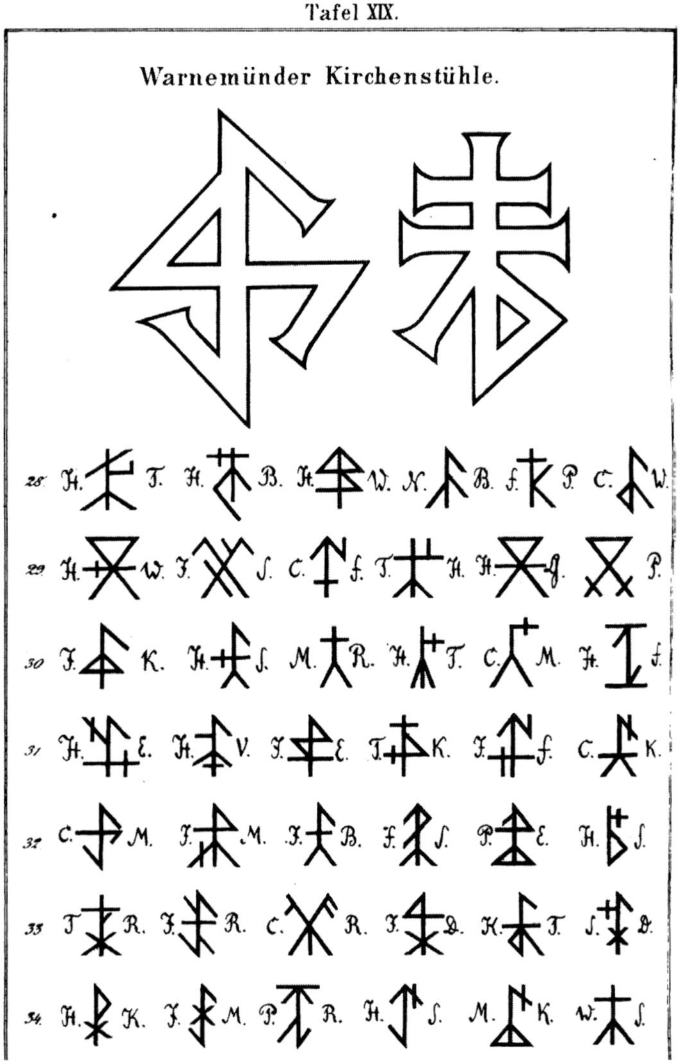

Figure 3. Carl Gustav Homeyer, drawings of house marks found on Warnemünde's church pews, most likely from the late sixteenth century. From Homeyer, *Die Haus- und Hofmarke* (Berlin, 1870).

Male, noninheriting family members, on the other hand, had to build and establish their own *Haus,* in both the material and symbolic senses of the word. Just as buildings would thus repeat and multiply with small variations in the layout, so too would house marks of offshoot family branches proliferate with subtle variations in the linework of the rune, productive of a surprisingly rich pictorial grammar, attested in the collection of marks carved into Warnemünde's old church pews (Figure 3). The arguably most crucial and fundamental repetition work was performed by the village's female population, not only through reproductive labor in the narrow sense, through childbirth and rearing, but also, alluded to by Barnewitz, through maintenance work: While fishermen were away on protracted seafaring trips, women worked on the making and mending of clothes and fishing nets, gardening, and the carpentry necessary for maintenance of the house.[16]

The deep entrenchment of these social scripts may explain why variations of an older, customary legal form echoed with relative poise through constant fires and storm surges, despite intermittent capture by the Duchy of Mecklenburg, the Danes, the Swedes, Rostock, and their often-hostile constitutions, from the Middle Ages all the way up to the eighteenth century. This was a property regime not dependent on state or municipal authority, but rather encoded in floor plans and house marks, both sustained through daily and generational reproductive labor, allowing for a collapse so reluctant as to preserve a semblance of stability.

Volkskunde in Mecklenburg

It was the apparent resilience of old life forms in Mecklenburg's villages—their insistent, stiff-necked cultural backwardness—that made them such beloved destinations for a group of scholars who, between the eighteenth and nineteenth centuries, established the arch-German discipline called *Volkskunde.*[17] Informed by ethnological studies in the colonies, a retraining of the ethnological gaze toward one's own backyard, they were concerned principally with the mundane cultural practices, or what they called the *Lebensformen,* of rural Europeans.[18]

Now, in Mecklenburg, some *Volkskundler* had the distinct impression of having come across cultural strata comparable to those uncovered in the great archaeological sites of the classical world.[19] The sense was that the ancient cultural praxes had been kept alive by generations of the local populace—gestures frozen in time, whose provenance could supposedly be traced back uninterruptedly to ancient Germanic tribal forms of life. The folk historian Carl Gustav Homeyer regarded the house mark, and its lasting use in some places well into the late 1850s, as one such fantastical, living fossil, and in the introduction to his treatise on the subject, Homeyer announces the topic in words that seem to spell out an indebtedness as much to ethnographical rigor as to Romantic nationalism: "It was the mystical, rune-like shape, the deep concealment from which this world of signs, which had remained almost alien to scholarly knowledge, now emerged in countless dots scattered according to time, space and trade, that attracted and drove me to carefully investigate its origin, its external and factual distribution, its significance for legal life, its gradual disappearance and its present-day remnants."[20] His subsequent discovery that the rune had not only been in use across Mecklenburg and Rügen but in the Netherlands, Austria, Switzerland, and Scandinavia pointed for Homeyer furthermore toward an ostensible mutual legal origin for the Germanic peoples, suggesting on fairly shaky grounds that the runes could be traced to Indo-European tribes, more specifically (and unsurprisingly, given the nationalistic tenor of mid-nineteenth-century ethnographic discourse in Germany following Fichte's *Addresses to the German Nation*) the Teutons.[21]

By 1868, however, that had all dramatically changed. Traveling Mecklenburg by train to map out the surviving uses of the house mark, he struggled to find a single living Warnemünder who had a clue what the signs carved into their houses and church pews meant, one interviewee mistaking them for "Hebrew letters."[22] Homeyer's clear exasperation at the confusion between the marks and Hebrew script has antisemitic overtones. We will shortly return to this aspect of the reception of the property regime of the house mark, and the discipline of Volkskunde more generally, but for now, suffice to say that the mark in mid-nineteenth-century Warnemünde, and the particular form of life it had represented, was about to entirely slip away to the benefit of a radically restructured and markedly more self-conscious social topos, the *lifestyles* of two arch-modern subjects: tourists and patients.

Lebensform to Lifestyle

Since the nineteenth century, increasing concern had been directed toward the storm floods that at irregular intervals swept away Warnemünde's houses. In 1802, a major campaign to stabilize the shoreline was initiated by the naturalist Adolph Christian Siemssen from the University of Rostock, beginning with the mass transplantation of trees from the forests surrounding the city to the tidal marshes near Warnemünde. Then, in 1853, the coastline was reinforced with a perpendicular pier that, beyond protecting against storm floods, caused dunes to accumulate along Warnemünde's shore.[23]

The unintended but not entirely unpleasant side effect of these two anti-flood interventions was thus that Warnemünde suddenly found itself in possession of two kinds of ecosystems whose stock had drastically risen in step with the intensification of nineteenth-century medical discourse: a forest and a beach. Already in 1843, resident physician and balneologist Friedrich Wilhelm Schütz had published a treatise on the benefits of the particular qualities of Warnemünde's air, and the mineral composition of its waters, for practically all ailments ranging from the respiratory to the nervous. When the Lloydbahn extended its railway line from Berlin to Warnemünde in 1863, it was a perfect storm: Industrialized Rostock and Berlin were teeming with hypochondriacs and neurotics who had surplus capital and free time to spend, smog-filled cities to withdraw from, and effective mass transportation of the steam locomotive to do so with.

Thus, if Homeyer in 1865 had trouble finding house marks in Warnemünde, he would, incidentally, have had no difficulty finding a place to spend the night. Since the 1840s, the people of Warnemünde had started to reapply their expertise in boatbuilding to raise seasonal pavilions in mastwood and canvas in order to accommodate a massive yearly influx of health-conscious summer tourists. By the early twentieth century, the verandas had ossified into permanent structures characteristic of Warnemünde today. Winter-garden-like in appearance, equipped with large pressed-pane windows that not only efficiently circulated air but also offered the perfect conditions for seeing, and being seen: Semi-transparent drapes in muslin, net, and voiles were in vogue and afforded tourists the ability to modulate their double visibility toward the now-teeming Warnow promenade (in a 1907 photograph, Munch has staged his ghostlike, double-exposed silhouette in the veranda, peering at the street through the curtain [Figure 4]).[24]

That illness and life in these resort towns was also becoming an aesthetic rather than purely medicinal concern, a self-conscious, fashion-oriented style of life rather than the supposedly more grounded, authentic form of life that had interested the Volkskundler, is best documented in the second chapter of Thomas Mann's Buddenbrooks, where Travemünde (which, roughly speaking, is to Lübeck what Warnemünde is to Rostock) serves as the mise-en-scène for a symptomatic voyeuristic doubling: The princely ideal of withdrawal turns, for Tony Buddenbrooks, into the social desire to be witnessed doing so.[25] And, if illness in *Der Tod in Venedig* had become a question of beauty, in the later *Zauberberg,* the time- and capital-intensive existence of the dying tubercular has intensified into a mode of life that stylizes every aspect of the self, from fashion and sexuality to career: a lifestyle, indeed.

Around the same time Mann writes Buddenbrooks, another dramatic transformation occurs along the Warnow river. Within the span of a few years a good portion of the old Fachwerkbauten had, in Potemkin-like fashion, tacked gables to their facades.[26] If it was still possible in the 1860s for Thomas Buddenbrooks to safely locate Hanseatic prestige in Lübeck's stepped gables ("die Nachbarschaft war sympathisch: gute Bürgerhäuser mit Giebeln"), now, in 1880s Warnemünde, they had become petit-bourgeois commonplace (Figure 5).[27] Behind the veneer disappeared not only the facades of the local Fachwerk but the house marks once engraved into their beams. For the mark, however, this was merely the coup de grâce. Its legal-signifying function had been in accelerating decline ever since jurisdiction over property claims in the nineteenth century had been assumed by municipal authorities and ownership came to be formalized through documentary title. Furthermore, the *Altenteil* was no longer set aside for the older generation but repurposed as a temporary summer residence

Figure 4. Edvard Munch, *Self-Portrait in Front of His Paintings in Am Strom 53, Warnemünde,* silver gelatin print, 1907. Courtesy of Munch, Oslo.

Figure 5. Facade of the house Am Strom 53, 1996. Photo: Angelika Fischer. Courtesy of Edvard-Munch-Haus e.V.

for the nuclear family as to make more room for tourists. The house mark's script of a slow, generational drift from front to back—birth in the *Voerstuv* and death in the *Altenteil*—had collapsed into a quick, seasonal retreat. (Munch left Warnemünde in 1908, calling the village, in a letter to the collector Gustav Schiefler, a "horribly bourgeois place"—an accusation, one has to believe, that would have been completely unthinkable some sixty years prior.)[28]

Unfinished, Unfinished Collapses

When the Edvard-Munch-Haus e.V. acquired the building in 1994, it was in a sorry state. The photographs taken by Angelika Fischer shortly before its renovation are marvelously surreal: exposed electrical cables dangling next to a Byzantine plumbing system, paint peeling off in impressive sheets from the living room ceiling. If inertia had carried the building on for a while, it was clearly nearing a point of complete exhaustion (Figures 5 and 6).

The collapse results from a rich mixture of events that will here only be briefly summarized: Lieselotte and her father, Albert, acquired the house in 1918, after the death of its previous owner, Albert Nielsen, who had inherited the building from the Lotse Karl Nielsen in 1908 (Munch returned from a trip to Berlin to find Karl dead on the veranda sofa, shortly after he committed himself into Dr. Jacobsen's nerve clinic in Denmark). In 1955, amid continuing postwar housing scarcity, the Council of Ministers of the GDR enacted the *Verordnung über die Lenkung des Wohnraums.*[29] The ordinance had two interconnected functions. First, it empowered municipal housing authorities to allocate living space to those in need, including by mandating private citizens to accommodate additional households if their dwellings were deemed underoccupied. Second, it authorized local housing offices to enforce repairs in cases where housing conditions were considered inadequate for cohabitation.

Lieselotte and Albert were affected by both aspects of the law. While it was in effect between 1955 and 1989, they took in at least seventeen families. On several occasions, they were forced to carry out modernization work on the house's plumbing and to reinforce its ceilings. Despite their unrelenting attempts at sabotage—ranging in degree of nuisance from last-minute cancellations of meetings with housing inspectors to outright refusals to take in tenants or to maintain or modernize the property—they yielded only at the threat of punishment. Albert passed away in 1966. When Lieselotte died in 1990, the house was practically derelict.

That Lieselotte refused to play the part a draconic socialist state expected of her is not to say she was some sort of antiauthoritarian hero. If anything, she was excessively human: Her letters reveal that her refusal to acquiesce to DDR rule—both to the repair orders and to the housing allocation program—was, at least in part, a kind of protest against her husband's killing during the Nazis' invasion of the Soviet Union in 1943, and the Soviets' later refusal to locate and return his body. Moreover, her letters to the local housing authorities make clear that she did not find a system in which she had no control over whom she had to show hospitality to, terribly appealing. Lieselotte

Figure 6. Living room of the house Am Strom 53, 1996. Photo: Angelika Fischer. Courtesy of Edvard-Munch-Haus e.V.

seems, instead, to have remained committed to another property regime: the one she had known under Nazi rule.

Remember that for Ernst Bloch, the concept of nonsimultaneity was deployed to explain the rise of reactionary movements in Germany during the Weimar Republic: why mildewed ideals reemerge to haunt modern states. For a large portion of the German intelligentsia, however, the problem was approached from the inverse angle. Modernization was articulated in negative terms, as the loss of authenticity, a fall from grace, of which Gustav Homeyer's indignant attitude to the waning of the house mark is just one example.

In the 1920s and '30s, a stock argument among antimodern, reactionary intellectuals was that the modern constitution, and its distribution of power across separate bodies, was disastrously disjointing state and society, nature and culture, *Volk* and *Land,* along with numerous other dyads that had ostensibly been unified in ancient Germanic forms of legal organization, such as the synthesis of governance, law, and kinship in the *Hausrecht,* which the house mark was seen to represent.[30] In response, the notorious first edition of *Land und Herrschaft* by Carl Schmitt's favorite historian, Otto Brunner, argues that the work of the *Volksgeschichtler* was precisely the careful editing away of any foreign or modern-liberal influences from their studies of Germanic cultures. Despite Brunner's important insistence on the close reading and reconstituting of past mentalities—rather than the reductive, teleological readings of history that back-project liberalism as the inevitable goal of history—he both erroneously and problematically believed not only that a purely Germanic customary law could, through this method, be reconstructed in its original, unadulterated form, but also that it should be projected forward as the legal and social foundation for a future Pan-Germanic state, one the Nazi regime was to bring to fruition (this projection is the part that, for good reason, is absent from later editions, but it remains the phantom destination of the book's itinerary).[31]

The path from these atavistic fantasies of ethnic law to a xenophobic legal form based on racial separation is both unsettling and short. And so, the house mark made an ungracious return when, on September 29, 1933, Joseph Goebbels enacted the *Reichserbhofgesetz,* a law designed to transform private property in Nazi Germany into a *res extra commercium:* an allodium that could not be traded on the free market, but only inherited within the same "racially pure" bloodline.[32] Emulating the form of property once symbolized by the house mark, estates governed by this law were affixed with cast iron runes, staging an artificial return to a racialized pastiche of the primogenital allodial system under which the house Am Strom 53 had once existed. While the house itself never formally came under its jurisdiction, Alexander von Brünneck has argued that the law's core concept of a racial cohesion between *Land* and *Volk* served as the model for the entirety of the Reich's property system, providing the judicial basis for the expropriation of "enemies of the state," Slavs, Jews, and communists, in particular.[33]

After the fall of Nazi Germany, it appears that Albert and Lieselotte remained committed to its core tenets—a claim supported not only by the excessive amount of Nazi literature and legal theory stored in the attic of the house, but also by their desperate attempts to sabotage the lives of a particular Jewish family assigned to them under the GDR's housing allocation ordinance. Between 1965 and 1966, they sent a barrage of letters to local authorities, ranging from accusations that the family was illegally receiving television from the West, to questions about their ethnicity and residency permit. Put in nonsimultaneous terms, in Fischer's photographs of the house Am Strom 53, in the flaking paint and the sagging infrastructure, we may observe the still-unfinished collapse of a racialized property regime. Moreover: The unfinished, unfinished collapse of the sixteenth-century house mark.

Dusty Provincial Museum

The claim that Edvard Munch had once lived in her house had been circulated by Lieselotte for some years by the time it came to the attention of art historian Petra Schmidt Dreyblatt.[34] The Edvard-Munch-Haus e.V. was convened shortly thereafter. Four years after Lieselotte's death in 1990, the organization had secured enough funds from private and public sponsors to acquire and renovate the house. Since the legal form eingetragener Verein (e.V.) uniquely confers upon the association the status of a juridical person, from that point onward, the house has, in a sense, been its own proprietor. Withdrawn from market circulation, the EMH has entered into a cultural economy, in which it is able, on account of its exemplary provenance, to apply for funding to host resident artists, produce exhibitions, commission research into its own history (this text is a case in point), and support ongoing maintenance and renovation work.

The first round of renovations, completed between 1995 and 1998, produced a curious hybrid. The *deel, vöörstuv* and *achterstuv* were then converted into a single open exhibition space, while the olendeel was repurposed into living quarters for visiting artists. The veranda, according to a different logic entirely, was restored into a period-room-style facsimile of what it might have looked like during Munch's stay in the house, partially based on the artist's own photographs of the space (whose experiments with black-and-white layered exposures make them an ambivalent record at best). When a house is turned into an artist's or writer's home, its history is typically collapsed into a single period, the eighteen months of Munch's past presence, in the case of the EMH. This sudden concentration of meaning produces a fascinating effect: Suddenly, seen through the rearview mirror of an exceptional provenance, the most jejune objects appear to take on great significance. A pear tree that stood in the house's courtyard for two hundred years becomes recast as the artist's still-living witness, while an old typewriter of dubious provenance, found in the attic during the renovation work, is presented to visitors as a potential index of his direct touch, a *medium* in both the technical and spiritual senses of the word.[35] Fredric Jameson spoke of the fallacies of such retrospective projections when he recalled Raymond Roussel's story of a scientist who discovers, "in a dusty provincial museum, under glass, the skull of Voltaire as a child."[36] In any case, the EMH is as much a historical index of its own time as of Munch's: a post-wall nineties when artist-in-residence programs proliferated and European investors were

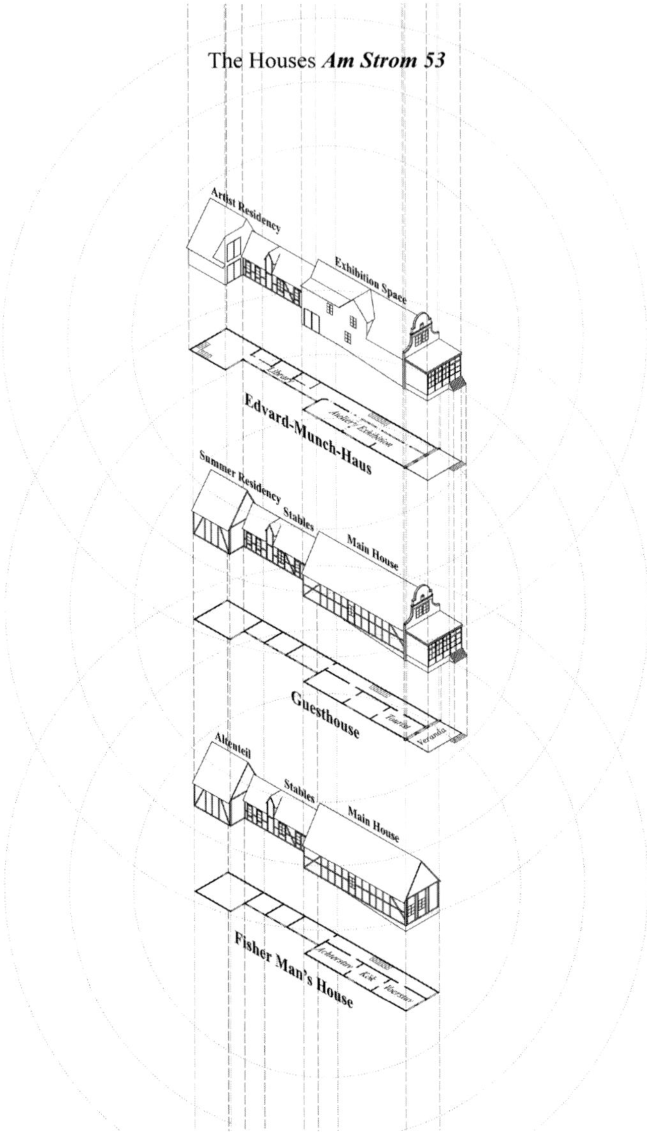

Figure 7. Katharina Wiedwald, *The Collapse of the House Am Strom 53* (2024). ISO-rendition of the collapse or co-lapse ("falling together") of three regimes: the fisher's house (Fachwerk), the guest house (veranda and Dutch gable), and the art institution (exhibition space, artist-in-residence studio). Courtesy of Katharina Wiedwald.

eager to support small-scale cultural projects—sometimes, no doubt, with a particular eye to getting a foot in the door of the Former East.

This is not to say that the EMH is any worse off for it. On the contrary, the institution's awkward, anachronistic hybridization of scripts—'90s art institution, commemorative artist's home, premodern fisher's house—makes it hesitate in precisely the overdetermined manner that makes dusty provincial museums worth researching, writing about, and exhibiting in. Though a reticence about the reductions of retrospective projections ought to explain why this text has been very careful to relegate Munch to footnotes and brackets: to avoid the kind of situation where a great artist is made to stand in as a surrogate for a missing architect, capital-B Building, or any other notion of a privileged, singular, and ultimately irretrievable origin.

Biography

Gustav Elgin is an art historian based in Oslo and Berlin. He holds an MA in Curating, Criticism and Cultural Heritage from the University of Oslo and the Humboldt University of Berlin, and a BA in art history from the University of Bergen and Freie Universität Berlin. The background of this article is the exhibition *Poetics of Property* at the Edvard Munch House in Warnemünde in 2024, curated by Elgin, Jenny H. Trømborg, and Katharina Wiedwald.

Notes

[1] In 1908, Munch leaves Warnemünde for Dr. Jacobson's nerve-clinic in Copenhagen, where he spends the next eight months.

[2] To press this point: There is no identifiable architect or *arkhi-tektōn*, as in "first builder" (though, as we will see, plenty of second, third, and subsequent builders), nor any discernible arche in the Aristotelian sense of an "origin" or "cause," precisely since there is no archive from which such an origin might be sourced.

[3] I am thinking of those concerned with authorial intent (there is no single author), vernacular styles (the links to a local vernacular *Handwerkskultur* have been inoperably severed), or conservation (piecemeal modifications have ensured that virtually none of the original material is left, no trace of an "original" state).

[4] De Certeau argues that there is a little neurosis in all forms of historiography—that the wish to murder the *Urvater* is the discipline's foundational desire. The term "archeo-logical" appears in his discussion of Joseph-François Lafitau's *Mœurs des Sauvages:* "it uses the procedures, therefore, of law or of exegesis. . . . Relative to another conception of history, they remain archaeo-logical; they make the *Arche* readable, the beginnings of Time." Michel de Certeau and James Hovde, "Writing vs. Time: History and Anthropology in the Works of Lafitau," *Yale French Studies,* no. 59 (1980): 41.

[5] *Provenance Projected. Architecture Past and Future in the Era of Circularity* at the Oslo School of Architecture and Design, in particular, from which this text takes its cue.

[6] A central premise of this text, the notion of repeating architectures and the idea of the cessation of repetition as revelatory, is taken from architectural historian Reinhold Martin. The full quote goes: "Infrastructure is what repeats. The dumbwaiter, bound to slave labor, carries bottle after bottle up to [Thomas] Jefferson's dining room. Its systemic properties tend to become visible only when the repetitions cease. If the wine ceases to appear, at some level and only for an instant, the entire apparatus of slavery comes into view. When you turn on the faucet and water does not flow, the entire water system leaps into the cognitive field." In "Do Media Determine Our Situation? Reflections on the Transatlantic Reception of Friedrich Kittler," a conversation with Reinhold Martin, Isabelle Graw, and André Rottmann, *Texte zur Kunst,* no. 98, "Media," edited by Isabelle Graw (June 2015): 37–64.

[7] Collapse is not to be understood here as a fall from grace or relative to some past greater state but—perhaps in the sense of Giorgio Agamben's irreparable—as pure presence, which disavows the notion of a more consummate past altogether. A collapse, then, describes the capacity of a building to become something else, to release and actualize potential energy, though never unaffected by an inertia of a past that unloads itself in the present.

[8] This is a paraphrase based on Marina Vishmidt's formulation that "broken infrastructures are loquacious." For the exhibition project, we took Vishmidt's conceptualization of infrastructural critique as a "critique based on contingent ruptures, with the interpretation and activation of these ruptures as the source of political meaning," and used the interpretation of these ruptures in infrastructures as the source, instead, of historical meaning. See Marina Vishmidt, "Between Not Everything and Not Nothing: Cuts Towards Infrastructural Critique," in *Former West: Art and the Contemporary After 1989,* ed. Maria Hlavajova and Simon Sheikh (MIT Press, 2017), 265–69.

[9] Regarding its specific uses in Warnemünde, see also Adolf Ahrens, "Warnemünder Hausmarken: Hakenkreuz und Wolfsangel," *Zeitschrift zur Pflege heimatlicher Art und Kunst* 10, no. 120 (1934): 589–91.

[10] Barnewitz's 1925 book is a fascinating and not unproblematic historical document in its own right. It is a book on the local culture of a tiny village, but it begins, in an almost cosmogonical gesture, at the very beginning: with speculations on the geological formation of Warnemünde's surroundings, followed by its flora and fauna. By the third chapter, the aim of this grand overture is revealed: Barnewitz wants to demonstrate that Warnemünde is, as the chapter's title puts it, down to the very geological core, "eine deutsche Pflanzung." To do so, he needed to blitz past an inconvenient fact: that the people he refers to as the "Wenden," a German term for West Slavic peoples, were the original settlers of both Rostock and Warnemünde. A brief, offhand section claims that the Wends likely did not interact with the Saxon population before they were driven away by them in the twelfth century,

and thus that the cultural habits practiced in Warnemünde in Barnewitz's day were unmingled with Slavic influence. But the displacement of the Slavic population and their customs was no clean or finished business. As late as the High Middle Ages, long after Barnewitz claimed that the last traces of the Wends had been uprooted, Rostock still had a so-called Wendisches Quartier, a Slavic district within the city. Stumbling across this deeper, Slavic substratum beneath the house at Am Strom 53 invites another reading of the house mark: as a symbolic infrastructure that aided in the ethnic codification of property and the Saxon colonization of Slavic territories—a form that then re-erupted, to use Bloch's term, along similar fault lines under Nazi property law, distinguishing between the "races" deemed capable of owning property and those who were not. Friedrich Barnewitz, *Geschichte des Hafenorts Warnemünde: unter besonderer Berücksichtigung der Volks- und Bodenkunde,* 2nd ed. (G. B. Leopold's Universitäts-Buchhandlung, 1925), 51–65.

[11] The ban placed a limit on the size of the Warnemünder fishing vessel and forced them to move their main residence to Rostock if they wanted to work in commercial trade.

[12] That Warnemünde could at all be "sold" by the local baron Heinrich der Löwen in 1323, signals that the allodial *Recht* was nominal already then.

[13] Ernst Bloch writes that Germany is even more "vulcanic," that is, marked by a more subcutaneously active history, than a country such as France. Ernst Bloch, "Nonsynchronism and the Obligation to Its Dialectics," originally published 1935, trans. Mark Ritter, *New German Critique*, no. 11 (Spring 1977): 22–38.

[14] One may glean the old sixteenth-century floor plan from the house's foundations, which follows a layout similar to the much more well-conserved neighboring house at the Alexandrinerstrasse 31, which today houses the local history museum. See Horst D. Schulz and Christoph Wegner, *Das Warnemünde-Museum* (ß Verlag & Medien GbR, 2023).

[15] This is obviously a truncation of the complex social life of the Warnemünder in the seventeenth century. We are only trying to make the point that, at the time, the generational movement script imposed by their buildings was heavily prescribed and formalized. For a more generous treatment of a Warnemünder's daily life during this period, see Barnewitz, *Geschichte des Hafenorts Warnemünde* (1925).

[16] See Barnewitz, *Geschichte des Hafenorts Warnemünde*, 223–24, 230, 234, 246–48, 251, 253.

[17] Mecklenburg is somewhat notorious for being one of the last regions in Central Europe to adopt a modern constitution, doing so only after the suicide of its Grand Duke in 1918 and the collapse of the German monarchies later that year.

[18] For one of the earliest and most influential attempts to systematize the field of *Volkskunde,* see Elard Hugo Meyer, *Deutsche Volkskunde* [Straßburg 1898] (Reprint-Verlag Leipzig, 1997).

[19] The most interesting of which is undoubtedly Richard Wossidlo, a *Volkskundler* who amassed an absurdly voluminous archive of local history in Mecklenburg (and a close friend of Adolf Ahrens, the first director of Warnemünde's local history museum). The archive is digitized and can be browsed online. Furthermore, many of the fairy tales in the Grimm brothers' *Kinder- und Hausmärchen* were sourced from Mecklenburg—a collection of regional stories was published in 2011 as *Grimms Märchen aus Mecklenburg-Vorpommern.*

[20] Author's translation. Original: "Die Hausmarke [hatte] für sich auf den eigenen Wegen, die mich zu ihr leiteten, eine ungemeine Anziehungskraft gewonnen. Es war diese mystische, runenähnliche Gestalt, die tiefe Verborgenheit, aus der diese der gelehrten Kunde fast fremd gebliebene Zeichenwelt nun in unzähligen, nach Zeit, Räumlichkeit und Gewerbe zerstreuten Punkten emportauchte, die mich reizte und trieb, dem Ursprunge, der äußeren und sachlichen Verbreitung, der Bedeutung für das Rechtsleben, dem Hinschwinden und den heutigen Überbleibseln sorgsam nachzugehen." Carl Gustav Homeyer, *Die Haus- und Hofmarke* (Verlag der Königlichen Geheimen Ober-Hofbuchdruckerei [R. v. Decker], 1870), 6.

[21] The link between the Teutons and the German people as an argument for national cohesion is articulated by Johann Gottlieb Fichte in *Addresses to the German Nation,* trans. Isaac Nakhimovsky (Cambridge University Press, 2013).

[22] Fichte, *Addresses*, 63.

[23] Aude Körfer, "Beach and Dune Management in Warnemünde," in *Coastline: Coastal Management in Germany,* ed. Rosa Reboreda, Aude Körfer, Gerald Schernewski, and Alan Pickaver (EUCC—The Coastal Union, October 2007).

[24] An aside: The setting of Munch's 1907 *Green Room* series has long been a subject of speculation. Paint analysis of the veranda walls at Am Strom 53—where Munch spent considerable time that year—reveals a green tone similar to the one used in the paintings. At the same time, Signe Endresen has proposed that the works may reference Munch's stage design for Max Reinhardt's *Kammerspiele* in Berlin, also from 1907. It could just as well be that paintings depict a sort of double exposure of both, and probably other, spaces.

[25] Thomas Mann, *Buddenbrooks: Verfall einer Familie* (S. Fischer Verlag, 1901), chapter 2.
[26] Stepped gables begin to appear sporadically in paintings and graphic depictions of Warnemünde in the 1860s, and by 1880 they cover most of the buildings along the Warnow.
[27] Mann, *Buddenbrooks,* 403.
[28] Munch writes: "Ich habe jetzt meine sämtlichen Arbeiten in Warnemünde eingepackt und werde wohl kaum dort mehr weilen. Es ist doch auch ein furchtbar bürgerlicher Ort und passt eben nicht für mich." See Edvard Munch and Gustav Schiefler, *Briefwechsel. 1902–1914,* ed. Verein für Hamburgische Geschichte (Verein für Hamburgische Geschichte, 1987), 125.
[29] The first regulation on housing allocation in the German Democratic Republic (GDR) was issued on December 22, 1955, and came into force on January 1, 1956. It replaced the previously valid Control Council Act No. 18 of March 8, 1946, which had established similar provisions for all occupation zones of Germany. *Verordnung über die Lenkung des Wohnraums, GBl. DDR I Nr. 100 (22 December 1955).*
[30] The notion of disjointment appears in everything from the state science of Carl Schmitt to the philosophy of Martin Heidegger, and the ecology of Jakob van Üexkull. For a recent discussion of the relationship between Nazism and Üexkullian ecology, see Gottfried Schnödl and Florian Sprenger, *Uexkülls Surroundings. Umwelt and the New Right* (Meson Press, 2022).
[31] Recent critiques of Brunner's book stress that the Germanic tribes were far more creolized and far less ethnically homogeneous than Brunner assumed. See, for instance, the brilliant translators' introduction to the English edition by Howard Kaminsky and James Van Horn Melton. Otto Brunner, *Land and Lordship: Structures of Governance in Medieval Austria,* trans. Howard Kaminsky and James Van Horn Melton (University of Pennsylvania Press, 1992), 13–61.
[32] *Reichsgesetzblatt,* 1933, Teil I, no. 108, 685–92.
[33] Alexander von Brünneck writes that Nazi jurists such as Ernst Rudolf Huber "repeatedly presented the hereditary farm legislation as a model for the overall development of the property regime." "Die Eigentumsordnung im Nationalsozialismus," *Kritische Justiz* 12, no. 2 (1979): 151–72 (160).
[34] Evident in the observation that visitors to Lieselotte frequently mention the artist in her guestbook.
[35] The tree now has a reception history of its own: depicted in Munch's *Old Man in Warnemünde* (1907), uprooted by a seasonal storm in 2020, three of its offshoots have been planted outside the new Munch Museum in Oslo.
[36] Fredric Jameson, "Itemised," *London Review of Books* 40, no. 21 (November 8, 2018). In a reply, Mark Ford has said that Jameson likely misremembered, explaining that it was rather "the French humorist Alphonse Allais (1854–1905) who put together a spoofy collection of rarities that included the skull of Voltaire at the age of 17, along with a genuine piece of the fake cross of Christ, and a left-handed Chinese teacup."

Figure 1. Marcel M. Celis, transfer of the Maison du Peuple pieces to the Horta Museum, undated. Courtesy of urban.brussels.

Alena Rieger

Usus, Fructus, Abusus

Roman law once controlled property by bestowing three rights upon its proprietors: *usus, fructus,* and *abusus,* the rights to use, enjoy the fruits, and dispose of, respectively.[1] One might have enjoyed property or harvested it, but usus and fructus alone did not constitute total ownership. In order to own something in ancient Rome, one must have been able to destroy or dispose of it.

Abusus was everywhere in mid-twentieth-century Brussels. Buildings were falling as fast as they were going up. A most-famous victim of this so-called "Brusselization" was Maison du Peuple (1896–99), the Belgian Socialist Party headquarters designed by the art nouveau architect Victor Horta (1861–1947).[2] Architects responded with outrage to the planned demolition: More than six hundred signed a petition against its destruction, and in Venice 1964 a congress of experts unanimously plead for its protection.[3] Nevertheless, in 1965, Maison du Peuple was demolished, save a few notable rooms that were marked, disassembled, and stored, until plans for their future use could be finalized. This disappearance sparked propagations of the building. Pieces were nearly sent to New York, Munich, Philadelphia, Baltimore, Berlin, and Turin, and each new future produced even more documentation.[4] Most plans for reconstruction never materialized. Instead, the pieces of Maison du Peuple, totaling three hundred forty tons of material, disappeared to disparate locations.[5] For years, remnants of Horta's masterpiece laid dormant in the cellar of the Saint-Gilles town hall, the backyard of the Horta Museum, a concrete frame in a public park, along railroad tracks, in bushes. A number of stone and iron pieces simply sunk into the swamp-like field where they were stored. Countless parts were looted from open storage in vacant lots.[6] And in 1983 seventy tons of iron elements were smelted in Japan.[7]

This "dark chapter" has been scorned, condemned, and averted by those devoted to Horta and his legacy.[8] But even as the building disappeared, the archives of Maison du Peuple proliferated. Today, there are tens of thousands of documents relating to Maison du Peuple spread among at least eight different archives and almost every document records affairs of the building in pieces. Within this extended interlude Maison du Peuple was sold, threatened, demolished, moved, stolen, divided, and multiplied by a whole new cast of characters. In the face of change, stability was obtained by marking

Future Anterior
Volume XXII, Numbers 1–2
Summer / Winter 2025

collections of objects to be saved, surveying their conditions and quantities, and writing agreements between parties involved in their movement. As the pieces of the building disintegrated, its documentation accumulated, and reputation was reinforced. In a fundamental discussion on provenance, art historian Anne Higonnet critically notes that we tend to fixate on the "meanings that cluster around an object at the moment it was created."[9] But if Maison du Peuple was made significant in its moments of crisis, then how might we pivot our focus?

A Dubious Provenance

A key thing about provenance is that it redirects attention from the author of a work to its custodians. In shifting from recounting a singular authorship to successive ownerships, we expand our gaze from the conception of an object to the reception of it. But this expansion in breadth can easily sacrifice depth. "Epic tales compressed into such dry lists," writes Higonnet. Time and space collapsed, "as if many decades never occurred and many miles never existed."[10] Studying "the social life of provenance," Higonnet focuses her critique on the compression of provenance research into reductive indexes of ownership. In thinking about these lists, she notices that the punctuation marks between names "replace verbs, replace history, and replace meaning."[11] Bloated with information, reductive in form, provenance lists conform the event of a transfer to two dots and a tail.

Transfers of ownership in Roman antiquity were events marked by the strike of scales, in the presence of a group of adult male Romans, alongside the utterance of a phrase. The ceremony, called *mancipatio,* required the vendor and vendee, someone to hold the balance, and five witnesses. Then came the words, the gestures, and a copper stick to strike the scales. The ceremonial transfer was made up of two parts: first the assertion of ownership by the seller followed by the assertion of purchase by the buyer.[12] If the semicolons in a provenance list are shorthand for events of transfer, then what happens when we expand those moments and describe them? Provenance is useful in widening our gaze to include ownerships, but it can also overlook the conditions of the transfers between. This becomes especially consequential when we look at what is typically excluded from provenance lists: the stuff of theft, power-play, and pillages, to paraphrase Higonnet.[13] But if we take the Roman definition of ownership as characterized by the power of abusus, then provenance is also the history of dispossession, exploitation, and destruction. To fully enjoy provenance as a method, this study works with a provenance that includes illegal acquisitions, custodianships, presumed, and misunderstood ownerships—in a story told through the legal hearings of one especially dubious transaction.

Figure 2. Maison du Peuple in storage at Jette, 1985. Unknown photographer. Courtesy of Brukselbinnenstebuiten.

Unidentified Objects

At the edge of Brussels, neighboring orderly suburban houses, was a grassy meadow waiting for development; an unfenced, unmonitored site frequented by passersby and collectors of all sorts.[14] When the pieces of Maison du Peuple were photographed at Jette in Brussels, they were rusted, sunken, littered about, and obscured by overgrowth. A pile of "broken stones" and "twisted irons" that had quickly integrated with their environment.[15] "The state of the pieces," now at home among the pleasantly named varieties of wildlife such as the short-toed treecreeper, the long-tailed tit, the red corn snake, and field forget-me-nots, was, according to its architectural custodians, "increasingly worrying."[16]

On a summer night in 1983, one Roland Devillers drove to Jette, where the pieces of Maison du Peuple appeared abandoned in the grass. Without raising suspicion, Devillers removed seventy tons of "scrap" from the open storage.[17] By the end of June, Devillers had found a buyer in Alphonse Stevens, described in later documents as "one of the most important scrap metal dealers in the area."[18] This esteemed dealer purchased the materials without a title deed, cut, sawed, broke, and bent the pieces to shrapnel, and immediately resold them. Stevens doubled his money on the scrap, which he purchased for two-fifty francs per kg and then resold for five.[19] According to court documents, most of the Maison du Peuple ironworks were then shipped to Japan, via Rotterdam, to be melted down.[20]

The first legal hearing ended in a fine, compensation to the owners, and fifteen months in prison for Roland Devillers, who was found guilty of grand theft, fraud, and driving without a license.[21] Devillers had stolen "unidentified objects" of "indeterminate value" to the detriment of an unclear owner, and in doing so had brought to light the topic of provenance, issues of ownership, and the question of material value.[22] In the sale from Devillers to Stevens, was it Devillers who forged the origin of the materials or Stevens who knowingly purchased the Maison du Peuple pieces? Who owned the dismembered Maison du Peuple? And how to determine damages? These issues had been neglected for nearly two decades as piecemeal, emergency measures were taken to face the increasingly urgent dilemmas of Maison du Peuple. But in the middle of a lengthy effort to find a dignified ending for the building, it was the theft and ensuing court cases that offered a moment of reflection. In its own legal fashion, the case would untangle difficult problems, record key elements of what had happened over the last two decades, and determine the consequences for the building, still in pieces.

The question of fraud was really a question of who understood the provenance of the scattered remains. The court ascribed responsibility to whichever party realized the provenance. If it was the thief Devillers who fraudulently claimed that they were unidentified, then he held responsibility. If it was the buyer Stevens who knowingly purchased the valuable pieces for the price of scrap, then it was he. In the court of first instance, the seller Devillers was found guilty on one count of misinforming the buyer Stevens "either by using false names or false qualities, or by using fraudulent means."[23] But this judgment was redirected toward the buyer Stevens on appeal. Lawyers argued that it was Stevens who had ignored the proper provenance of the materials and quickly resold them with intent of "unjust enrichment."[24] The acquittal of the seller Devillers on one count of fraud also came to the detriment of its caretakers. The judge implied that they had enabled the theft through "une certaine légèreté" in their sloppy supervision for the pieces.[25] This was a polite, but condemning, way of acknowledging that they had not been diligent in their care of the objects (for example, by failing to erect a fence). But in the dense and distributed post-demolition provenance at stake here, who was responsible for the pieces of Maison du Peuple?

Unknown Owners

The ownership of Maison du Peuple had been disputed from the start. In the early 1960s, proponents of demolition came from within the Socialist Party itself.[26] The party was outgrowing their tenancy at Maison du Peuple: The building already wrapped the perimeter of the site, a six-story addition already closed in all unused space, offices had long since replaced production areas, and still, more room was needed.[27] At the same time, former Socialist Prime Minister Camille Huysmans (1871–1968, served as prime minister 1946–47) went on public rants, describing Maison du Peuple as a "pathetic structure," not worth taking care of.[28] This publicly declared dissatisfaction, along with the fact that the party was the most notable tenant of the building, led to a popular assumption that the land was property of the Socialist Party itself. It was in 1981, nearly twenty years later, that this fallacy was corrected, when a high-up bureaucrat clarified that the owners of the building were, in fact, the Socialist Cooperatives.[29] They had purchased the land in 1895 and constructed Maison du Peuple in the following years. What might seem a futile distinction is fairly significant from the perspective of provenance: while the party gained power through votes, the cooperatives were sustained by purchases.[30] By the 1960s, the cooperatives were struggling financially, and in a bid to save themselves, sold the land to the developer, Blaton.[31]

The Blaton company was a veritable dynasty in Belgium.[32] The firm was founded in 1865 as Blaton-Aubert, and by 1963 it was a fourth-generation family business that had changed its name many times.[33] Blaton-Aubert was highly regarded and constructed many of Horta's buildings, but during the era of "Brusselization," Blaton became synonymous with demolition. This was a period of mass demolition made possible by a lack of building regulation and made lucrative by the Brussels World's Fair in 1958 and the establishment of Brussels as the European Union capital around the same time.[34] As the desire for a unified Europe emerged, large swaths of the Brussels building mass were destroyed. It was in this context of real-estate speculation in 1963 that Blaton purchased the land below Maison du Peuple, demolished the building, and constructed a twenty-six-story tower in its place.

Once the court had determined the facts of the theft at Jette, it remained to be seen to whom it was harmful. But determining a single owner was difficult. Misunderstandings of ownership only increased once Maison du Peuple was

Figure 3. Robert Courtois, Maison du Peuple in storage at Tervuren, c. 1981. Courtesy of CIVA Collections, Brussels.

deconstructed. At various points in the trial, the court found that the theft resulted in damages to the city of Brussels (where Maison du Peuple was built, demolished, and stored), the state (who had provided the subsidy), the Société centrale d'architecture de Belgique [SCAB] (who was under contract with the state to conserve the pieces), the architects (who, under contract with SCAB, were responsible for the reuse of the elements) and specifically local architect Jean Delhaye, who the court documents refer to as the "custodian of the Maison du Peuple."[35]

Jean Delhaye had once worked for Horta, lived in a house designed by Horta, and spent the years after Horta's death fighting for his legacy. In his quest to salvage Maison du Peuple, Delhaye was joined by well-known architects in Brussels such as Victor Gaston Martiny, father-and-son Robert and Pierre Puttemans, Louis Herman De Koninck, and Robert Courtois. But even if these custodians were working in the name of Horta, their personal archives tell the story of a post-Horta frenzy to salvage his legacy. Horta was conferred a baron in 1932 and Maison du Peuple had received praise in three seminal books on architecture: Nicolaus Pevsner's *Pioneers of the Modern Movement* (1936), Sigfried Giedion's *Space, Time and Architecture* (1941), and Bruno Zevi's *Storia dell'architettura moderna* (1950). Yet Horta's works were depreciating.[36] Many structures were at risk and in this period of uncertainty Jean Delhaye emerged as a main proponent of Horta's work.[37] Delhaye personally acquired buildings, deposited Horta's work in institutions, and convinced officials of the

Figure 4. André Dartevelle, stills showing Pierre Puttemans in *La Maison du Peuple de Victor Horta*, 1996. Courtesy of Sonuma.

value embedded in his architecture. When news of the demolition of Maison du Peuple emerged, Delhaye began a campaign to save the building that would last until his own death.

The first proposal to classify Maison du Peuple as a monument had landed on the desk of the Commission royale des Monuments et des Sites back in December 1963. The thinking went that if Maison du Peuple acquired heritage status, the acquisition by Blaton could be usurped. The commission had been distinguishing what should be kept from what could be lost in the midst of large-scale urban renewal in Brussels since 1835, but even their hands were tied. A building permit for the tower to replace Maison du Peuple had already been approved.

The campaign began with a postcard, sent to at least seven hundred architects and historians in at least twenty-four different countries. In prewritten French, English, and German, it laid out support for the preservation of Maison du Peuple: "deeply moved at the thought of the menace threatening the Brussels 'Maison du Peuple' I associate myself to the protest . . . to ask for the safeguard of this capital work of modern architecture."[38] It was this collection of return-to-sender postcards that formed the basis of a petition printed in *Rhythme,* the monthly publication of the society of architects, SCAB, in April 1964. A manifesto laid out the grounds for preservation. The fragility of the building under individual ownership was countered by a greater-good argument that undermined the abusus-power of Blaton by discussing ownership in a broad sense. The manifesto exalted Horta's work, declaring that it was "to History, therefore to the common good, that Horta's work now belong[ed]."[39]

Common ownership of Maison du Peuple would be discussed again just one month later, when, over seven days in May 1964, attendees of the Second International Congress of Architects and Technicians of Historic Monuments would share knowledge, meals, and tours of the Venetian canals. The congress aimed to assert the "unity of human values" and find a common understanding of their "common responsibility" for safeguarding "common heritage."[40] The outcomes were summarized in thirteen documents. Document one became the famous Venice Charter.[41] Document two founded the International Council on Monuments and Sites.[42] Document thirteen was the only to mention a building or architect by name. It read: "RESOLUTION CONCERNING THE PRESERVATION OF THE 'MAISON DU PEUPLE' IN BRUSSELS." A total of 792 participants from 61 different nations, "profoundly touched by the threatened destruction," applauded to appeal "most urgently to the Belgian authorities to do everything in their power to save as much as possible of this major work by Victor Horta."[43]

Ambiguous Transfers

Changes of ownership and plans for reconstruction offered means to secure Maison du Peuple when heritage authorities failed to do so. Ownership for the architects meant architectural authorship and Jean Delhaye, Pierre Puttemans, Robert Courtois, and Louis-Herman De Koninck worked tirelessly, without much success, toward reuse. From May 1965 until February 1966, Maison du Peuple was subject to a sometimes-careful, otherwise-brutal demolition. Following international dissent, the Belgian state agreed to provide SCAB with the necessary funds to deconstruct notable sections of the building.[44] This resulted in a complex assignment for the contractor A. Antoine, who, by way of a demolition contract with Blaton, was now owner of the building.[45] When Blaton hired Antoine, demolition was the task and speed was the measure of success. The remains from destruction were a problem to be dealt with rather than objects to be saved. But when international dissent spawned action from architects and money from the state, a new nonprofit organization was born.[46] Under the purview of SCAB, the Comité Horta assumed responsibility for the deconstruction of particular fragments. They, in turn, hired the contractors R. Adam, G. Leclercq, and F. Decuyper to carry out the disassembly and transport operations.[47] It is worth noting that while Antoine, the demolisher, became owner of the building, Adam, Leclercq, and Decuyper, charged with deconstruction, did not. Likely because they were taking care of the elements, not destroying them, they did not require the status of owner to complete their work.

Maison du Peuple became especially subject to the whims of its various caretakers during this demolition. Pieces that had been earmarked for restoration were distributed throughout, meaning that every element to be deconstructed was attached to, supported by, holding up, or integrated with sections to be turned into rubble. And so the act of undoing the building swung between a ruthless destruction and an emergency antiquarian deconstruction. This messy task was documented by the constant presence of Jean Delhaye. Through his thousands of photographs, the building site appears shockingly precarious.[48] Delhaye would later remark that he had "rarely seen a building so hard to bring down."[49] Every tool in the toolbox—wrenches, wrecking balls, cranes, and sledgehammers—was used to take Maison du Peuple to the ground.

As it was taken apart, Maison du Peuple was thoroughly documented. Together with Delhaye's photographs came drawings that captured parts to be undone and then reassembled and receipts accounted for the crews working toward contradictory goals. The last four photographs in Delhaye's demolition collection capture a stack of stones and ironworks in storage. Each element is unique, every angle is at play, and sizes range from dinner plate to dining table. Each stone was cut from the quarry, its form finessed on site in the center of Brussels, wedged into place in Maison du Peuple, and then more recently, oil-painted with a number, pulled apart, transported, and stacked here.[50] The storage site at the *Musée royal de l'Afrique centrale* in Tervuren made use of a building that had halted mid-construction, leaving only the foundation and a concrete frame. When in 1971, members of SCAB were made aware of ongoing thefts from the stockpile, they reached out to the Municipality of Saint-Gilles to restart an old deal.[51] It had been six years since the pieces were moved to storage and no reconstruction was in view.[52] The municipality agreed to

Figure 5. Jean Delhaye, Maison du Peuple in storage at Tervuren, 1966. Courtesy of Hortamuseum, St-Gilles/Gillis.

acquire doors, railings, balustrades, and columns, as well as the grand staircase, but it would take over a decade for the municipality to retrieve their goods.[53] At Tervuren for fifteen years, the two buildings kept company while each waited for funds to secure their construction. By early 1981, plans for resuming construction on the concrete skeleton were in motion.[54] Maison du Peuple had to move once again.

Indeterminate Value

It was the Socialists who built Maison du Peuple, Blaton who traded it for something new, and the demolishers who took it apart. Sure, the state had provided funds, the city of Brussels was left with spare parts, and the architects had spent many unpaid hours on the case. But it was the architects' association SCAB, who had purchased the elements from Antoine with support from the state, who the court of appeals finally assumed to be owner of the elements.[55] Concrete numbers for what was then owed to them could be gleaned from the sale from Antoine

Figure 6. Maison du Peuple in storage at Jette, 1985. Unknown photographer. Courtesy of Brukselbinnenstebuiten.

to SCAB (1.50 francs/kg), the illegal sale from Devillers to Stevens (2.50 francs/kg), or the sale from Stevens to the Japanese smelter (5 francs/kg).[56] While these amounts were clear, they remained insufficient.[57] A different sum came from tallying potential sales offered by museums and other institutions, but this still ignored broader notions of value.[58] Civil courts determined that the elements could not be reduced to their material resale value. The actions of Devillers prevented SCAB from achieving its objective of "restoring the essence of the work of Horta," lead to a loss of value for any remaining pieces, voided all costs incurred by the deconstruction and conservation of those pieces, and caused "moral and artistic loss" that was "incalculable" but obvious.[59] Using some combination of metrics, damages were estimated at fifty million francs.[60]

Fundamentally, the court cases attempted to settle whether the architectural remains constituted architecture or scrap, and to whom those remains belonged. Still, it is not the conclusions of the court that are most useful but the questions it wrestled with. The case paralleled disagreements that took place between architects, preservationists, and developers throughout the long interlude of Maison du Peuple: questions of architectural copyright against the rights of owners, of the slippage between buildings and materials, and of movability and mutability.

After the 1983 Devillers theft presented a serious threat to reconstruction, attitudes toward reconstruction began to change. Only "most of the stones" and a "few pieces of truss" remained.[61] Iron beams, after years of rust and ruin, no longer had load-bearing capacity. Horta's unique means of merging structure with ornament were now reduced to the latter. Beyond financial need, space requirements, and the lack of complete building blocks, the condition of the pieces seemed a real setback to reconstruction. Newspapers continued to publish articles on the robbery and its consequences while, Delhaye, for the first time, seemed to lose his stamina for the battle. In an article headlined "The Second Death of Victor Horta," he claimed that "thefts over these 18 years have ruined the possibility of any solution. I am very pessimistic."[62] This pessimism was evident in the unsentimental, unambitious proposals that followed: a small stone monument, a few metal pieces as railings in a metro station, the sale of stones to stonecutters or schools. A final note from meeting minutes says to write "a history of Maison du Peuple since 1964."[63] The era of possibility seemed at an end.

A Monument in Pieces

Today, a commemorative plaque in the entrance to the Grand Café Horta in Antwerp tells a story of death and "wederopstanding" (resurrection). The death of Maison du Peuple, it suggests, began in 1963. But the resurrection sputtered starts in decadal intervals from the moment of the theft onward. The 1984 exhibition *Vrij gedacht in ijzer* (freely thought in iron) used two iron trusses from Maison du Peuple as an entrance portal.[64] A weeklong business center for the Flanders Technology Fair in 1991 made use of the skeletal frame, which was test constructed, deconstructed, and reconstructed for the one-week "évocation" of Maison du Peuple.[65] Realization came as a result of the theft, out of lowered ambition for the project and clarified ownerships. Once SCAB had been ridiculed in court for their handling of the pieces, they were eager to rescind control of the materials that had been haunting them for over twenty years. In 1988, through a contract signed by seven involved parties, SCAB was dismissed from all "obligations and responsibilities whatsoever concerning the safeguarding of the remains of the Maison du Peuple."[66] In the following years, elements were restored, reconstructed, and retained by veritable institutions in secure locations. Through the agreement, the remains were distributed to a museum, a municipality, and an archive. The provenance of the pieces was so persistent that even though deconstructed, rusted, and incapable of holding themselves up, they remained worthy of collection.

The Delhaye archives conclude at the 1991 fair, just two years before the collector's death. Martiny's archives taper out over this same period; he died in 1996. As a result, details of the ensuing period are obscured, leaving many questions to be answered. What is certain is that since the year 2000, one can

Figure 7. Remains of the Maison du Peuple retrieved from Jette, 1998. Unknown photographer. Courtesy of CIVA Collections, Brussels.

choose between an "art nouveau" or "continental" breakfast in a reconstruction of the former festival hall. One might take public transport from a platform with Horta's stained glass and iron balustrades. One may visit the Horta Museum, where people continue to donate fragments found in private possession, and where columns and stairs from Maison du Peuple provide structural and circulatory support.[67] One can find balustrades

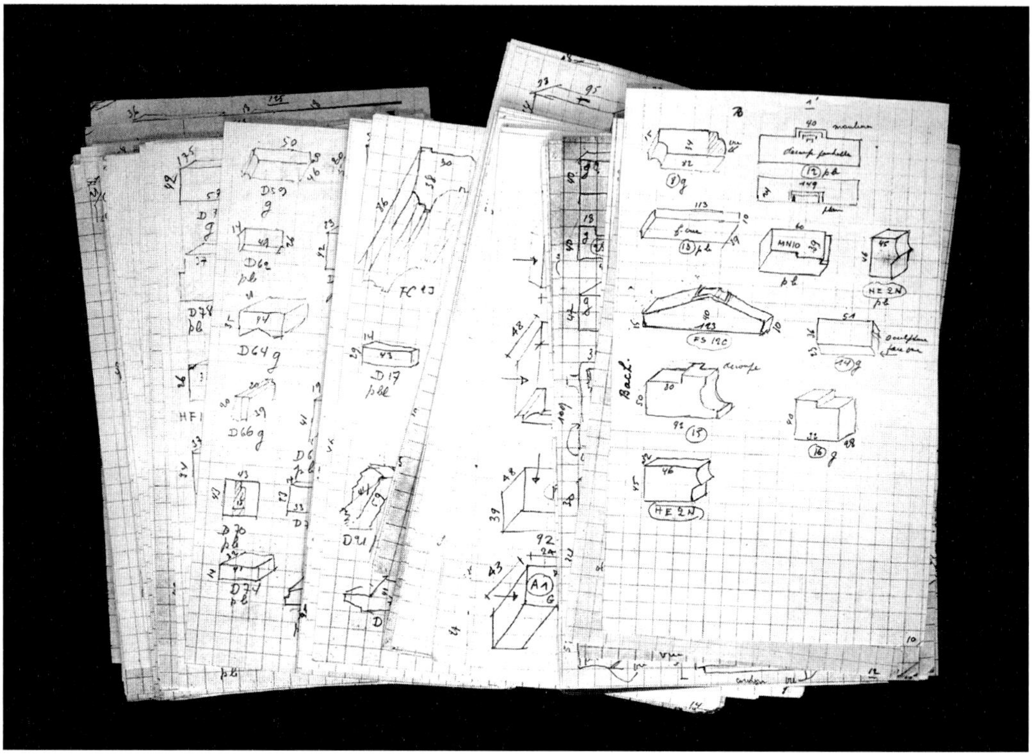

Figure 8. Jean Delhaye, drawings of Maison du Peuple pieces during move to Jette, c. 1981. Courtesy of Hortamuseum, St-Gilles/Gillis.

from the facade of Maison du Peuple wrapped in bubble wrap in an office at the Université Libre de Bruxelles. At CIVA, one can see chairs and tables and railings kept among documents in three subterranean levels of storage. In the winter of 2023, one could visit the Palais des Beaux-Arts where five pieces of the building were displayed, still rusting enough to flake onto their plinth.[68]

Even if every effort has gone into preserving this monument in pieces, the significance of Maison du Peuple lies not in its ending but in its interlude. Histories of Maison du Peuple have often divorced the building from its unsavory ownerships, but it was precisely during these moments of crisis and bad behavior that its reputation was reconfigured. Exchange, effort, and transfers of ownership transformed the building from something worth the cost of the land it sat on into an invaluable monument in pieces. Possession of the vulnerable building, even under the care of those coordinating its protection, often ended in further degradation, spoliation, decline, or decay. Yet, this material entropy led to the inverse in knowledge: Each transfer, whether real, illegal, or potential, produced materials and attracted attention. It was in these moments of crisis when the objects' provenance was especially precarious that its potential was debated. Surveys, photographs, drawings, assessments, reports, historical analyses, and plans for new assemblages accumulated in the archives of its custodians. Even as newspapers constructed fiction from fact, plans went undeveloped, attempts at protection were rejected, and pieces went missing, the reputation of Maison du Peuple advanced. The imperative of this article is not a conclusion for Maison du Peuple but a proposal for understanding its convoluted history. Provenance enables us to remain in moments of contingency. In the history of Maison du Peuple, provenance is not only a method for parsing history but one that actively redefined it.

Biography
Alena Rieger is a PhD fellow at the Oslo School of Architecture and Design. Her dissertation examines twentieth-century building demolitions and material provenance and is supervised by Mari Lending as part of the international research project *Provenance Projected: Architecture Past and Future in the Era of Circularity.* Rieger's work has been supported by grants and fellowships from the Canadian Centre for Architecture, the Canada Council for the Arts, and the Manitoba Arts Council. She was awarded the J.B.C. Watkins Award in Architecture (2023) and is a recipient of the SSHRC Doctoral Fellowship (2023–27).

Notes

[1] In Roman law, ownership is described as "ius utendi fruendi abutendi." W. W. Buckland, *A Text-Book of Roman Law from Augustus to Justinian* (Cambridge University Press, 1921), 188; Utendi (usus) was the right to use; Fruendi (fructus), the right to harvest from; Abutendi (abusus), the right to fully consume or abuse. As defined by a well-regarded dictionary, abusus is "the right to do exactly as one likes with property, or having full dominion over property." "Jus Abutendi," in *Black's Law Dictionary,* 2nd ed. (West Publishing Company, 1910), 676.

[2] There is a good introduction to Brusselization in Isabelle Doucet, "Making a City with Words: Understanding Brussels Through Its Urban Heroes and Villains," *City, Culture and Society* 3, no. 2 (2012).

[3] The petition against the demolition of Maison du Peuple was published in S.C.A.B., "Destruction de la Maison du Peuple de Bruxelles : Manifeste," *Rythme : l'œuvre de Victor Horta,* April 1964, 32. The IInd International Congress of Architects and Technicians of Historic Monuments took place in Venice May 25 to May 31, 1964. *A propos de la Maison du Peuple de Bruxelles,* August 1964, Lutte contre la destruction de la Maison du Peuple 1963–1965, Archives Delhaye, Horta Museum, Brussels.

[4] The Museum of Modern Art (New York), the Neue Sammlung (Munich), the Philadelphia Museum of Art, the American Institute of Architects (Baltimore), the Staatliche Museum (Berlin), and the Städelsches Kunstinstitut (Frankfurt) were among the interested institutions. Letters from L. Wittamer to Jean Delhaye, December 8–9, 1964, Lutte contre la destruction de la Maison du Peuple 1963–1965, Archives Delhaye, Horta Museum, Brussels; These potential relocations are also listed in Marcel M. Celis, "Van Volkshuis tot schroot. Achtergronden van een kwarteeuw falen," *Monumenten en Landschappen* 10, no. 2 (1991): 25.

[5] Minutes from meeting with the Cabinet du Ministre de la Région Bruxelloise, February 24, 1981, Maison Peuple 1965–1987, Archives Delhaye, Horta Museum, Brussels.

[6] Letter from the Horta Committee to the Ministry of French Culture, 1971, Démontage de la Maison Peuple 1965–1972, Archives Delhaye, Horta Museum, Brussels.

[7] Summary of the Devillers case, 1983, Réutilisation des éléments de la Maison du Peuple 1971–1991, Archives Delhaye, Horta Museum, Brussels.

[8] "Dark chapter" quoted from an email with an employee at Amsab Institute of Social History, Brussels. January 28, 2025. It should be mentioned that Marcel Celis chronicles the post-demolition affairs of Maison du Peuple in Celis, "Van Volkshuis tot schroot," and Franco Borsi claims the significance of the demolition in Franco Borsi, "Victor Horta et la Maison du Peuple de Bruxelles," in *Architecture pour le Peuple: Maisons du Peuple* (Archives d'Architecture Moderne, 1984).

[9] Anne Higonnet, "Afterword: The Social Life of Provenance," in *Provenance: An Alternative History of Art,* ed. Gail Feigenbaum and Inge Reist (Getty Research Institute, 2012), 198.

[10] Higonnet, "Afterword," 195–97.

[11] Higonnet, 202.

[12] "Mancipatio," in *Black's Law Dictionary,* 753; Buckland, *A Text-Book of Roman Law from Augustus to Justinian,* 236.

[13] Higonnet, "Afterword," 197.

[14] Letter from Pierre Puttemans to SCAB, September 2, 1981, Réutilisation des éléments de la Maison du Peuple 1971–1991, Archives Delhaye, Horta Museum, Brussels.
[15] Original quote reads: "Des pièces ayant été entreposées à Tervuren en bon état sont arrivées fort détériorées à Jette : pierres cassées, fers tordus." Letter from Pierre Puttemans to SCAB, September 2, 1981, Réutilisation des éléments de la Maison du Peuple 1971–1991, Archives Delhaye, Horta Museum, Brussels.
[16] Original quote reads: "la situation des pièces est de plus en plus préoccupante." Letter from SCAB to Commission Royale des Monuments et des Sites, 1982, Maison Peuple 1965–1987, Archives Delhaye, Horta Museum, Brussels; "Jette—Parc Roi Baudouin," *Observations Belgium,* accessed March 5, 2024.
[17] *Tribunal, o6655,* November 4, 1983, Réutilisation des éléments de la Maison du Peuple, 1971–1991, Archives Delhaye, Horta Museum, Brussels.
[18] Original quote reads: "Alphonse Stevens, présenté à l'audience correctionnelle comme l'un des importants marchands de mitraille de la place." Summary of the Devillers case, 1983, Réutilisation des éléments de la Maison du Peuple 1971–1991, Archives Delhaye, Horta Museum, Brussels.
[19] Summary of the Devillers case, 1983, Réutilisation des éléments de la Maison du Peuple 1971–1991, Archives Delhaye, Horta Museum, Brussels.
[20] *Tribunal o6655,* November 4, 1983; Letter from Pierre Puttemans to Michel Van Doosselaere, October 25, 1983, Réutilisation des éléments de la Maison du Peuple 1971–1991, Archives Delhaye, Horta Museum, Brussels.
[21] "Ferronnerie Horta : 15 mois de prison," *La Cite,* November 5, 1983, Clipping in Réutilisation des éléments de la Maison du Peuple 1971–1991, Archives Delhaye, Horta Museum; Summary of the Devillers case, 1983, Réutilisation des éléments de la Maison du Peuple 1971–1991, Archives Delhaye, Horta Museum, Brussels; *Tribunal, o6655,* November 4, 1983, Réutilisation des éléments de la Maison du Peuple, 1971–1991, Archives Delhaye, Horta Museum, Brussels.
[22] Original quote reads: "frauduleusement soustraire des objets non identifiés, d'une valeur totale indéterminée, qui ne lui appartenaient pas." *Tribunal, o6655,* November 4, 1983, Réutilisation des éléments de la Maison du Peuple, 1971–1991, Archives Delhaye, Horta Museum, Brussels.
[23] Original quote reads: "soit en faisant usage de faux noms ou de fausses qualités, soit en employant des manoeuvres frauduleuses pour abuser de la confiance ou de la crédulité." *Tribunal, o6655,* November 4, 1983, Réutilisation des éléments de la Maison du Peuple, 1971–1991, Archives Delhaye, Horta Museum, Brussels.
[24] Original quote reads: "d'enrichissement sans cause." Summary of the Devillers case, 1983, Réutilisation des éléments de la Maison du Peuple 1971–1991, Archives Delhaye, Horta Museum, Brussels. Page 6.
[25] *Tribunal, o6655,* November 4, 1983, Réutilisation des éléments de la Maison du Peuple, 1971–1991, Archives Delhaye, Horta Museum, Brussels. Page 3.
[26] The party existed as the Parti socialiste belge from 1945 to 1978. It was preceded by the Parti ouvrier belge (1885–1940) and split into separate Flemish and Francophone parties after 1978. For sake of clarity, it is referred to here as they were in the 1960s, as the Parti socialiste belge (the Belgian Socialist Party).
[27] Françoise Aubry notes that the tenants of Maison du Peuple had already outgrown the space by 1911, when renovations to add and adapt Horta's building began without him. Françoise Aubry [translated by Barbara Harshav], "Victor Horta: Vicissitudes of a Work," *Yale French Studies*, no. 102 (2002): 180. For a detailed description on the various additions, see Lucia van der Horst, "Het proces rondom de afbraak van het Maison du Peuple in Brussel" (Bachelor Utrecht University, 2012), 6–9.
[28] Original text reads: "Laissez donc Horta en paix! Il ne vaut pas qu'on s'occupe de lui. La Maison du Peuple de la Place Emile Vandervelde est une construction lamentable." Camille Huysmans, *Le Peuple,* October 16, 1964. This quote has become part of the history of Maison du Peuple and is cited frequently, including in Aubry, "Victor Horta"; and Celis, "Van Volkshuis tot schroot. Achtergronden van een kwarteeuw falen."
[29] According to Marcel Celis, it was L. Denonne, director at the Ministry of Labor and Employment, who corrected the claim. Celis, "Van Volkshuis tot schroot," 30.
[30] Roger Ramaekers, President of the fédération belge des coopératives, notes this distinction in an interview (1:04:54) in Dartevelle, André, dir., *La Maison du Peuple de Victor Horta.* To Do Today productions, 1996, 79 minutes.
[31] The cooperatives sold the land to Blaton for twenty-five million francs. Celis, "Van Volkshuis tot schroot," 30.
[32] For more on the Blaton family and its companies, see Maurice Culot et al., eds., *Blaton. Une dynastie de constructeurs,* Éditions AAM (Archives d'architecture moderne, 2018).

[33] Today, the company is CIT Blaton (1988–). Bernard Espion, "The Belgian Company Blaton," in *Changing Cultures:* European Perspectives on the History of Portland Cement and Reinforced Concrete, 19th and 20th Centuries, ed. Bernard Espion, Rika Devos, and Michel Provost (CRC Press, 2023).
[34] T. Jozef Hermans et al., "Brussels." *Encyclopedia Britannica,* Updated January 7, 2024; For more on Brusselization, see Katarzyna M. Romanczyk, "Transforming Brussels into an International City—Reflections on 'Brusselization,'" *Cities* 29, no. 2 (2012).
[35] In court documents, Delhaye is referred to as "Conservateur de la Maison du Peuple Horta." *Tribunal, 06655,* November 4, 1983, Réutilisation des éléments de la Maison du Peuple, 1971–1991, Archives Delhaye, Horta Museum, Brussels. Page 1.
[36] Françoise Aubry writes that Horta "saw his glory decline" between World War I and World War II. Aubry, "Victor Horta," 176.
[37] Delhaye studied under Horta at the Académie des Beaux-Arts de Bruxelles. He worked in Horta's office from 1934 to 1939 and then again after the war. Description of Jean Delhaye's life and work, Jean Delhaye (1908–1993), 1993, J Delhaye 1, Library Holdings, CIVA, Brussels.
[38] Postcard to save Maison du Peuple, November 1963, Lutte contre la destruction de la Maison du Peuple 1963–1965, Archives Delhaye, Horta Museum, Brussels.
[39] Original quote reads: "Or, sans conteste, c'est à l'Histoire, donc au bien commun, qu'appartient désormais l'œuvre d'Horta." S.C.A.B., "Destruction de la Maison du Peuple de Bruxelles : Manifeste," 32.
[40] ICOMOS, "International Charter for the Conservation and Restoration of Monuments and Sites (The Venice Charter)," Second International Congress of Architects and Technicians of Historic Monuments, Venice, 1964, 1.
[41] "Decisions and Resolutions," Second International Congress of Architects and Technicians of Historic Monuments, Venice, 1964.
[42] "Decisions and Resolutions."
[43] Newspaper Clipping, "Un appel mondial en faveur du maintien de la Maison du Peuple à Bruxelles," August 29, 1964, Comité Horta, SCAB, Victor Horta B5–B6, Fonds Victor G Martiny, CIVA, Brussels; "Decisions and Resolutions," May 1964, SADBr and Congrès architectes et techniciens des monuments historiques, Fonds Victor G Martiny, CIVA, Brussels. Page 30–31.
[44] The subsidy was formally granted by Council of Ministers, French and Dutch Ministries of Education and Culture, on September 1, 1965, four months after the start of the demolition. Celis, "Van Volkshuis tot schroot," 25.
[45] Contract between SCAB and Antoine, undated (likely 1965), Démontage de la Maison Peuple 1965–1972, Archives Delhaye, Horta Museum, Brussels.
[46] The Victor Horta Committee was founded on January 28, 1960, within the fold of the Société Centrale d'Architecture de Belgique. Renamed Comité Horta in 1965, the association was dissolved in favor of the nonprofit organization Musee Horta on March 22, 1981. Official document announcing the dissolution of the Horta Committee, March 22, 1981, Maison Peuple 1965–1987, Archives Delhaye, Horta Museum, Brussels.
[47] Contract with Adam, May 5, 1965, Lutte contre la destruction de la Maison du Peuple 1963–1965, Archives Delhaye, Horta Museum, Brussels; Maison du Peuple, Report from the site visit, September 22, 1965, Démontage de la Maison Peuple 1965–1972, Archives Delhaye, Horta Museum, Brussels.
[48] Photographic negatives by Jean Delhaye are held at the Horta Museum, Brussels.
[49] "The Second Death of Victor Horta," *The Bulletin,* July 15, 1983, 17.
[50] White oil paint was used for the numbering of stones. "The Second Death of Victor Horta," 15.
[51] Letter from Horta Committee to the Ministry of French Culture, 1971, Démontage de la Maison Peuple 1965–1972, Archives Delhaye, Horta Museum, Brussels.
[52] Letter from Horta Committee to the Ministry of French Culture.
[53] Contract between SCAB, MIAT, AAM, and Saint-Gilles, March 2, 1988, Réutilisation des éléments de la Maison du Peuple 1971–1991, Archives Delhaye, Horta Museum, Brussels.
[54] Letter from Public Works to SCAB, March 27, 1981, Maison Peuple 1965–1987, Archives Delhaye. Horta Museum, Brussels.
[55] To establish ownership, the court worked from an undated agreement between the Ministry of French Culture and architects working on behalf of the SCAB. Summary of the Devillers case, 1983, Réutilisation des éléments de la Maison du Peuple 1971–1991, Archives Delhaye, Horta Museum, Brussels. Page 4.
[56] SCAB purchased the building elements from Antoine for 1.50 francs per kilo of iron and 1.30 francs per kilo of stones. Invoice from A. Antoine, November 4, 1965, Démontage de la Maison Peuple 1965–1972, Archives Delhaye, Horta Museum Brussels; Invoice from A. Antoine, October 12, 1965, Démontage de la Maison Peuple 1965–1972, Archives Delhaye, Horta Museum Brussels.

[57] Summary of the Devillers case, 1983, Réutilisation des éléments de la Maison du Peuple 1971–1991, Archives Delhaye, Horta Museum, Brussels. Page 3–4.
[58] Summary of the Devillers case, 1983, Réutilisation des éléments de la Maison du Peuple 1971–1991, Archives Delhaye, Horta Museum, Brussels. Page 3.
[59] Devillers case conclussions, 1983, Réutilisation des éléments de la Maison du Peuple 1971–1991, Archives Delhaye, Horta Museum, Brussels. Page 2.
[60] "Ferronnerie Horta: 15 mois de prison," *La Cite,* November 5, 1983, Clipping in Réutilisation des éléments de la Maison du Peuple 1971–1991, Archives Delhaye, Horta Museum; *Tribunal, 06655,* November 4, 1983, Réutilisation des éléments de la Maison du Peuple, 1971–1991, Archives Delhaye, Horta Museum, Brussels.
[61] Original quote reads: "actuellement, il ne reste que la plupart des pierres (environ 1500) et quelques morceaux de fermes." SCAB meeting minutes, August 24, 1983, Réutilisation des éléments de la Maison du Peuple 1971–1991, Archives Delhaye, Horta Museum, Brussels.
[62] "The Second Death of Victor Horta," 17.
[63] SCAB meeting minutes, August 24, 1983, Réutilisation des éléments de la Maison du Peuple 1971–1991, Archives Delhaye, Horta Museum, Brussels.
[64] The portal was designed by Hendrik Hendrickx and stood in front of the Centrum voor Kunst en Cultuur Sint-Pietersabdij, in Gent. The exhibition ran from October 28, 1983, until January 15, 1984.
[65] The test construction of the hall took place on February 28, 1991. The "évocation" was designed by architect W. Slock and open to the public April 21–28, 1991. Letter from E. Goedleven to Jean Delhaye, January 29, 1991, Réutilisation des éléments de la Maison du Peuple 1971–1991, Archives Delhaye, Horta Museum, Brussels.
[66] Contract between SCAB, MIAT, AAM, and Saint-Gilles, March 2, 1988, Réutilisation des éléments de la Maison du Peuple 1971–1991, Archives Delhaye, Horta Museum, Brussels. Page 3.
[67] Françoise Aubry and Barbara Van der Wee, *Vingt ans de travaux de restauration au Musée Horta, Saint-Gilles—Twintig jaar restauratiewerken in het Horta Museum, Sint-Gillis* (Musée Horta, 2011).
[68] The exhibition "Victor Horta and the Grammar of Art Nouveau" ran from October 18, 2023, to January 14, 2024.

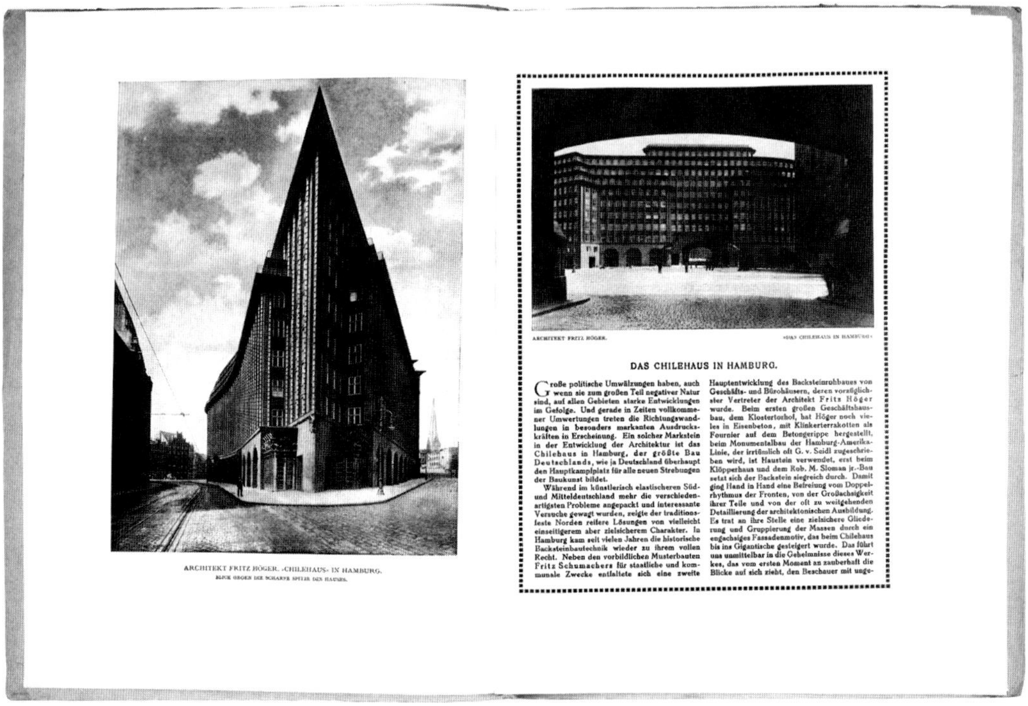

DAS CHILEHAUS IN HAMBURG.

Große politische Umwälzungen haben, auch wenn sie zum großen Teil negativer Natur sind, auf allen Gebieten starke Entwicklungen im Gefolge. Und gerade in Zeiten vollkommener Umwertungen treten die Richtungswandlungen in besonders markanten Ausdruckskräften in Erscheinung. Ein solcher Markstein in der Entwicklung der Architektur ist das Chilehaus in Hamburg, der größte Bau Deutschlands, wie ja Deutschland überhaupt den Hauptkampfplatz für alle neuen Strebungen der Baukunst bildet.

Während im künstlerisch elastischeren Süd- und Mitteldeutschland mehr die verschiedenartigsten Probleme angepackt und interessante Versuche gewagt wurden, zeigte der traditionsfeste Norden reifere Lösungen von vielleicht einseitigerem aber zielsicherem Charakter. In Hamburg kam seit vielen Jahren die historische Backsteinbautechnik wieder zu ihrem vollen Recht. Neben den vorbildlichen Musterbauten Fritz Schumachers für staatliche und kommunale Zwecke entfaltete sich eine zweite Hauptentwicklung des Backsteinrohbaues von Geschäfts- und Bürohäusern, deren vorzüglichster Vertreter der Architekt Fritz Höger wurde. Beim ersten großen Geschäftshausbau, dem Klostertorhof, hat Höger noch vieles in Eisenbeton, mit Klinkerterrakotten als Fournier auf dem Betongerippe hergestellt, beim Monumentalbau der Hamburg-Amerika-Linie, der irrtümlich oft G. v. Seidl zugeschrieben wird, ist Haustein verwendet, erst beim Klöpperhaus und dem Rob. M. Sloman jr.-Bau setzt sich der Backstein siegreich durch. Damit ging Hand in Hand eine Befreiung vom Doppelrhythmus der Fronten, von der Großachsigkeit ihrer Teile und von der oft zu weitgehenden Detaillierung der architektonischen Ausbildung. Es trat an ihre Stelle eine zielsichere Gliederung und Gruppierung der Massen durch ein engachsiges Fassadenmotiv, das beim Chilehaus bis ins Gigantische gesteigert wurde. Das führt uns unmittelbar in die Geheimnisse dieses Werkes, das vom ersten Moment an zauberhaft die Blicke auf sich zieht, den Beschauer mit unge-

Figure 1. The iconic status of the Chilehaus can be largely credited to a series of photographs taken by the Dransfeld brothers, capturing its eastern tip from a low angle. These images circulated worldwide, generating significant attention. From Dr. Alexander Koch, *Deutsche Kunst und Dekoration. Sonderdruck: Das Chilehaus in Hamburg* (Darmstadt, 1924).

Alfredo Thiermann, Pedro Correa, Ella Neumaier, and Xavier Nueno

Office Work

Architecture and Extraction Between Atacama and Hamburg

The politics of memorialization are as much about remembering as they are about selective forgetfulness.[1] In 2015, UNESCO granted world heritage status to the Speicherstadt and Kontorhaus districts of Hamburg, with special mention to the Chilehaus as the most iconic monument of these two quarters. In characteristic UNESCO jargon, the report highlighted this district's technological and stylistic advancements, described as "the consequence of the rapid growth of international trade in the late 19th and early 20th centuries."[2] Built in three successive phases between 1885 and 1927, the Speicherstadt, with its fifteen large warehouse blocks, was one of the global logistical centers of its time, linking the port of Hamburg with the confines of colonial empires and new Atlantic markets.[3] Meanwhile, the Kontorhaus district, built in the aftermath of World War I, was to become one of the administrative centers of global trade. Designed by architect Fritz Höger and completed in 1924, the Chilehaus, considered one of the first tall office buildings in Europe, created a new type of architecture to govern over the ebbs and flows of the world economy through paperwork.[4]

Despite occasional mentions of these colonial histories, little—if anything—of them is made legible in the more than eight hundred pages of the UNESCO report. Instead, the emphasis is on the buildings' stylistic, structural, and tectonic qualities or the constructive prowess of these massive centers of power. In the "Criteria for Justification of Universal Value," we read that "while international office block architecture was still influenced by the Beaux-Arts style and other forms of Historicism, Hamburg's buildings already displayed modern brick facades in expressionist forms, which, in the Chilehaus and the Sprinkenhof were unsurpassed in the virtuosity of their design and craftsmanship."[5] With its east facade resembling the bow of a ship, the Chilehaus had given Hamburg—and German architecture in general—one of the most iconic architectural perspectives of the 1920s.[6] Often regarded as the pinnacle of brick expressionism in Germany, the building was celebrated for its cost-effective and rationalized plan, made possible by the reinforced concrete skeleton combined with traditional brickwork patterned in a repetitive and decorative manner.

The making of modern monuments by institutions such as UNESCO involves operations of "framing" and "disentangling," which allow the reconstruction of buildings as emblems of

Future Anterior
Volume XXII, Numbers 1–2
Summer / Winter 2025

world history by selecting certain aspects to be memorialized while obfuscating others.[7] In the case of the Chilehaus, framing operations are visible in suppressing all the reactionary gestures that loomed large over this project. Since its conception, the building was imagined as a cornerstone in the restoration of the German *Geist,* severely wounded by the defeat of the German Empire in World War I. Capitalists like Henry B. Sloman, a financier and owner of the Chilehaus, and architects like Fritz Höger proposed counteracting the alienation of German craftsmanship, a product of industrialization, with brick structures like this one. While brick was widely used across the Hanseatic League for centuries, Höger's identification and self-promotion as the country's foremost *Backsteinbaumeister* (master of brick building) was significantly fueled by his association with the Northern German Heimatschutz movement that tried to resemantisize brick Gothic architecture as the highpoint of "Aryan German culture" in the interwar period.[8] This connection would be made clear by the unambiguous political and financial support that Höger and the Sloman family would give to the Nazi Party from its earliest moments.[9] By remaining silent on these aspects, the UNESCO report offers a narrowly crafted view of the Chilehaus and its relationship to modernity, repressing its political, financial, and ideological origins and motivations through the sublimation of its programmatic, stylistic, or constructive features.[10]

In turn, the disentanglement operations involved the active concealment of the provenance of both the financial means and the working culture, which served as the conditions of possibility for the Chilehaus in the first place. Only once, and in passing, is there a reference to the biography of its developer and the global trade that generated the entirety of the more than four billion marks necessary to achieve this construction. Buried on page 137 of the report, we read that the building was commissioned by "Henry Brarens Sloman, who owned saltpetre mines in Chile, and therefore had a ready supply of foreign currency, which is why he was able to construct the building during the inflation years."[11] Indeed, as biographers of Sloman indicated already in 1939, to acquire the funds necessary to build the Chilehaus, Sloman had sold large parts of his saltpeter mines in the Atacama Desert after the British Pacific blockade during World War I had made it virtually impossible for his product to reach German shores.[12] In all its complexity, this peculiar brick building embodies an alchemical transubstantiation of sorts: namely, the transformation of the capital accumulated after decades of mining the Atacama Desert in Chile for saltpeter into office real estate and brick expressionism in Hamburg.

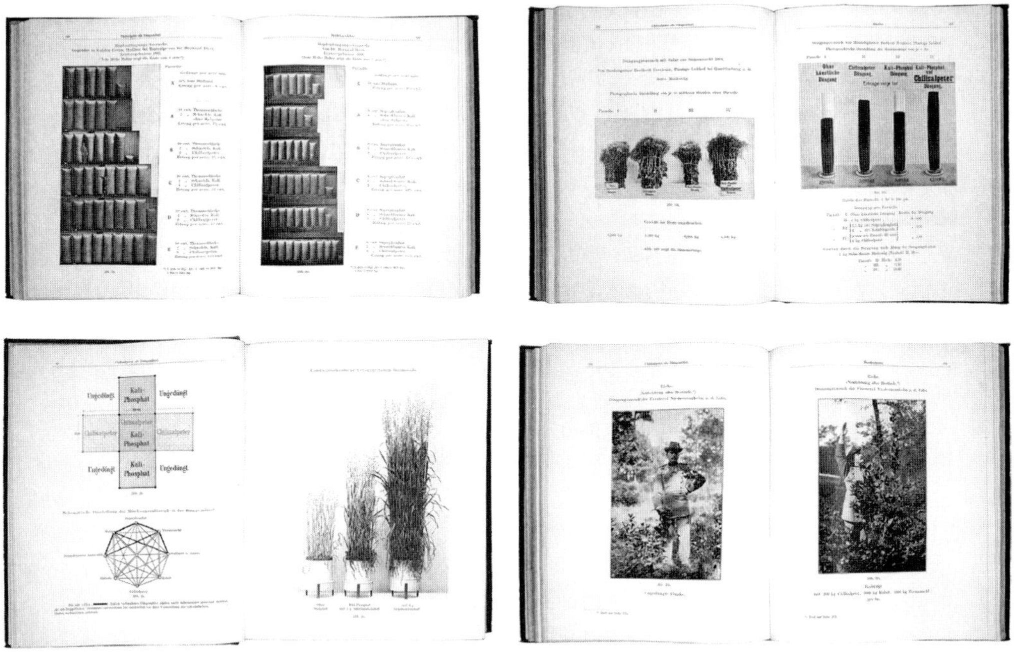

Figure 2. From Dr. M. Weitz's *Der Chilisalpeter als Düngemittel* (Verlagsbuchhandlung Paul Parey, 1905).

Henry B. Sloman made his fortune in one of the booming businesses at the turn of the twentieth century: extracting and refining saltpeter from the Atacama Desert and importing it to Europe. The great expansion of the nitrate industry in the Atacama region followed the *Guerra del Pacífico* (also known as the Saltpeter Wars) in which Chile, backed by the British Empire, was confronted with Peru and Bolivia between 1879 and 1883.[13] Saltpeter, or potassium nitrate, is a mineral that can be used as a powerful natural fertilizer or as an essential component for fabricating gunpowder. At a depth of about one and a half meters below the Atacama Desert floor, the driest place on earth, there was a mineral with an extraordinary capacity to fertilize agricultural land. The demographic expansion that followed the second industrialization in Europe was largely fed using this resource, which exponentially multiplied the output of an ever more limited agricultural land. European soil, the condition of possibility of human life in Europe, was largely produced by the exploitation of these geological deposits, whose composition was, at the time, variously theorized to derive from dinosaur bones, stardust (atmospheric sediments), millennia-old volcanic ash, and all rich organic substances that accumulated in what was once the ocean floor.[14]

By framing and disentangling the Chilehaus from these global historical dynamics, UNESCO not only eclipsed the building's provenance from neocolonial networks of extraction, but in doing so it missed the exceptional opportunity that buildings like the Chilehaus offer to understand the mechanisms through which architecture connects—and separates—

the rise of white-collar work in one part of the world with the industrialization of mining in the other. These two transformations were symmetrical, and their shared history crystallizes as much in the Chilehaus as it does in the landscape of the Atacama Desert. Simultaneously observing two apparently disconnected sites, we articulate an idea of modern architecture that is not limited to the formal, stylistic, and technological advancements of a particular building, but one that recognizes the techniques of mineral extraction in the "periphery" and the administration of financial and symbolic capital at the "center" as equally modern.

Management

There is a semantic connection between the Chilehaus, considered by UNESCO as "the first modern office building unlike any other that had existed before,"[15] and the mining sites in the Atacama Desert, also known as "oficinas." Before emerging in the context of modern bureaucracies, the term *oficina* (inherited from the Latin *officina* or "workshop") referred to mining concessions from the state and included the grounds from which minerals were extracted as well as the housing for workers, the machinery and industrial infrastructure required to process the minerals, the warehouses to store them, and all other facilities linked to the extraction process. Preserving this ancient cognate, saltpeter mining settlements in the Atacama Desert were called oficinas to distinguish them from the itinerant system of "paradas" that characterized the exploitation of minerals such as silver or nitrates by indigenous and mestizo free miners. If oficinas had remained relatively small operations until the 1870s, the arrival in the region of investment from England and Germany (often with local capital, advanced by Chilean banks) initiated the industrialization of these sites well before the arrival of Sloman.[16] With heavy capital investment came a culture of labor management hitherto unfamiliar in local mining culture. The semantic polyvalence of the term *oficina* points to a historical synchronicity: Just as managers invaded factories before inhabiting white-collar high-rises, Hanseatic managers began their operations in faraway mines before finding a home in the Chilehaus in Hamburg.[17]

Managerial culture in the desert entailed not only a newfangled regimentation of work but also the introduction of new social differences. As historian Sergio González Miranda has argued, the workers of modern saltpeter oficinas emerged as a new social class. Many of them were families who had long lived in the same region and territory, which had been incorporated into the production cycle of nitrates since preindustrial times. While many followed the labor opportunities that accrued with the concentration of national and foreign capitals, others were migrants from the south of Chile who had been expelled from the hacienda economy with the increase of intensive agriculture and mechanized farming.[18] As shown by numerous testimonies in unionized newspapers, workers lived in near-enslaved conditions inside the oficinas. The power that managers held over their captive populations was nearly total. Workers were not paid with money but with tokens to spend exclusively in company-owned stores. Oficinas were perceived as insulae within the state, areas of exception where the rule of law was suspended in favor of the regulations dictated by administrators. These managers, in turn, increasingly controlled who could come in and who could go out; who would receive an education and who would not; how much water every worker should get; the cost of labor and basic goods.[19]

Although the paper trail of this story tends to perpetuate managerial perspectives, often reproduced by memorial documents like the UNESCO report, the imprint that it left on the surface of the earth discloses a different story. The Atacama Desert is one of the most sophisticated storage devices on the planet. Indeed, the unique concentration of nitrates right below its surface is the product of its very mnemonic capacity. The extreme aridity and other environmental conditions have kept with precision not only the deep-time sedimentations that constitute the nitrates and other minerals, but also an extraordinary record of all the activity that ever occurred on its surface, as if they were drawings. Dryness, in this case, is memory, and all human and nonhuman traces in these landscapes have been registered on the surface, creating a millenary archive. This memory device is as vast as it is precise. Despite attempts to construct the desert as an uninhabited and forsaken environment, the omnipresence of traces reveals that there is no part of the desert that has not been marked by humans or animals.

In May 2024, our team went to the pampa in the Atacama Desert, in the former Cantón del Toco, the hinterland of the port of Tocopilla, to research the five mining sites Henry B. Sloman owned. Although the sites had been largely dismantled in the 1950s—Sloman had sold them to other investors already in 1920—the contours of the industrial infrastructures, housing, and mining grounds were made visible by a concatenation of lines, holes, debris, and accumulation deposits that appeared under the aerial view of a commercial drone. With the help of local historians and a wealth of archival resources on both sides of the Atlantic, we could appreciate the extraordinary storage capacities of the desert and began to read its patterns and lines literally as an archive, helping us reconstitute some of the most salient aspects of the social and territorial transformation enacted by the Henry B. Sloman Saltpeter Company, which was in activity between 1892 and 1920.[20]

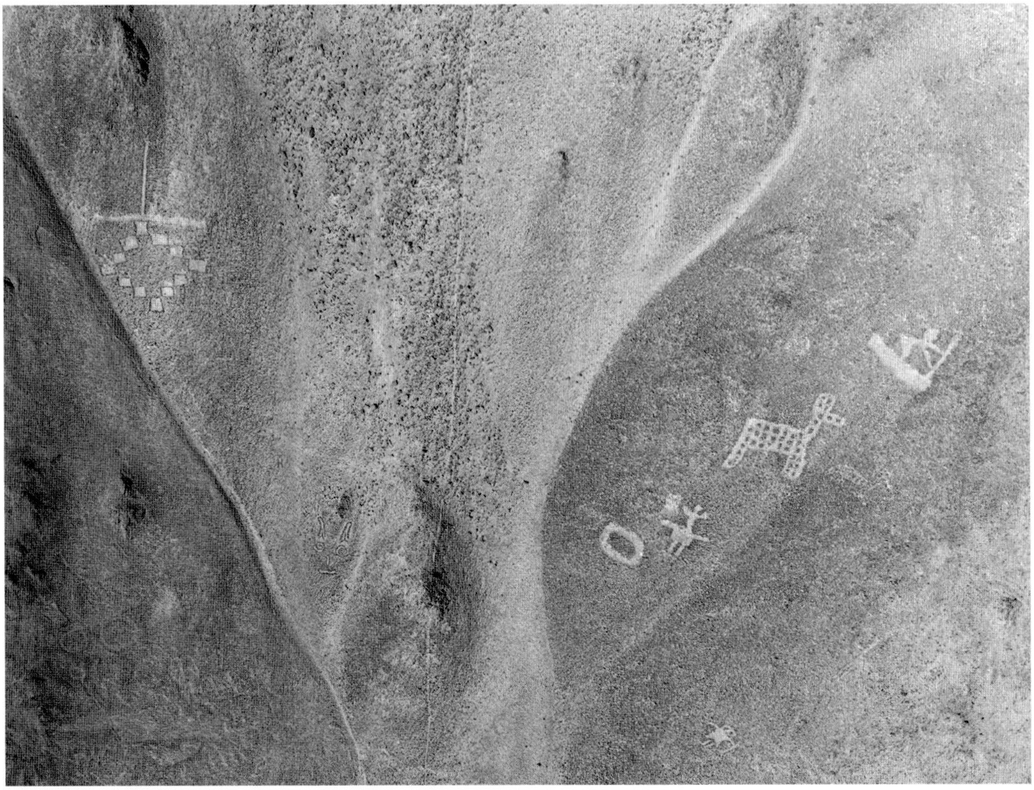

Figure 3. 20°37'34.9" S 69°39'50.9" W. Geoglifos de Pintados. Geoglyphs created by indigenous merchants between 700 and 1500 AD to serve as guides in the caravan routes. Pampa del Tamarugal. Comuna de Pozo Almonte. Courtesy of Alfredo Thiermann.

For instance, the constant struggle between industrialists and workers is registered perpetually in Atacama's salty crust. On the left part of this photograph, we see Oficina Buena Esperanza, the first oficina administered by Sloman. In 1892, shortly after Sloman had acquired the mining site, workers attempted to burn the entire facility in a big labor strike at this site. This was possible because the premises of Buena Esperanza, as most of the oficinas until the early twentieth century in Atacama, were built out of imported Oregon Pine wood.[21] On the right, we see the foundations of what would become the massive structure of Rica Aventura, the first oficina designed by Sloman, which introduced steel as its principal construction material for the first time.[22] As a direct response to the workers' strikes experienced a few years earlier, here, steel's modernity derives not only from its structural properties, lightness, and constructive malleability but also from its ability to drive a wedge between workers and capital. While the columns and beams used for the construction of Rica Aventura were reutilized for the construction of shanti towns in the region after the structures were finally dismantled in the 1950s, they left a grid-like pattern of holes in the ground that, like scars, register the entangled histories of workers struggle and technological development of the region.[23] These metal structures, as much as the shanties that were built with their remains, belong to the same historical constellation as the brick monument that Höger

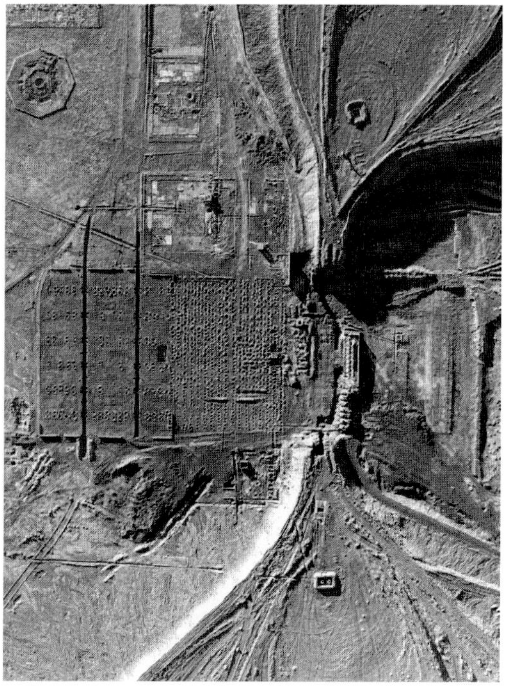

Figure 4a (*left*). 22°1'11.2' S 69°37'3.8' W. View of Oficina Buena Esperanza, the first saltpeter works bought by Henry B. Sloman from Eduardo Squire in 1892. Oficina Buena Esperanza, Cantón del Toco. Courtesy of Alfredo Thiermann.

Figure 4b (*right*). 22°2'18.1' S 69°37'18.1' W. Traces of the foundations of the steel structure that supported the cachuchos and chancadoras of a lixiviation plant using the Shanks method. The saltpeter drying ponds can be seen immediately to the left of the picture. Oficina Empresa, Cantón del Toco. Courtesy of Alfredo Thiermann.

designed, simultaneously, to house managers allegorizing the persistence of the German Geist through craftsmanship.

While office buildings in Hamburg provided the modern separation of reproductive from productive labor for managers, the industrial organization of the extraction of nitrates employed a new type of settlement in which the same industrialists managed, on site, both kinds of labor practices. These "saltpeter cities" (ciudades salitreras) aimed to organize and mobilize the greatest concentration of capital and labor to maximize the production of a commodity with a nearly infinite demand. A new type of biopolitical power emerged from this crucible, one that coincides with the development of company towns. It was common for oficinas to include civic infrastructures such as hospitals, churches, schools, libraries, theaters, and orchestras. In this image, we can see the imprint of an octagonal covered plaza at the bottom left. Slightly to its right, we see the footprint of a Catholic church that Sloman, of Protestant faith, built for the workers of Oficina Rica Aventura. On top of it, we find the trace of the hospital and, in front of it, the perimeter of the school in which, ironically, children were partially instructed in German.[24]

In 1908, the reformist politician Manuel Salas Lavaqui was commissioned to study the saltpeter works in northern Chile. In a chapter titled "Displays of Affection" (*muestras de afecto*), he praised Sloman for introducing two important reforms in his oficinas. The first was to turn the owners of the company stores or *pulperías* into salaried employees to avoid them making too big a profit from workers. The other was to put a list of prices

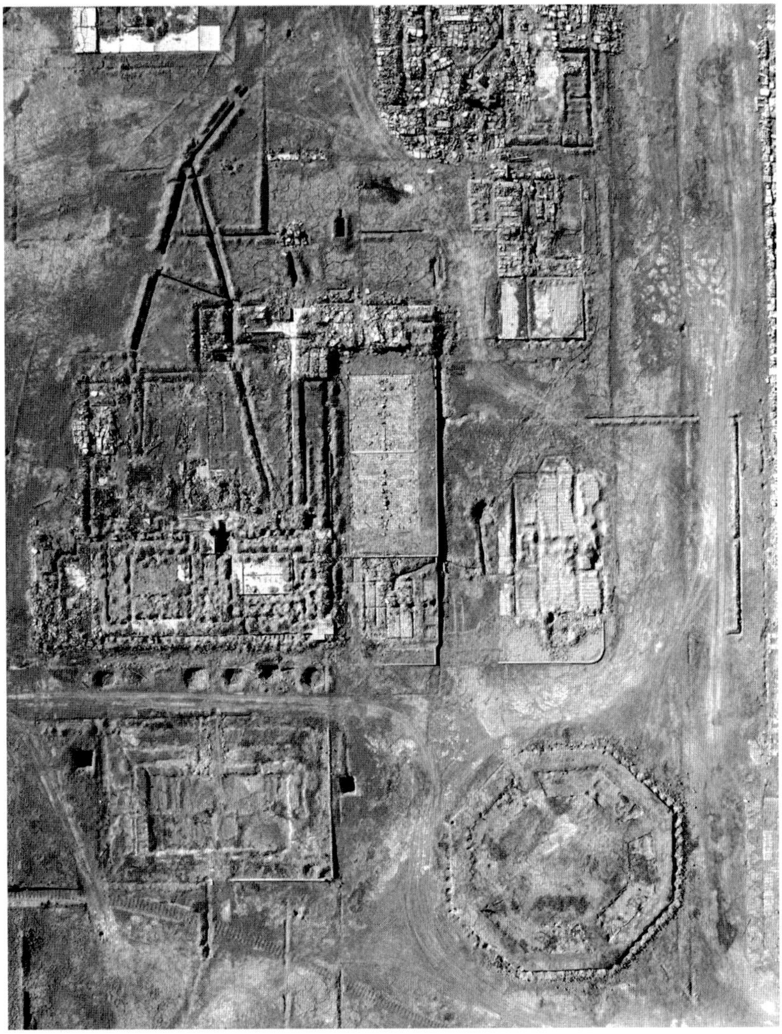

Figure 5. 21°59'7.7" S 69°36'32.8" W. Detail of public buildings including traces of the church, the school, the hospital and a covered plaza. The nonorthogonal geometry of the ditches suggests the presence of sanitary infrastructure. Oficina Rica Aventura, Cantón del Toco. Courtesy of Alfredo Thiermann.

outside the store to ensure collective supervision over the cost of goods. However, Salas Lavaqui also described many situations in which the "generosity" of the owners was outweighed by the cruelty of the managers and owners of pulperías, making clear that the workers' affection for the owners implied a generalized acceptance of the status quo. "Love, the proverb goes," wrote Salas Lavaqui, "tames the wild beasts."[25]

Class divisions have been inscribed endurably and unmistakably in these landscapes. On the left side, we see an overview of the workers' housing quarters of Oficina Rica Aventura. This was one of the largest camps run by Sloman. It could house up to two thousand workers simultaneously. On the upper half of the image, we see ten lines of barracks. These barracks were divided into narrow, long units, semi-attached to their neighbors on both ends. Each unit had one or two rooms without any internal circulation. They were intended for families—bachelors lived in communal barracks. These units had no access to electricity, water, or sewage facilities. The

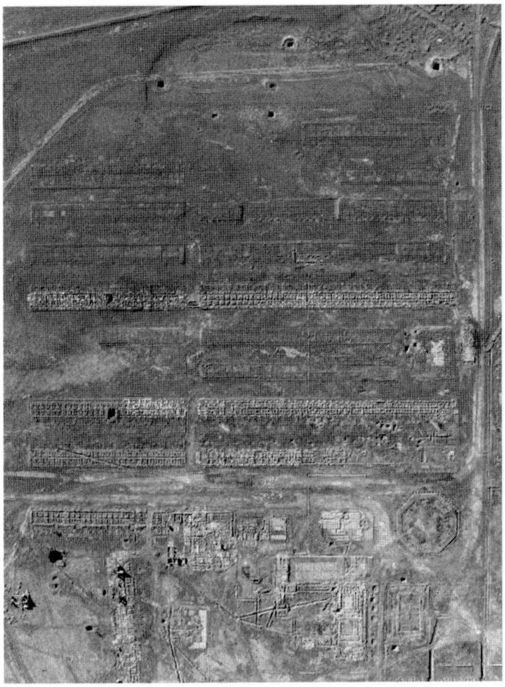

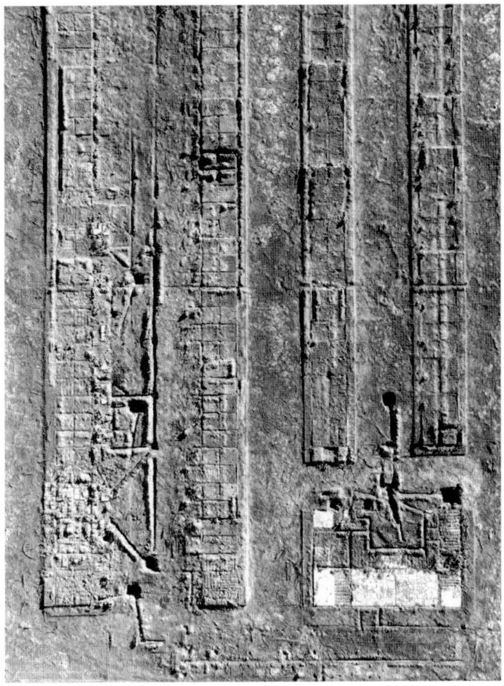

Figure 6a (*left*). 21°59'6.8" S 69°36'26.8" W. At the top of the image are several rows of workers' houses bordered at the bottom by public and administrative buildings. This oficina had a population of eighteen hundred workers. Oficina Rica Aventura, Cantón del Toco. Courtesy of Alfredo Thiermann.

Figure 6b (*right*). 22°2'13.9' S 69°37'7.9' W. Floor plans of the managers' houses, where the typical sewer system is also in view. Oficina Empresa, Cantón del Toco. Courtesy of Alfredo Thiermann.

photograph on the right, on the other hand, shows a network of deeper lines—some vertical, some diagonal. The housing units of employees and administrators did have access to sewage and water, occasionally even to electricity, as we can tell from archival pictures. The traces left in the desert cannot lie in this respect. Nor will they ever be erased. They register class divisions and asymmetries in ways that official documents and corporate archives actively conceal. They have become part of the landscape. Seen from far enough, not unlike the geoglyphs that preceded them by hundreds of years, they are a register of work and life, etched into the crust of the desert.[26]

Extraction

At what scale is the history of the Chilehaus told? The scale of the building, at which Fritz Höger reasonably developed his project, is less reasonably repeated in countless history books. This reaffirms its status as world heritage while blurring the historical synchronicity and material ties linking and separating the rise of office intellectual work in Hamburg with shovel labor in the South American desert. To understand the exorbitant amount of human labor employed in Sloman's operations, it may be useful to pay attention to this photograph (Figure 7). A line demarcating two types of territory shows what we have deemed the frontier of industrial capitalism. At the bottom of the image, we can see the unexploited desert. At the top, we see the expanding territory of extractive capitalism. The slight change in tone and the patterned plough lines reveal the traces of extraction. Each of these lines has around a meter and a

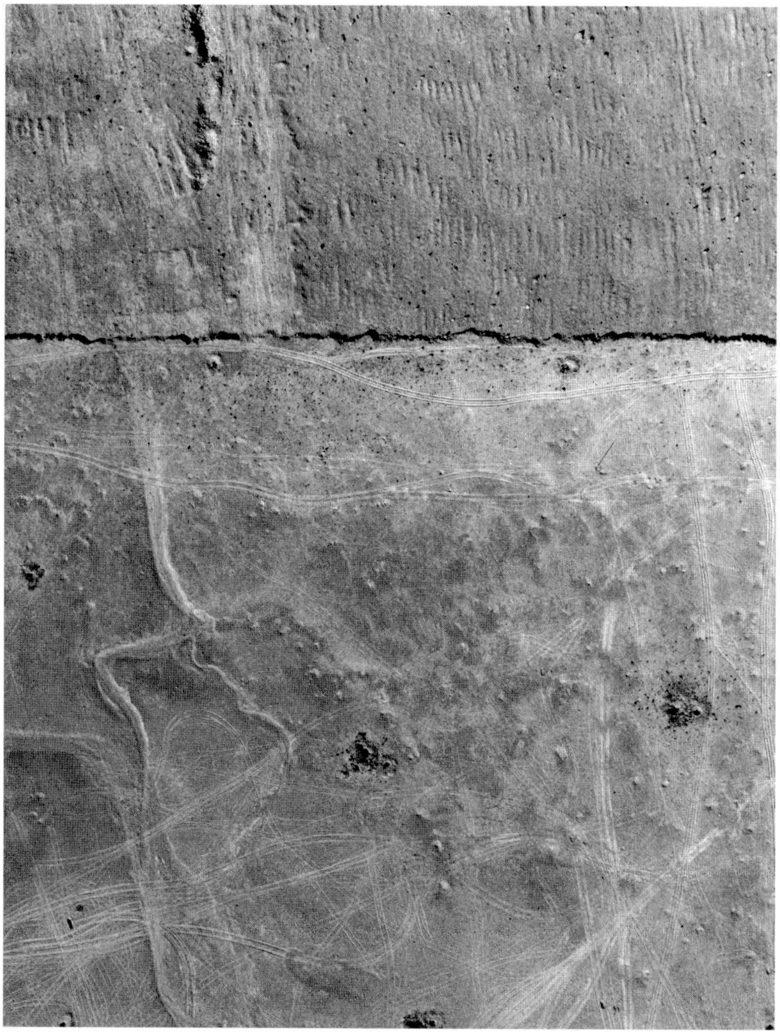

Figure 7. 22°1'2.6" S 69°38'42.5" W. The frontier line extends for dozens of kilometers and marks the areas of untouched desert from those that have already been exploited by Sloman. At the lower end of this line, drill holes can be seen in the untouched chuca. Fields between Oficina Buena Esperanza and Rica Aventura. Courtesy of Alfredo Thiermann.

half in width, enough to install a railway with a cart that was pushed manually or pulled by mules to transport the mined resources from the fields to the site where they were industrially refined. The unevenness between the two terrains may not be as visible in this aerial image: The exploited land is one and a half meters below the unexploited. This frontier extends over hundreds of kilometers and reveals the crude fact that tens of thousands of square kilometers of the surface of the desert were literally turned upside down by shovels and human hands. The Atacama Desert, one of the most uninhabitable places on the planet, was turned into a profitable geography through a metabolic process whereby fossilized nutrients—extracted with the sweat of the saltpeter workers—significantly increased the fertility of soil in Europe, enhancing, in turn, the nutrition of European bodies.[27]

Following the plough lines, we can learn how the extraction process was increasingly rationalized in the desert to maximize returns. Elevating several dozen meters above the

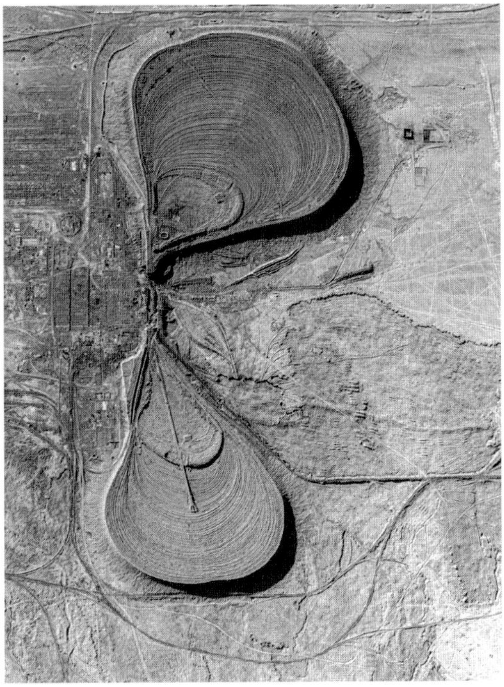

Figure 8a (*left*). 22°1'11.2" S 69°37'3.8" W. View of the Buena Esperanza office, the first saltpeter works bought by Henry B. Sloman from Eduardo Squire in 1892, with the irregular geometry of the ripio torta visible. The shape became common in later saltpeter works with the introduction of new industrial processes, imported from Germany from 1895 onward. Oficina Buena Esperanza, Cantón del Toco. Courtesy of Alfredo Thiermann.

Figure 8b (*right*). 21959'20.5" S 69°36'43" W. View of the ripio torta of the saltpeter works torta Aventura, founded in 1902 by Henry B. Sloman. Oficina Rica Aventura, Cantón del Toco. Courtesy of Alfredo Thiermann.

ground, the mounds growing outward from the steel structure are called *tortas* and are made of accumulated refuse from the extraction process. At eye level, these mounds of depleted soil may seem like fortuitous geographic accidents, perceived as part of the site's geography. However, from above, the size and shape of each torta reveal the size of the adjacent saltpeter work and the type of process that was implemented.[28] The left image shows the mining grounds of Oficina Buena Esperanza, as mentioned above, the first saltpeter work that Sloman owned. Sloman's company did not design this mining site; it was acquired in 1892 from another entrepreneur, essentially adopting the process of production used by its former owner.[29] The torta with the shape of a flower growing irregularly hints at an equally erratic extraction and refinement process. The image on the right shows the torta of Oficina Rica Aventura, the first saltpeter works fully designed by Sloman's company. Here, in contrast, the regular shape of the torta and grooves resembling tree rings reveal the adoption of a more systematic production process that confines refuse within regular and predictable geometries. This artificial landscape carries traces of the intensity and regularity of the work's activities. The shape of each of these rings may conceal stories about changes in production, strikes, or output regulations due to external reasons such as commercial agreements or wars.[30]

We can see another example of landscape transformation when we investigate the plough lines in Oficina Santa Fe and those made years later in Oficina Rica Aventura. Unlike the latter, Santa Fe was a saltpeter factory owned and designed by German entrepreneurs Fölsch & Martin (where Sloman was employed as a manager before starting his business). As seen on the left, the lines in Santa Fe trace paths of least resistance, organic shapes left by the erratic track of mules and other cargo animals. While extraction and transportation relied on artisanal techniques, the Oficina Santa Fe introduced multiple technological fixes in energy production for the industrial processes. In fact, this was the first oficina to build an electric dam on the Loa River, the only water source in the surrounding desert. In 1906, Sloman would build a second, much larger dam, with a thirty-eight-meter canted stone wall and a diameter of sixty-one meters, substantially transitioning the energy regime for his operations. This dam created a great artificial lake with a six-million-cubic-meter capacity, described by historian Damir Galaz-Mandakovic as "a refreshing artificial lacustrine irony amid so much desert."[31] Sloman used the dam to power three top-of-the-line 500 HP turbines that were connected to a Siemens-Schuckertwerke (SSW) generator with 525 volts, 370 kilowatts, and 375 revolutions per minute (all provided by German companies).[32] Rica Aventura's straight plough lines, seen on the right, are the traces of the machine in the desert. Parallel and repetitive, they show a systematic rhythm of extraction that is indifferent to paths of least resistance, like those left by animals in Santa Fe. These lines advance for tens of kilometers at a time without quivering. It was due to Europe's "compost hunger," as one German engineer wrote at the time, that "this production process had to be thoroughly rationalized": "instead of mule transport, the saltpeter area was opened up by rail; instead of the simple boiling process by which only very rich 'caliches' (saltpeter rocks) could be economically exploited, complicated lixiviation processes were adopted in industrial installations with high-precision machines; instead of wood combustion, coal combustion was used."[33]

These technical improvements required heavy capital investment in comparison with previous extraction methods. This rationalized method also demanded a more specific and rigorous division of labor: *calicheros, barreteros, corraleros, cafeteros, particulares, carreteros, carrilanos, boleteros, herramenteros, botarripios, canarios* are only a few of the different roles that workers could have in these camps. In these sites, which developed their own popular cultures, the struggle between workers and industrialists was permanent. They saw the emergence of workers' unions (*mancomunales*) as well as brutal mass killings, such as the one that occurred in Santa María de Iquique in 1907, where four thousand saltpeter workers were killed by their patrons in collaboration with the Chilean army after they protested for better working conditions. Although that event did not happen in Sloman's mining

Figure 9a (*left*). 21°52'12.8' S 69°33'20' W. Calichera in the pampa with organically shaped cracks caused by mining. Oficina Santa Fe, founded in 1886 by Fölsch & Martin. Courtesy of Alfredo Thiermann.

Figure 9b (*right*). 22°0'58.8' S 69°37'18.3' W. Calichera with linear and standardized plough lines. There is a change from Oficina Santa Fe; the lines are now systematic and parallel. Oficina Buena Esperanza, acquired in 1892 by Henry B. Sloman. Courtesy of Alfredo Thiermann.

sites, it directly affected his operations, as can be read in the annual report the company circulated among its investors. In 1908, the Sloman company reported that although it had been a challenging year, "unlike other neighboring mining sites, ours suffered no grievous affliction, or only tangentially, from labor tumult and other elemental upheavals," suggesting that what differentiated his company from his competitors' was the investment in technology, proudly adding that "the engine hall operates without mishap, and the dam upon the River Loa, brought into service this past year, has met all expectations in full measure."[34]

Further rationalizations of the extraction process become visible when we examine the explosions required to turn the desert mantle on its head. To extract saltpeter, it was necessary to blow up the desert soil with explosives—often potassium nitrate mixed with sulfur. On the left is a photograph of the mining grounds called *calicheras* in Oficina Santa Fe (Figure 10a). The perforation pattern is extremely erratic—almost a glyph of the maddening striving for profit in the desert. On the right, we see the precise grid of holes of the extraction sites owned by Sloman that were done years later. As planetary minesweepers, Sloman's workers drew grids of holes, each situated at about fifty meters from the next, to test the nitrate concentration on the ground at each given point. This type of territorial organization, which served to hierarchize the extraction process, had first been introduced to the desert by the government's Oficina de Guaneras y Salitreras to systematize the prospection and appraisal of land sold to investors at periodical auctions after

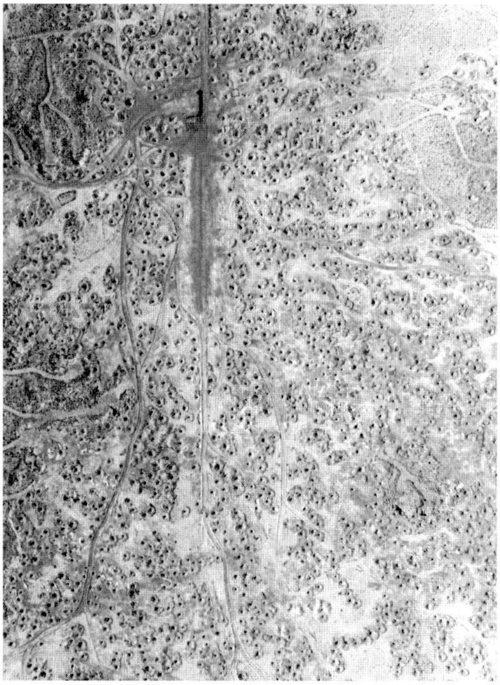

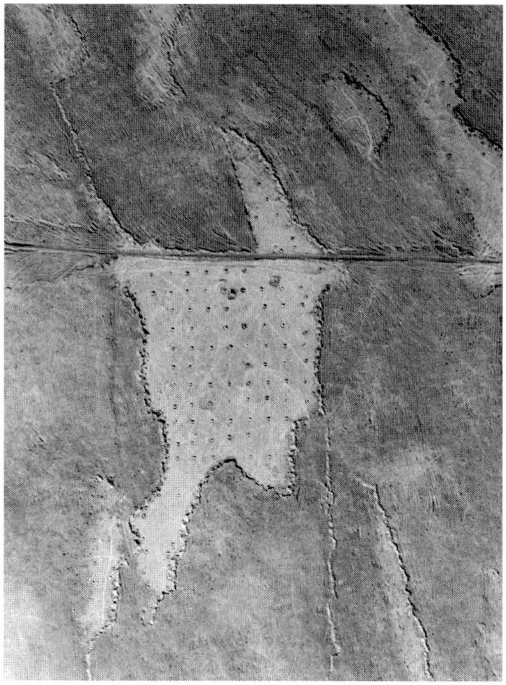

Figure 10a (*left*). 21°51'9.2" S 69°33'36.3" W. Calichera in the pampas with numerous detonation holes. In view are the paths over which the caliche was transported. Oficina Santa Fe, Cantón del Toco. Courtesy of Alfredo Thiermann.

Figure 10b (*right*). 22°0'10.1" S 69°38'5.3" W. Field with cateo holes in a grid pattern, each about fifty meters apart. Oficina Buena Esperanza, Cantón del Toco. Courtesy of Alfredo Thiermann.

the Guerra del Pacífico. It is often the case that we see patches of land, such as this one, that were left unexploited due to the low nitrate concentration revealed by these surveys. The entire territory, nature itself, was rationalized by a grid—one that could be further abstracted in printed tables used, in turn, by managers to anticipate risks and maximize returns statistically.[35] It is this very process which eventually allowed capitalists like Sloman, and his employees, aided by telegraphs and telephones, to govern their business from office buildings at a distance.

Office Work

The Chilehaus was often perceived as a solid and stable masonry building, aspiring to link traditional craftsmanship and brick with immaterial national values. Against the grain of that narrative is the fact that the Chilehaus crowned a boom of high-rise office buildings in reinforced concrete underway in Hamburg since the 1880s.[36] While the smooth, continuous curves of the building's perimeter that we observe in the floor plan make for its expressionist monumentality, the dotted intercolumniation of the concrete frames supports its outward grandeur by bracing the unpredictability and inherently unstable reality of transnational trade. The plan of the Chilehaus, impermeable, rhythmic, and stable in its outline, absorbed the intrinsic volatility of transnational mining with its internal flexibility.

Contemporary descriptions of the precarious lives of white-collar employees disclose this regime of perpetual fluctuations. In 1930, soon after the Chilehaus was completed and critically

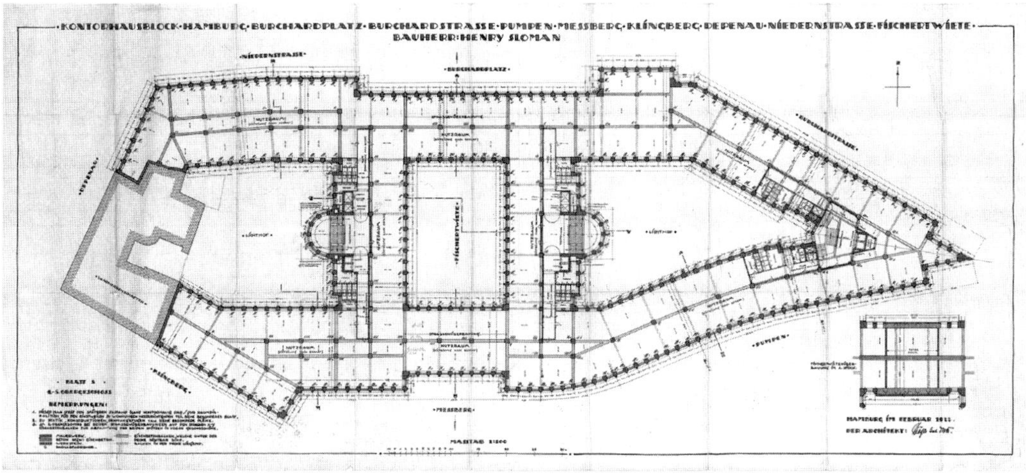

Figure 11. Fritz Höger, Typical plan Chilehaus, Hamburg, floors 1–5. Dated February 1922. Amt für Bauordnung und Hochbau, Hamburg.

acclaimed, Siegfried Kracauer published his influential essay *The Salaried Masses,* in which he investigated the rise of white-collar labor throughout the 1920s in Germany. As businesses grew larger and more complex, control fell into the hands of managers rather than owners. The Chilehaus—which UNESCO describes as a "modern office building architecture unlike anything that existed anywhere before"[37]—was designed to house this new type of salaried worker. This white-collar employee managed records, logistics, statistics, and paperwork. According to Kracauer, the highly repetitive and mechanized nature of bureaucratic work created a culture of conformity in which workers were expected to adhere to strict routines and norms—"an industrial reserve army of salaried employees," he argued, "has come into being." [38] To cope with the monotony and pressure of office work, Kracauer argues, many turned toward mass culture, such as cinema, to distract themselves from the repetitive patterns experienced in their daily routines. However, this docile and obedient class, which hungered for norms, also risked turning deeply reactionary if their privileges were endangered, as happened after the 1929 financial crisis.

One can extrapolate Kracauer's descriptions to the lives of the workers inside the Chilehaus, as they manage companies and operations, through paperwork, on the other side of the Atlantic. After all, the development of the Kontorhaus district in Hamburg aimed to create an administrative center for the logistics companies that used the Speicherstadt warehouse infrastructure. In fact, despite supposedly selling most of his mining grounds in Chile after World War I, Henry B. Sloman continued to manage most of his operations in the Southern Cone through his offices located inside the Chilehaus.[39] Understood in such a way, buildings like the Chilehaus were the data centers of their day. Within them, the accumulation of global information on things such as soil composition, the weather, or nautical routes could be gathered and mobilized toward calculating significant gains. But as we have seen, the drawings in the desert, no less than this building's layout, kept registry of the tension between modernity's unpredictability and its mirages of control and stability. As in an unbalanced double-entry ledger, they reveal this tension as two apparently separate and incompatible stories.

By framing and disentangling this building from its colonial origins, UNESCO buried under the narrative of material progress the nature of a truly global and modern event: the simultaneous destruction of the Atacama Desert and the indigenous culture and lives it supported, and the rise of the managerial class in cities such as Hamburg. Understanding these two events as simultaneous and codependent demands a different politics of memorialization from such institutions. Despite UNESCO's selective forgetfulness, it is a blessing for the historian that the desert can truly not forget. Dry, salty, rugged, and silent, everything that has ever touched its surface is condemned to eternal memory. Walking on its crust, one treads on the surface of a millennia-old archive, a memory device that stores everything that world heritage has decided to forget.

Biographies

Alfredo Thiermann is assistant professor of History and Theory of Architecture at the École Polytechnique Fédérale in Lausanne, where he directs the Laboratory for History and Theories of Architecture, Technology and Media. He previously taught at Harvard University and the Pontificia Universidad Católica de Chile.

Pedro Correa is a research assistant at the Laboratory for History and Theories of Architecture, Technology and Media at the École Polytechnique Fédérale in Lausanne, where he also teaches architecture history. He is a doctoral candidate in architecture history at Columbia GSAPP.

Ella Neumaier is a doctoral candidate at the Laboratory for History and Theories of Architecture, Technology and Media at the École Polytechnique Fédérale in Lausanne. She holds an MA in architecture (Cultural Heritage, History, and Criticism) from TU Munich.

Xavier Nueno is a postdoctoral researcher at the Laboratory for History and Theories of Architecture, Technology and Media at the École Polytechnique Fédérale in Lausanne, where he also teaches architecture history. He holds a PhD in Film and Visual Studies from Harvard University.

Notes

[1] This research was supported by the Swiss National Science Foundation (SNSF) under grant no. 10003568, for the project Data Centers: An Environmental History of Information, 1850s–1950s.

[2] UNESCO, *Nomination for the UNESCO World Heritage List: The Speicherstadt and Kontorhaus District with Chilehaus* (UNESCO, 2015), 26.

[3] While recent studies have explored the relationship between Hamburg's architecture and its colonial past, Germany's colonial expansion in South America remains largely overlooked. Jürgen Zimmerer and Kim Sebastian Todzi have produced one of the most thorough accounts of Hamburg's colonial history, yet their work makes almost no mention of the mining enterprises in Chile, the Chilehaus, or the Sloman family—key actors in Germany's imperial entanglements. See Jürgen Zimmerer and Kim Sebastian Todzi, *Hamburg: Tor zur kolonialen Welt: Erinnerungsorte der (post-)kolonialen Globalisierung* (Wallstein Verlag, 2021).

[4] On the architectural history of the Kontorhaus district, see Ralf Lange, *Das Hamburger Kontorhaus. Architektur, Geschichte, Denkmal* (Hamburg: Dölling and Galitz Verlag, 2015). On the Chilehaus and Fritz Höger, see Claudia Turtenwald, ed., *Fritz Höger (1877–1949) Moderne Monumente* (Dölling and Galitz Verlag, 2003).

[5] Lange, *Das Hamburger Kontorhaus*, 27.

[6] The building was famously photographed by the Hamburg-based brothers Adolf and Carl Dransfeld, who in the 1920s had turned to architecture photography, staging projects for architects like Fritz Schuhmacher and Fritz Höger. Circulated in the media before the Chilehaus was even unveiled, the image with its low perspective resulted in a dynamic, exaggerated gesture that immediately elevated it to its iconic status. Supported by Höger's ambitions, the photograph became the illustration to imputations of the Chilehaus as a "laughing, victorious formation of a gigantic thought." Rudolf G. Binding, "Das Chile-Haus in Hamburg," *Deutsche Kunst und Dekoration* (2025). The most comprehensive overview of Adolf and Carl Dransfeld's oeuvre is Matthias Müller Prove, "Hamburg Reloaded—Architekturphotographie der Gebrüder Dransfeld, 1919 bis 1932," http://photo.mprove.net/dransfeld/index.html (accessed March 5, 2025).

[7] We take the terms "framing" and "disentanglement" from the economic sociology of Michel Callon. To account for how goods or services are created, Callon uses "framing" to refer to the process of defining the boundaries of an economic or social interaction. Meanwhile, disentanglement refers to the process of separating goods, services, or individuals from the social, cultural, or network ties that surround them. Something similar we see occurring in UNESCO World Heritage monuments that become a new kind of currency in the symbolic economy of world history. Michel Callon, "The Embeddedness of Economic Markets in Economics," *The Sociological Review* 46, no. 1 (1998): 1–57.

[8] See Hans Much, *Norddeutsche Backsteingotik Ein Heimatbuch* (Georg Westermann, 1923), 6. For pre twentieth-century brick buildings in the Hanseatic League, see, for example, Hans Josef Böker, *Die mittelalterliche Backsteinarchitektur Norddeutschlands* (Wissenschaftliche Buchgesellschaft, 1988); and Ernst Badstübner et al., eds., *Früher Backsteinbau zwischen Ostsee und Alpen*, Studien zur Backsteinarchitektur, 8 (Lukas Verlag, 2024).

[9] Höger ardently believed that the "Volksseele" (soul of the nation) could be cured by ridding the German building spirit of foreign influence. He saw this as committing to the "idealistic world view of the forming spirit of the Third Reich," and in 1934 he promoted to ban all "evil formations of Bolshevism" like the Weissenhofsiedlung in Stuttgart or the Bauhaus Dessau. Gerhard Kaldewei, "'Zu dienen Volk und Vaterland'—Der 'niederdeutsche Backstein-Baumeister' Fritz Höger und sein Werk im Kontext der Nordischen Kunsthochschule Bremen im Dritten Reich," in *Stadtmuseum Delmenhorst*, ed. Gerhard Kaldewei (Isensee Verlag, 1999), 95–96. The Chilehaus and other buildings by Höger also appeared in the *Nazi Monthly Bulletin* in 1937. The article praises Höger for his immunity to foreign architectural styles and as the ideal of the Lower German tradition. *Nationalsozialistische Monatshefte*, Heft 92, Jahrgang 8 (November 1937). However, to Höger's dismay, he never established himself as part of the architecture elite in the Nazi era. Hitler preferred classicist buildings by architects such as Albert Speer or Paul Ludwig Troost over Höger's "North German Expressionism," which was soon considered "degenerate." See Kaldewei, "Zu dienen Volk und Vaterland," 108.

[10] The most thorough research on Höger's Nazi past is David Templin, "Wissenschaftliche Untersuchung zur NS-Belastung von Straßennamen. Abschlussbericht, erstellt im Auftrag des Staatsarchivs Hamburg," November 30, 2017. https://www.hamburg.de/resource/blob/50388/1cfc0532ce77788d3193501fb16485db/d-st-ueber-uns-verkehrsflaechen-templin-abschlussbericht-ns-belastete-strassennamen-data.pdf (accessed October 1, 2024).

[11] UNESCO, *Nomination*, 137.

[12] "The Chilehaus was built entirely with money from Chile. However, as these funds had to be converted into marks beforehand, as the authorities stipulated that all payments to suppliers and workers could only be made in the national currency, and as the mark was devalued very quickly due to the slow conversion process, new foreign currency had to be obtained again and again, which made construction very expensive. This shows once again how the Germans channeled their foreign-acquired assets into the German economy and encouraged it in this way." Hildegard von Marchtaler, *Die Slomans. Geschichte einer Hamburger Reeder- und Kaufmannsfamilie* (Kommissionsverlag bei Hans Christians Verlag, 1939), 238.

[13] The conflict started when Bolivia attempted to raise taxes on Chilean-controlled nitrate companies. British investors, with significant stakes in the region, indirectly supported Chile, despite Britain's neutrality. Chile's victory resulted in the annexation of vast nitrate-rich territories from Bolivia and Peru, greatly benefiting the interests of foreign investors in the region, particularly from Britain. For a synthetic account, see John Bellamy Foster and Brett Clark, "Ecological Imperialism and the Global Metabolic Rift: Unequal Exchange and Guano/Nitrates Trade," *International Journal of Comparative Sociology* 50, no. 3–4 (2009): 311–34.

[14] The main reference on the business of saltpeter in Chile remains: Dr. Semper and Dr. Michels, *Die Salpeterindustrie Chiles* (Verlag von Wilhelm Ernst & Sohn, 1904). There is a Spanish translation that was widely used in the early twentieth century: *La industria del salitre en Chile,* trans. and expanded by Javier Gandarillas and Orlando Ghigliotto Salas (Imprenta, Litografía i Encuadernación Barcelona, 1908). See also Enrique Kaempffer, *La industria del salitre i del yodo. 1907–1914* (Imprenta Cervantes, 1914). The literature on the uses of Chilean nitrates in Germany includes: Dr. M. Weitz, *Der Chilisalpeter als Düngemittel* (Verlagsbuchhandlung Paul Parey, 1905); and *Delegation Der Vereinigten Salpeter Producenten.* Berlin-Charlottenburg, n.d.

[15] UNESCO, *Nomination,* 18.

[16] Damián Lo Chávez, "Tarapacá, 1718–1875. La Larga era del beneficio proto-industrial de minerales," *Iqueique* (March 2024): 49.

[17] This is most strikingly illustrated by the professional life of Henry Sloman's sons Enrique and Ricardo and other employees from the Hanseatic mercantile elite. They started their career overseeing operations and workers in the desert before eventually retreating to Germany, moving up within the company and simultaneously acting as board members or expert advisors to trading corporations, banks, or even divisions of the German Empire. See biographical company records, 1954, Henry B. Sloman Archive, uncatalogued. The close relation between neocolonial entrepreneurship and the multilevel managerial apparatus in the German Empire is present in figures from the West German mining elite as well, such as Ruhr industrialist Theodor von Möller. His company K. & Th. Möller built at least one of Sloman's oficinas while Möller acted as Prussian minister of trade from 1901 to 1905. He had been a protagonist in economic interest associations since the 1870s and became one of the loudest advocates for German colonial ambitions. Möller's activities for the Sloman enterprise are documented in photographs depicting the building site of Oficina Rica Aventura, ca. 1902, Henry B. Sloman Archives, uncatalogued. For biographical information on Theodor von Möller, see Stefan Hartmann, "Möller, Theodor Adolf von," in *Neue Deutsche Biographie,* vol. 17 (1994), 634–36, online version. Accessed May 25, 2025. https://www.deutsche-biographie.de/pnd117083186.html#ndbcontent. See also Eckhard Hansen and Florian Tennstedt, eds., *Biographisches Lexikon zur Geschichte der deutschen Sozialpolitik 1871 bis 1945,* vol. 1, *Sozialpolitiker im Deutschen Kaiserreich 1871 bis 1918* (Kassel University Press, 2010), 110.

[18] Sergio González Miranda, "La presencia indígena en el enclave salitrero de Tarapacá: Una reflexión en torno a la fiesta de la Tirana," *Chungara. Revista de Antropología Chilena Tarapacá* 38, no. 1 (2006): 36.

[19] Take, for instance, this letter sent to the workers' newspaper *El Trabajo:* "During the work stoppages which took place at the Empresa office last week, nearly all the peddlers in the various German saltpeter offices were taken prisoner. By what right are the peddlers apprehended? By none, it is certain, since no provision of the law authorizes the administrators to become policemen or judges capable of issuing arrest warrants. The insula of the Toco [mining canton] is the greatest sarcasm introduced into the territory of the republic." *Semanario El Trabajo* (May 21, 1905). Or this other letter in which a worker states: "These abuses border on the unbelievable. In the pampa the only authority is the administrator to whom the police obey as servants to the master." *Semanario El Trabajo* (April 3, 1905). We thank historian Damir Galaz-Mandakovic for facilitating us these sources.

[20] Technically, the Henry Sloman Saltpeter Company was only founded in 1904. Prior to this, Sloman was operating with multiple limited companies. Here we take the date 1892 as the founding date only because it corresponds to the first acquisition of an entire saltpeter works. On the foundation of the limited company in 1904, see *Jahresbericht der H.B. Sloman & Co. Salpeterwerke Aktiengesellschaft in Hamburg. Für das zweite Geschäftsjahr vom 1. Januar bis 31. Dezember 1905.* Staatsarchiv Hamburg. 231–7_B 1964–29. Band 1.

[21] See von Marchtaler, *Die Slomans,* 225; and Adriana Capaldo, "Expansión imperialista y su particularidad en la explotación alemana de las salitreras del cantón El Toco 1880–1930" (Master's thesis, Universidad de Chile, 2010), 34.

[22] Sloman collaborated with Friedrich Kraemer, an engineer for K. & Th. Möller, to design the steel structures. The import of material and the construction management on site was executed by the same firm, which quickly became the leading engineering company for the German saltpeter industry. Based in Brackwede, by 1914 they had built twenty-two oficinas spanning five regions of the desert, including six in the Tocopilla area. See Paul Haubrock, *Chemie-Vortrag "Salpeter" von Paul Haubrock* (Manuscript, 1914): 102. Stadtarchiv Bielefeld. 200,162/FamArchiv Haubrock.

[23] On the dismantling of the oficinas, see Sergio González, *La Pampa Escrita. Cartas y fragmentos del desierto salitrero. Fuentes para la historia de la república XXVI* (Ediciones de la Dirección de Bibliotecas, Archivos y Museos, 2006), 74.

[24] The main architectural study to date of the "ciudades salitreras" is Eugenio Garcés Feliú, *Las Ciudades del Salitre. Un estudio de las oficinas salitreras en la región de Antofagasta* (Orígenes, 1999). On the relation between oficinas and company towns, see Damir Galaz-Mandakovic, "De comunidad política a comunidad im-política: El fin del company town (Tocopilla, Chile, 1915–1996)," *Urbano* 26, no. 47 (2023): 58–69.

[25] Manuel Salas Lavaqui, *Trabajos y antecedentes presentados al Supremo Gobierno de Chile recopilados por encargo del Ministerio del Interior* (Imprenta Cervantes, 1908), 880–883.

[26] "The absolute lack of electricity, water and sewage facilities and services in the workers' housing was striking, but not in the employees' housing. The absence of toilets meant that they had to resort to public toilets, when there were any, and the water supply had to be obtained from the only water through on the block, and in some cases the lack of a kitchen meant that a fire had to be improvised in the courtyard, in the shade." Garcés Feliú, *Ciudades del salitre,* 42.

[27] John Bellamy Foster, "Marx's Theory of Metabolic Rift: Classical Foundations for Environmental Sociology," *American Journal of Sociology* 105, no. 2 (September 1999): 366–405. See also John Bellamy Foster, Brett Clark, and Richard York, *The Ecological Rift: Capitalism's War on the Earth* (Monthly Review Press, 2010). And more recently: John Bellamy Foster and Brett Clark, *The Robbery of Nature. Capitalism and the Ecological Rift* (Monthly Review Press, 2020).

[28] See the testimony of Sloman's grandchild Hans-Jürgen Sloman's trip to Chile in 1953 on the orographic landscape of the tortas: "The torta keeps growing every year, so that the edge rails have to be constantly moved. These mounds of baked earth are the typical sign of all saltpeter offices, where you can still recognize the place where an office once stood many decades later, even if there is not much else to remind you of it, apart from the foundations left behind and the plundered fields around it. The importance of the offices can be judged by the size of their tortas." Hans-Jürgen Sloman, *Reisebericht aus Chile* (Manuscript, 1953), 29. Staatsarchiv Hamburg. 621–1/46_625.

[29] "Mr. Eduardo Squire sells Mr. Enrique B. Sloman sixteen 'estacas' of the saltpeter-rich lands he owns in Toco, which constitute a part of the forty 'estacas' granted to him by the Chilean Government, by decree of May 12, 1883, as final settlement of the rights which Mr. Juan J. Meiggs [legally succeeded by Squire] had in that region. It is noted that the 'estacas' to which reference is made measure 1,600 meters on each side, constitute a total area of 2,560,000 square meters, each 'estaca' in accordance with Bolivian legislation." Contract of sale of the Buena Esperanza office. Herr Eduardo Squire to Enrique B. Sloman. Third quarter of 1892. Translated from Spanish into German and contained in the file of documents accompanying the formation of the joint stock company that Henry B. Sloman formed in 1904. Staatsarchiv Hamburg, 231–7_B 1964–29 Band 1.

[30] "The price of the entire sale is the sum of twenty-five thousand pounds sterling, which the buyer will distribute among the sellers as follows: to Mr. Otto Harnecker, seventy percent, to Mr. Juan Federico Haefliger, twenty-one and a half percent, and to Mrs. Carmen Ruiz, widow of Sáez, the remaining seven and a half percent. . . . The sale includes the shares and rights of all kinds directly or indirectly related to the saltpeter exploitation, the active or passive services (*easements*) and the concessions, enjoyments or privileges of any kind, which are to be related to it. The sale also includes machinery and buildings." Contract of sale of the Rica Aventura office. Herr Otto Harnecker and others to Banco Mobiliario. First quarter of 1895. Translated from Spanish into German and contained in the file of documents accompanying the formation of the joint stock company that Henry B. Sloman formed in 1904. Staatsarchiv Hamburg, 231–7_B 1964–29 Band 1.

[31] While providing electricity to Sloman's oficinas, the dam also had severe ecological and socioeconomic consequences for the downstream village of Quillagua. On the tranque Sloman and its impact on the Loa River, see Damir Galaz-Mandakovic, "Río, murallas y turbinas. Innovación hidroeléctrica en el cantón El Toco: Tranque Santa Fe y Tranque Sloman," *Revista de Ciencias Sociales* 28, no. 43 (2019): 80.

[32] *Die Anlagen der Chile Exploration Company in Tocopilla und Chuquicamata. Ausgeführt von den SSW in den Kriegsjahren 1914 bis 1916* (Siemens-Schuckertwerke, 1920).

[33] M. Weitz, *Der Chilisalpeter,* 23.

[34] "Annual Report of the Hamburg Saltpeter Company H. B. Sloman & Co, from 1 January to 31 December 1908," translated from German into English, presented to the Board of Directors chaired by Henry Sloman. Staatsarchiv Hamburg, 231–7_B 1964–29 Band 1.

[35] On the practice of prospection: "The irregular extension of the caliche deposits, the great difference in thickness from one point to another, and their varying *lei* [quality], require that before acquiring a piece of land or before starting to exploit

it, the existence of usable saltpeter must be revealed with precision by means of a meticulous survey of the deposits. On a flat terrain whose surface is not subject to erosion caused by alluvial deposits, test pits are taken 100 to 300 meters apart, in parallel lines, and placed in such a way that the pits in each row fall between two pits in the next. If of two neighboring shots, one gives good quality caliche and the other does not, another shot is drilled in the center to delimit the useful ground." Semper and Michels, *Die Salpeterindustrie Chiles*. The state surveys of saltpeter plots in the Cantón del Toco can be found in *Delegación Fiscal de Salitreras y Guaneras. Décimo remate de terrenos salitrales de Tarapacá y el Toco* (Imprenta-Litografía Barcelona, 1918).

[36] A detailed account of the Kontorhaus' turn-of-the-century development can be found in Architekten- und Ingenieur-Verein zu Hamburg, *Das Hamburger Kontorhaus* (Boysen u. Maasch, 1909). At the latest in the 1890s, concrete frames, open floor plans, and facades with increasingly repetitive window schemes became an economic consideration that organized rentable space and maximized profit.

[37] UNESCO, *Nomination*, 18.

[38] Siegfried Kracauer, *The Salaried Masses. Duty and Distraction in Weimar Germany* (Verso, 1998), 30.

[39] In 1920, Sloman transferred his holdings in the Atacama Desert to a new company under Chilean law, Compañia Salitrera de Tocopilla (CST), to avoid impending expropriation of his German assets after the war. From 1925, he also held the majority shares to an agriculture, livestock, and coffee plantation in Brazil, Companhia de Viação de São Paulo, a connected transport company, Companhia de Viação de São Paulo Matto Grosso, and from 1927, the Cia. Sudamericana de Colonizacion y de Comercio, which like the CST was founded to protect and manage Sloman's holdings in the turbulence of the 1920s Chilean saltpeter politics. To finance and manage both his plans for the Chilehaus and his trading activities, Sloman also founded a bank, Sloman Finanzbank A.G., which had its offices in the building. Ricardo Sloman, *Das Entstehen, Entwickeln und teilweise Erlöschen des Sloman'schen Besitzes* (Manuscript, 1954). Henry B. Sloman Archive.

Figure 1. Langøya south crater, drone photo, 2019. Courtesy of NOAH.

Thomas McQuillan

An Island, Translated
A Geology of Provenances

In the fjord, some fifty kilometers south of the city of Oslo, an island is nearing completion. After "100 years of extracting limestone and 30 years as a landfill, Langøya is being restored to one of Oslofjord's natural gems," according to the Norwegian waste management company NOAH.[1] By 2030, NOAH is set to have restored the island by reproducing its original form, positioning it as a demonstration of the company's ambition for circular resource management. This essay explores the island's layered history, tracing its multiple transformations over time, an archaeology unfolding at the scale of geological time and mirrored in the landscape's shifting regimes of ownership across modernity. Langøya illustrates the malleable conceptions of resource extraction, terraforming, and landscape restoration, forming a paradoxical local model of the Anthropocene, in which human activity becomes inseparable from geological transformation. In a prescient 2009 essay, Dipesh Chakrabarty argues that "anthropogenic explanations of climate change spell the collapse of the age-old humanist distinction between natural history and human history."[2] On a planetary timescale, the island is a process more than four hundred million years in duration, during which it was slowly built up through biostratigraphic layers. Obliterating it through extraction took a mere century. From 1895 to 1985, the island served as a limestone quarry for the Christiania Portland Cementfabrik (CPC), whose product was the major source of concrete for the building of the city of Oslo. The history of the island is one of inversion: As the city expanded, the island shrank—its matter blasted out to build the architecture and infrastructure that enabled the city's growth. Its roads and highways, rail infrastructure, and public and private buildings between 1950 and 1980 owe their existence to the cement that the island provided when blended to concrete. Emptied of its contents, the island found new use as a dumping ground for toxic waste. Now, as the mounting waste is reaching capacity, this landfill is being reconceptualized as a natural restoration. In the process, the island is *translated,* in the dual sense of this word, from one idiom into another, and as a passage between sites and material states, akin to the ceremonial transfer of relics, conferring renewed meaning, status, and place.

The history of Langøya prompts a broadening of the scope of provenance research, which typically documents chains of ownership, emphasizing objects' legitimacy and economic

Future Anterior
Volume XXII, Numbers 1–2
Summer / Winter 2025

and cultural value. Recent work in the field of art history has expanded the use of the concept beyond simple ownership and transfer, employed to assure authenticity and just ownership. While the traditional "expression of provenance in words has developed into a formula to articulate systematically and 'scientifically' the litany of past owners and record the means by which an object passed from one to the next," recent work in provenance is blazing fresh trails, by considering material histories, their contexts, and the forces that shape artifacts and transform landscapes.[3] Reframing provenance in this way allows it to be understood as a complex interaction between materiality, location, valuation, and the forces that interact with each, making the concept particularly apt for describing the layered transformations landscapes of extraction.

Langøya's provenance is geological, industrial, and now ecological, each phase reframing its perceived value, illustrating that landscapes, like artifacts, accumulate multiple and at times conflicting histories, and move beyond linear accounts of origins to become laminates of use, ideology, and environmental transformation. Transitions such as these demonstrate the contending ideologies of the value of infrastructures and landscapes on the scale of Langøya. For early geologists, this was a place of scientific discovery. For capitalists, a material resource to be extracted, while for architects, a source of responsive modern material. In its current process of transformation, the island is emerging as an emblem of our anthropogenic moment in which boundaries between the natural and artificial are increasingly intermixed to create a hybrid form, a simulacrum of a landscape disappeared.

Ownership

In his seminal 1986 study of the cultural biography of things and commoditization processes, Igor Kopytoff provides a useful lens to understand the way that ownership influences the status of things being exchanged. From an economic perspective, anything exchanged is simply an item of value that can be traded for another in an abstract way, while from a cultural perspective the production and flow of these items are culturally and cognitively constructed: "Shifts and differences in whether and when a thing is a commodity reveal a moral economy that stands behind the objective economy of visible transactions."[4] This process, which Kopytoff describes as the movement between commoditization and singularization, helps explain how certain objects—or even landscapes—can shift from priceless to mere resource. "To be a non-commodity is to be 'priceless' in the full possible sense of the term, ranging from the uniquely valuable to the uniquely worthless."[5] For Kopytoff, something is commoditized when it is removed from a state of singularity and channeled into the domain of exchange, its value no longer defined by cultural or social meaning but by its potential for trade, extraction, or economic gain.

Langøya's history of ownership illustrates this movement. The earliest records from 1624 show Langøya as part of a feudal estate owned by a Margrethe Brockenhuus, its value tied primarily to landownership rather than resource exploitation. Brockenhuus died unmarried and in the absence of kin, the property transferred to *Norges rikes kansler* (chancellor of Norway) Jens Bjelke in 1637, the country's wealthiest landowner. Records of a "Peder the Limeburner" living on the island attest to its use at this time as a source of lime mortar.[6] As limestone extraction became a profitable activity on the island, its value increasingly came to be measured not just as land but in terms of the materials it could yield. Purchased in 1732 by an Arent Kjerulf for 252 riksdaler, it was sold on in 1737 to King Christian VI of Denmark and Norway at a handsome profit for 2,000 riksdaler. Under royal ownership, the island supplied cement and mortar for Denmark's royal works and Norway's coastal defenses. However, royal finances, strained by the Napoleonic Wars, led to the auction of the site in 1806, where it fetched a paltry 1163 riksdaler to a Norwegian landholder.

What had once been a site of small-scale production now became increasingly integrated into expanding networks of industrial material supply. Throughout the first half of the eighteenth century, the island passed through a succession of hands before the mineral rights were purchased by an Ignas Wankel in 1845, who extracted the rock for the production of lime mortars, agricultural soil treatment and the production of lye for the burgeoning paper industry, extracting some six thousand tons annually.[7] In 1895, the island was acquired by the CPC, who held it for ninety years, and excavated nearly fifty million tons of limestone. The island, once singular, had now been entirely eradicated by the logic of extraction, its form dissolved into raw material. Following the closure of the aging cement works at Slemmestad, some thirty kilometers south of Oslo, in 1985, the island was sold for 137 million Norwegian crowns to the government-led waste disposal consortium NOAH of which the Norwegian state held a majority share.[8] With this, the island began to reattain singularity anew—not as a source of commodity but as a scar in the landscape, a visible remnant of decades of extraction, repurposed as a receptacle for society's toxic by-products. In 2003, both the island and the waste processing business were sold for 280 million crowns to Bjørn Rune Gjelsten, one of Norway's richest industrialists. This shift in ownership marked a new phase in the island's *longue durée:* As it transitioned from industrial infrastructure to speculative asset, its value was no longer tied to resource extraction or waste injection, but to the promise of future development. As the refilling draws to a close, his company Gjelsten Holding recasts the island's future as a return to public use, framed within the company's broader claims of circular resource stewardship. The role of the island shifted as it changed hands, from an eighteenth-century quarry, first artisanal and then industrial, to a twentieth-century landfill intended to deposit toxic waste, to a twenty-first-century showcase for circular restoration, promoted as a future public asset even as its speculative value continues to shape its fate.

Geology

Langøya first enters the literature as a touchstone for scientific inquiry, becoming a foundational site in the development of local biology and geology. In 1826, the pioneering Norwegian botanist Mathias Numsen Blytt surveyed the island and collected herbarium samples, now held by the Oslo Botanical Garden. In the same year, it became the focus of geological study, through the work of the founding figure of Norwegian geology, Balthazar Keilhau, whose 1838 work, *Gaea Norvegica,* first mapped the geology of the entire country and laid the basis for geological research in Norway. But a decade earlier, his 1826 *Darstellung der Uebergangs-formation in Norwegen,* centered around Langøya as a natural case study of the complex geological dynamics that shaped the region.[9] This area, today known as the Oslo Formation—in Keilhau's time as the *Christiania Silur-Becken*—had a unique geological significance in the nineteenth century, providing an exceptional record of both Paleozoic sedimentary rocks and extensive igneous activity, and offering the opportunity to study the interactions between these formations. The unique fossil record, volcanic features, and tectonic structures of the island made it a key site for advancing stratigraphy, paleontology, and emerging theories of Earth's geological processes. Keilhau theorized that geological events could cause the transubstantiation of rock, from one form to another through chemical alteration, effectively transforming its composition and structure. At Langøya, the Silurian sedimentary layers, deposited by the slow decomposition of marine organisms such as trilobites, brachiopods, and corals between 440 and 420 million years ago, are marked by sharp zig-zagging intrusions of Permian era feldspar and hornblende, of far greater youth.[10] How did they arrive there?

For Keilhau, the jagged bands in the rock reflected a chemical transformation influenced by geological processes. Langøya, with its striking formations, served as an important case for the "Neptunist" interpretation, which posited that all rocks, including ones later understood to be volcanic, had originally formed as sedimentary deposits from primordial seas. In 1837, Keilhau

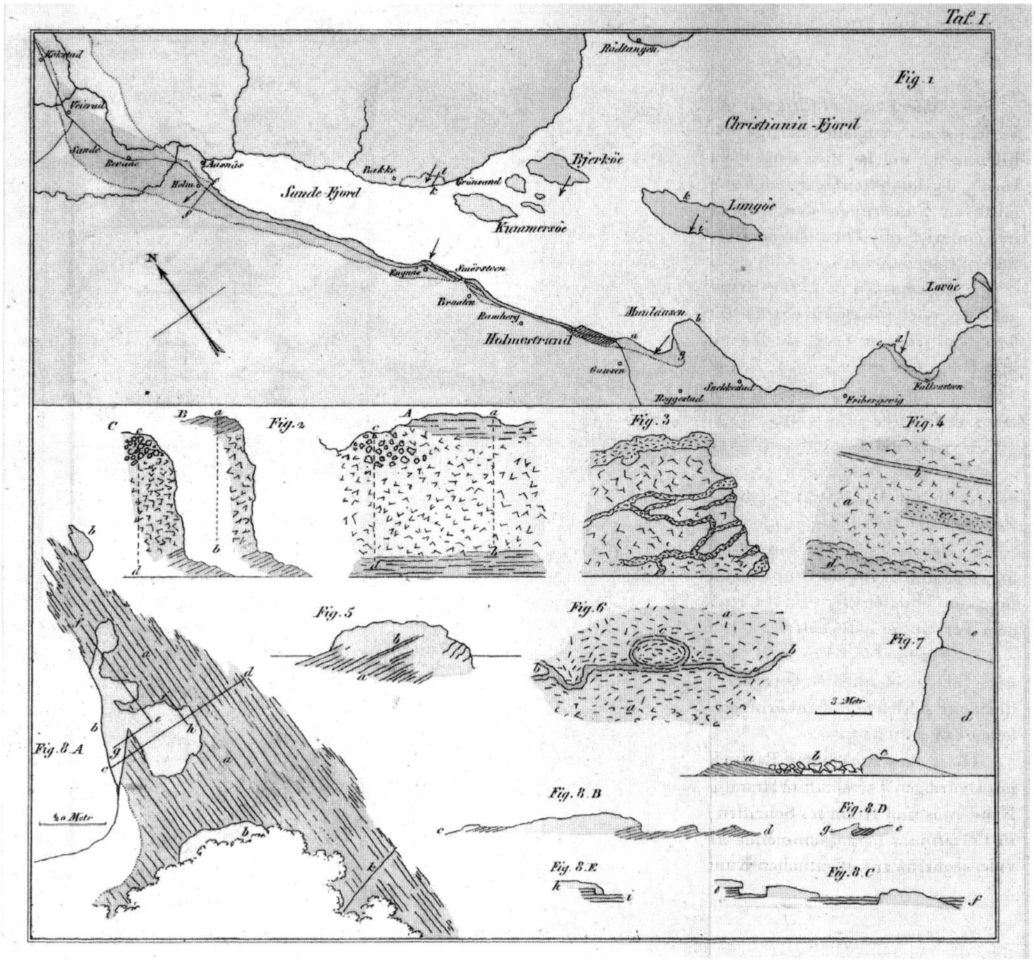

Figure 2. Map of Langøya from Balthazar Keilhau, *Darstellung der Uebergangs-formation in Norwegen* (Verlag von Johann Ambrosius Barth, 1826).

invited the groundbreaking English geologist Charles Lyell to Christiania (Oslo) for a geological tour of the fjord, including a boat tour to Langøya. While Keilhau believed that the evidence they found there supported the view that sedimentary rock could be transubstantiated into crystalline, Lyell—whose "Plutonist" interpretation, introduced by James Hutton fifty years earlier, that volcanic magma could shoot through older sedimentary rock—saw at Langøya a vivid demonstration that igneous and sedimentary rock were chemically distinct and complexly interwoven by volcanic processes.[11] Lyell's view ultimately became the standard, forming the foundation for modern geology's understanding of Earth's dynamic crust and the processes of intrusion, crystallization, and contact metamorphism.

The island remained a touchstone for geological research in the next century. Keilhau's student, Theodor Kjerulf, broke with his mentor in "one of the bitterest conflicts in Norwegian scientific history," and later succeeded him in the professorship, where he further advanced the Plutonist perspective, solidifying the modern understanding of the so-called Oslo Formation.[12] Kjerulf saw Langøya as a clear refutation of Keilhau's "romantic" notion of transubstantiation, noting in his 1857 *Ueber die Geologie des südlichen Norwegens* that "anyone doubting the true volcanic nature of our porphyry mountains must visit this area."[13] In this intellectual contest, Langøya served as evidence in the dispute over the provenance of geological knowledge—whether rooted in Neptunist or Plutonist traditions. The minute fossilized layering and fracturing intrusions provided clues to the geological history of the world—clues that, in retrospect, resemble what Carlo Ginzburg would later describe as a microhistorical examination of "the most trivial details" to understand the larger-scale historical fabric: "By this method, details usually considered of little importance, even trivial or 'minor,' provided the key for approaching higher aspects of the human spirit."[14] The island's stratigraphy became an index to the shifting authority of the scientific paradigm, the minutiae of sedimentary layers revealing the history of the world. While Kjerulf's work destined Keilhau's interpretations to the dustheap, it also laid the groundwork for future research. In 1871, Kjerulf led a group of students on an excursion to the island for further fieldwork. Among them was a student of zoology, Waldemar Brøgger, whose interest lay in the rich fossil layers of the Silurian period found there. For Brøgger, the visit was a turning point, which led him instead to pursue geology as his primary field of study. Brøgger would become a monumental figure in Norway, first as a prolific and exacting geological scientist, and later as professor and rector, instrumental in the establishment of the University Library and the Botanical Garden in Christiania, both realized in *Drammensgranitt,* a stone whose name he had coined.[15] As we will see, Brøgger would be instrumental in recommending and acquiring the island for the CPC.

The legacy of Langøya as an open-air laboratory for geological research culminated with the contributions of Johan Kjær, a mining engineer and geologist whose meticulous fieldwork and mapping complemented the foundational studies of his predecessors, helping to refine the broader understanding of the geological complexity of the Oslo basin. Kjær, who studied under Brøgger at the Kongelige Frederiks Universitet, today the University of Oslo, conducted extensive research at Langøya, dedicating to it sixty-nine pages of his 1908 *Das Obersilur im Kristianiagebiete,* in which he reviewed and extended Kjerulf's work on its geology. Kjær's research provided an extremely detailed reckoning of the Silurian layers, in which he identified six distinct periods (Stages 8α, 8β, 8γ, 9α, 9β, and 9γ) on the basis of the fossils found within. Kjær also had drawn up the first accurate topographical map of the island as a color plate, showing the nearly original contours of the topography prior to the CPC's extensive mining, and exhibiting traces of only

Figure 3. Photograph of the Northwest edge of Langøya, from Johan Kjær, *Das Obersilur im Kristianiagebiete. Eine-Stratigraphisch-Faunistische Untersuchung* (Kristiania, 1908).

scattered sites of extraction. Johan Kjær's work on Langøya provided foundational insights into the island's geological and paleontological significance as well as the Oslo Formation as a whole. As a result, Langøya remains a key site for understanding the dynamic processes of the Silurian period, from sediment deposition and fossil preservation to magmatic intrusions and tectonic deformation. This work helped establish its place as a scientifically valuable geological location.

Nonetheless, the island represented a different resource for the building industry, having long been recognized locally as a source of limestone for the production of quicklime mortars. Early techniques for firing the lime were small in scale and artisanal in character. In rough stone ovens, chunks of limestone broken by hand from the ground were stacked in alternating layers with wood and fired to achieve calcination. This process was both labor intensive and protracted, requiring days or even weeks of tending. Technological advances in the mid nineteenth century led to the development of a more industrial methodology. The Portland process, developed in England by Joseph Aspdin in the 1820s, produced a cement that far surpassed the old artisanal method in both appearance and strength. The key to this process was temperature. While earlier kilns had produced mortars at heats of around 900°C, innovations in oven technology—namely Frederick Ransome's 1873 rotary kiln—allowed temperatures of up to 1450°C. At this heat, gaseous carbon is released in greater quantity into the atmosphere, and the lime forms spherical nodules, known

Figure 4. Map of Langøya from Johan Kjær, *Das Obersilur im Kristianiagebiete* (1908).

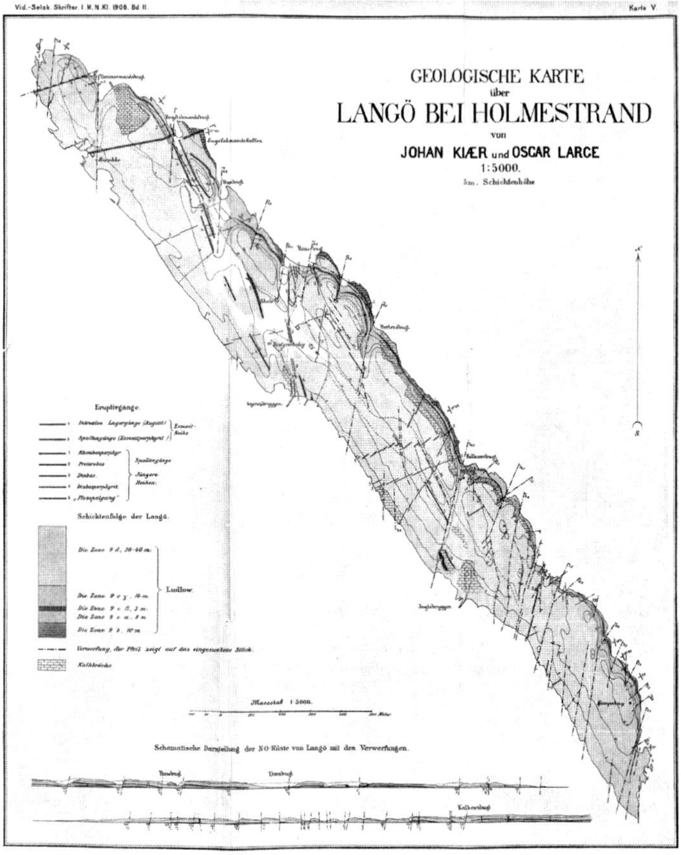

as clinker. This process, fed by pulverized coal, is the very image of carbon pollution, expressed chemically in this way: $CaCO_3(s) \dashrightarrow CaO(s) + CO_2(g)$, or in prose: Calcium carbonate (solid) is fired, producing calcium oxide (solid) and carbon dioxide (as a gas). The cement produced, and the concrete that it enables, is thereby a major source of carbon emissions. In this way, we can trace the provenance of the carbon emissions that threaten the present-day climate to the technological and industrial transformation of the island from geological history to an extractive process whose ramifications are only recently fully coming into view.

Acquisition

As the industrial potential of Langøya's limestone became apparent, it drew the interest of investors seeking to capitalize on the island's resources. In 1892, a group of local investors purchased a failed cement factory at Slemmestad. Their initial plan to extract limestone from the site proved difficult, and expensive. They turned to the day's leading expert in geology, Waldemar Brøgger, whose transformative experience during his 1871 excursion to Langøya had changed the course of his academic career. In the company of his colleague professor Johan Vogt, Brøgger acted regularly as a consultant to business, frequently advocating enthusiastically for the potential of resource development and the importance of a national conception of natural resources—particularly stone—ensuring that foreign owners did not gain control over Norwegian quarries.[16] Extraction was in the national interest. The CPC engaged Brøgger to evaluate the site as a source of limestone for their product, and his report to the board formed the basis of the company's decision in 1895 to purchase the island. He was also retained as a go-between, negotiating the price with the current owner Ignas Wankel, and setting terms and conditions for the use of the site. Rumors swirled that Brøgger had inquired only about a site for a country house, and kept the name of the company anonymous, to assure a lower price.[17] Despite his personal experience with the island, Brøgger apparently had few qualms about recommending its exploitation. In the end, the acquisition of Langøya by the CPC set the stage for a wholesale demolition of the fossil record for profit. In the process, millions of years of terrestrial history was transformed into an industrial product, reduced to little more than clinker for the production of cement.

Following its acquisition in two tranches in the 1890s, the island became the CPC's near total source of limestone. Early extraction was performed by manual labor, breaking the stone with hand tools and charges of dynamite to blow out larger chunks for further processing. But demand was rising, as concrete became ever more attractive in the building industry and its engineering methods more developed. In the beginning, 246 men were employed in the quarry, many of whom rowed themselves in small boats to the island for work. By 1920, this number had grown to 584.[18] A community grew up on the island, a company village, with a school for children. Still, the island possessed no source of water, which had to be gathering from rainwater pools or freighted over from the mainland in barrels. Not until 1956 was a line drawn from the mainland for fresh water.

Business boomed for the CPC in the postwar period. Road building, rail lines, and public buildings all received the limestone from Langøya, burned to cement. An electric cable was laid from the mainland in 1920, allowing for mechanized equipment and greater rapidity in extraction; only thirty-six years later would a water main be drawn to the island for its inhabitants. In 1927, rail cars and locomotive were installed to more efficiently freight broken stone to its shipping quay. There, a silo fed the stone onto purpose-built vessels, obviating the old method of barrel transport. By the 1950s, greater efficiency halved the number of workers. While in 1913, 1,000 tons of broken stone required 7,643 hours of labor; by 1965 this figure had sunk to 1,182 hours.[19]

Figure 5. *Manual Boring*. Photo album, early twentieth century. Courtesy of Slemmestad bibliotek, geologisenter and cementmuseum.

Figure 6. *Serial Detonation*. Courtesy of Slemmestad bibliotek, geologisenter and cementmuseum.

The process of the production of cement on the wet method utilized by the CPC essentially anonymizes the biological and geological traces from the Silurian era, preventing any precise account of where the historical biological remnants that created the stone ended up, once utilized in building. In this course, its lithic identity is blurred, its provenance reset. The limestone, once extracted, is robbed of much of its geological specificity as it is transformed into generic cement. This chemical transmutation exemplifies Tim Ingold's notion of material transformation as an active and ongoing process, complicating

Figure 7. *Waterline to Langøya.* Courtesy of Slemmestad bibliotek, geologisenter and cementmuseum.

Figure 8. *Dangerous Work.* Courtesy of Slemmestad bibliotek, geologisenter and cementmuseum.

Figure 9. Christiania Portland Cement Headquarters, Oslo, early 1960s. Courtesy of Slemmestad bibliotek, geologisenter and cementmuseum.

traditional notions of provenance based on the traceability of the origins and structure of the findspot, and revealing instead the lived experience of the extractive process. For Ingold, "the properties of materials, regarded as constituents of an environment, cannot be identified as fixed, essential attributes of things, but are rather processual and relational. They are neither objectively determined nor subjectively imagined but practically experienced. In that sense, every property is a condensed story."[20] The mineral powder procured, a blendable raw mix burned at Slemmestad, was ferried by barge thirty kilometers to city terminals at Filipstad and Sjursøya for further distribution by truck and mixer. The flow of these materials was under control of a governmentally sanctioned cement cartel (A/S Norsk Portland Cementkontor), a collaborative office manned by the three major Norwegian cement producers and headquartered in CPC's main offices downtown facing the city hall.[21] This building, designed by John Engh from 1959 to 1961, was constructed in prefabricated concrete panels and in situ placement, cast from Langøya limestone whose "essential" qualities were supplanted by the use they provided to architecture.

The growth of Oslo was paralleled by the diminishment of the island in the Oslo fjord. By 1953, fifteen meters had been excavated under sea level. In 1964, a level of thirty meters was reached. By the apex of production in the late 1970s, work con-

Figure 10. *Limestone Wall.* Courtesy of Slemmestad bibliotek, geologisenter and cementmuseum.

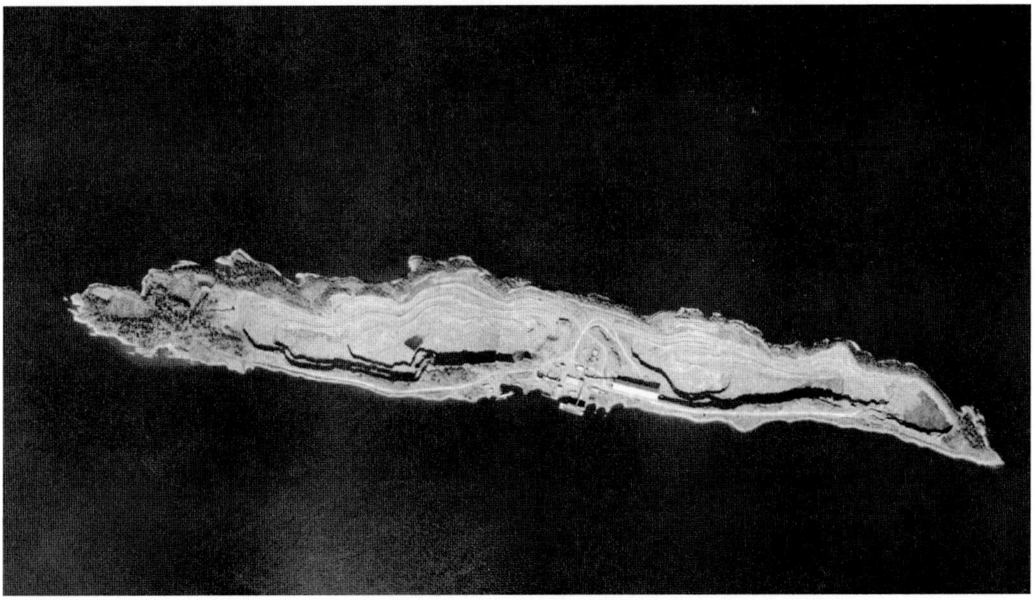

Figure 11. Langøya, aerial photo, 1986. Photographer unknown. Courtesy of Kartverket.

tinued fifty meters below sea level. The expansion of extraction left little room for those who once lived and worked on Langøya. As the craters widened, homes were demolished and the small community that was once found on the island dwindled and disappeared. By the 1960s, the last of the remaining houses were removed to accommodate further quarrying, and as extraction expanded, the workforce itself dwindled. By 1985, only thirty-one workers remained; two years later, just nineteen.[22] By the closure of the cement works at Slemmestad in 1985, a total of forty-seven million tons of limestone had been broken from the island and burned to cement. The quarry abandoned, an island hollowed out, created a paradoxical void: once a valuable source of national material, now, suddenly an environmental scar, and a hole in the sea that needed to be filled.

A Plaster Cast

The conglomerate Norcem, into which the CPC had been folded in 1968, explored alternatives to the problem of what to do with the hole that they had inherited—a charged and contested site, bearing the layered claims of multiple actors, a geological artifact shaped both by deep time and by the interventions of modern industry. Across the fjord, it became publicly known that the industrial enterprise Kronos Titan had for years exceeded the legal limit of discharge of sulfuric acid into the fjord and was facing penalties.[23] The factory had been a pioneer in the production of titanium dioxide (TiO_2)—or titanium white—since its founding in 1916. This pigment produces a white unmatched in brightness, opacity, and durability, and became an essential feature of modernist spaces, enabling the white aesthetic of the era.[24] Its production, however, produces a significant amount of toxic byproduct: sulfuric acid. Since its founding, this waste had simply been released into the wild. Increasingly stringent laws on pollution required them to find a safer way to discard it. More than eight million liters of sulfuric acid, in addition to hundreds of tons of chromium, copper, nickel, zinc, cobalt, and mercury were released annually. For Norcem, Kronos Titan's waste offered profitable new use for their hole, repurposing the pillaged island as a hazardous materials disposal site. There was ample space, and the cavity was presumed leakage-proof, but another reason—related to chemistry—recommended the site for the Kronos waste. In an unexpectedly serendipitous fashion, the acid from titanium white production (H_2SO_4) would react with the calcium carbonate ($CaCO_3$) in the limestone, which under the site's aqueous conditions hydrates to form calcium sulfate dihydrate ($CaSO_4 \cdot 2H_2O$), otherwise known as gypsum. By depositing this waste product into the cavities, a plaster filling could be constructed, layer by layer, resulting in one of the world's largest plaster casts, poured into a form shaped by geological forces and explosive extraction, vast in both temporal depth and spatial extent.

This reversal in fortunes mirrored a reversal in process. While for a hundred years the landscape had been emptied of its contents, providing mortars and cements for building cities and roads, now the waste products from its industries could be channeled back into the void. Adoption of the EEC Council Directive on Hazardous Waste in 1991 necessitated that the Norwegian state develop comprehensive waste management plans, including the identification and approval of sites for the safe disposal of toxic and hazardous matter.[25] In 1991, NOAH was created to meet this demand, and purchased the island in 1993 as a hazardous materials disposal site. Echoing Brøgger's imperative to keep quarries in Norwegian hands, Minister of the Environment Thorbjørn Berntsen, authorized the purchase by the Norwegian state to prevent the American firm Waste Management from acquiring it.[26] Virtually any kind of inorganic toxic waste could be mixed into the gypsum slurry being produced by the mixture of acid and lime. Fly ash from the burning of household refuse in the generation of district heating was admixed into the deposit. Asbestos from the decontamination of buildings followed. Heavy metal-contaminated soil excavated during construction, such as that of the Oslo Opera House, completed in 2008, found a new resting place here. Indeed, as the reception of contaminated materials developed into a profitable business, toxic waste from Sweden, Ireland, Italy, and elsewhere was dumped into the craters. But the process was not without risks. On at least two occasions, careless addition of volatile chemicals to the mix resulted in runaway reactions, boiling over and releasing massive clouds of toxic gasses to the nearby town of Holmestrand, where residents reported burning eyes and difficulties breathing.[27]

When the island again changed hands, from the state-led consortium to a corporate entity headed by Bjørn Rune Gjelsten, this transference also signaled a change in identity for the island. No longer simply a site to deposit toxic waste, it became an advantageous business, and reportedly the most profitable unit in Gjelsten's portfolio.[28] A recent report details a yearly import of waste into the island of more than a million tons, roughly half of which was toxic—mainly ash from burning garbage for district heating in Sweden, Denmark, Norway, the Baltics and Ireland, mixed with sulfuric acid from Kronos Titan, and sundry asbestos and industrial detritus—while the other half was "ordinary" garbage: polluted soils, demolition waste, and sludge.[29]

In a striking manner, the cavities of Langøya inscribe the cost of extraction as a reciprocal landscape, to use Jane Hutton's term, in which any urban development "is materially linked to another place: a largely invisible yet very connected *elsewhere*."[30] The history of the building of the modern concrete society was laid bare there as the absence that resulted from its construction. Here are layers of translation: from geology to resource and from industry to urban history. Now as the site fills, it has become a prosthetic island, an imprecise reproduction of a landscape that bore the traces of geological history. The island now taking shape owes only the most notional correspondence with the topography obliterated. For its future value, the replication of the lost island is an

Figure 12. *Crater Lake.*
Photo: Astrid Westvang.
Public domain.

important step in concealing the memory-hole whose presence, rich in cultural and historical value, remained a hinder to its real estate. This process, paradoxical as it might seem, is also somehow inevitable. Society demanded building, and in turn, a place to hide its waste, creating archaeologies of extraction that is a spatial and material model of modernity itself. The island, closed to the public for one hundred years, is once again reopening. But what is jarring is that in the quest to solve the problem of the whole and restore a natural area, a simulacrum of a landscape lost is being created.

But there is another, more precise and telling simulacrum produced in this process: that of the boundary between the excavated quarry and the hardened slurry that has filled it. While the International Geological Society declined in 2023 to officially designate an "Anthropocene" era in the geological record, citing the difficulty in establishing a global 'golden spike' to mark it, here at Langøya, a very precise and identifiable geological threshold has been created and preserved—that of the interface between the craters of excavation and the molded face of the plaster cast.[31] We might speak of an Oslo local Anthropocene marker: an instance of reverse archaeology, indicative both of the terraforming that occurred here as well as the sedimentary deposition of societal waste into solid form. This *plaster monument,* to employ Mari Lending's apt phrase, lies cached, a solid cradled still in its form: a monumental plaster cast, forever concealed.[32]

Biography

Thomas McQuillan has been a professor of architecture at the Oslo School of Architecture and Design since 2020, where he teaches the design studio Subject Matter. He previously served as the head of the Institute of Architecture (2013–20) and maintains a private practice. His research explores the intersection of modernism, technology, and material resources. Recent publications include "Currency" in *AsBuilt 25,* "Concorde" in *Extinct: A Compendium of Obsolete Objects,* "À chacun son paradis" in the Nasjonalmuseet catalog *Becoming Anna-Eva Bergman,* and his selection and afterword for the Norwegian edition of Lina Bo Bardi's writings, *Fra Brasil*. He contributed the entries "Quarry" and "Material" for *Provenance in Architecture: A Dictionary of Terms*.

Notes

[1] "Langøya—NOAH's History," accessed January 5, 2025, https://www.noah.no/en/langoya/noahs-historie/.
[2] Dipesh Chakrabarty, "The Climate of History: Four Theses," *Critical Inquiry* 35, no. 2 (2009): 201. https://doi.org/10.1086/596640.
[3] Gail Feigenbaum "Manifest Provenance," in *Provenance: An Alternate History of Art*, ed. Gail Feigenbaum and Inge Reist (Getty Research Institute, 2012), 19.
[4] Igor Kopytoff, "The Cultural Biography of Things: Commoditization as Process," in *The Social Life of Things: Commodities in Cultural Perspective*, ed. Arjun Appadurai (Cambridge University Press, 1986), 64.
[5] Kopytoff, "The Cultural Biography," 75.
[6] Sigurd H. Unneberg, *Langøya* (Jarlsberg, June 24, 1954).
[7] W. C. Brøgger, *Norske forekomster af malme, nyttige mineraler og bergarter* (Jacob Dybwad, 1894), 60.
[8] It is notoriously difficult to compare historical currencies over centuries, but the 1985 sale price represents an estimated twenty-five-fold increase.
[9] B. M. Keilhau, *Darstellung der Uebergangs-formation in Norwegen* (Verlag von Johann Ambrosius Barth, 1826).
[10] Keilhau, *Darstellung der Uebergangs-formation in Norwegen*, 28.
[11] Geir Hestmark, "The Meaning of 'Metamorphic'—Charles & Mary Lyell in Norway, 1837," *Norwegian Journal of Geology* 91 (2011): 247–75.
[12] Geir Hestmark. *Vitenskap og nasjon: Waldemar Christopher Brøgger, 1851–1905* (Aschehoug. 1999), 45.
[13] Theodor Kjerulf, *Ueber die Geologie des südlichen Norwegens* (Christiania, Verlag von Johan Dahl, 1857), 114.
[14] Carlo Ginzburg, "Clues: Roots of an Evidential Paradigm," in *Clues, Myths, and the Historical Method* (Johns Hopkins University Press, 1992), 101.
[15] W. C. Brøgger, *Die Eruptivgesteine des Kristianiagebietes II. Der Eruptionsfolge der triadischen Eruptivgesteine bei Predazzo in Südtirol*. Vitenskabsselskapets Skrifter. I. Matematisk-naturvidenskabelig Kl., 1895, nr. 7.
[16] Anne Kristine Børresen, "1800-tallets modus 2," *Forskningspolitikk*, no. 2 (2004), 14–15.
[17] *Farmand* (Christiania) 8, no. 9, 179, and no. 11, 229 (1898).
[18] Aktieselskabet Christiania Portland Cementfabrik: 1892–27. Mai. 1942 (Fabriken, 1942), 122.
[19] Morten Magnus, "CPCs utvikling fra 1942–1957," in *Ved en milepel: utgitt i anledning av A/S Christiania Portland Cementfabriks 75-års jubileum* (Fabrikken, 1967), 44
[20] Tim Ingold, "Materials Against Materiality," *Archaeological Dialogues* 14, no. 1 (2007): 14. https://doi.org/10.1017/S1380203807002127.
[21] Peter Lorange, *Anatomy of a Complex Merger: A Case Study and Analysis. Journal of Business Finance* 5, no. 2 (1973): 32–38.
[22] Hans Lindemann, ed., *Langøya: en helt spesiell øy i Oslofjorden* (NOAH, Almater, 1999), 107.
[23] *Klassekampen*, May 23, 1987.
[24] Ingrid Halland, "With-On White: Inconspicuous Modernity with and on Aesthetic Surfaces, 1910–1950," *The Aggregate Architectural History Collaborative* (January 2023), https://doi.org/10.53965/CLXI6947.
[25] Council Directive 91/689/EEC on Hazardous Waste, *Official Journal of the European Communities*, December 12 (1991), https://eur-lex.europa.eu/eli/dir/1991/689/oj/eng.
[26] Anonymous, "Noah kjøper Norcems anlegg på Langøya," *Gjengangeren*, March 5, 1993.
[27] Anonymous, *Den komplette skandalen, Dagbladet*, April 27, 1993.
[28] Lars Kristian Solem, "Gjelsten fikk nesten en halv milliard i overskudd—tjener mest på giftig avfall," *Dagens Næringsliv*, June 4, 2020.
[29] NOAH, "NOAH Mottak Langøya 2020,"https://www.noah.no/wp-content/uploads/2021/06/NOAH-mottak-Langøya-2020.pdf https://www.noah.no/wp-content/uploads/2021/06/NOAH-mottak-Langøya-2020.pdf.
[30] Jane Hutton, *Reciprocal Landscapes: Stories of Material Movements* (Routledge, 2019), 218.
[31] International Union of Geological Sciences, *The Anthropocene: IUGS-ICS Extended Statement*. Report. March 21, 2024.
[32] Mari Lending, *Plaster Monuments Architecture and the Power of Reproduction* (Princeton University Press, 2017).

Figure 1. Félix Bonfils, the Acropolis site in the 1860s, still covered in rubble in need of classification and storage. Courtesy of Gallica BnF.

Nikos Magouliotis

Between Archaeologies
Kyriakos Pittakis and His Wall of Spolia on the Acropolis

An Amateur in Charge

The London Protocol of February 3, 1830, declared Greece as an independent, sovereign state after four centuries of Ottoman rule. Soon thereafter, the Great Powers of Europe decided that this state would be governed by a foreign monarch: Otto, son of Ludwig I of Bavaria, who was appointed king of Greece in 1832. Two years later, Athens was appointed capital of this Greek state. These were crucial steps for the beginning of Western archaeology in modern Greece. King Otto arrived together with a retinue of architects and archaeologists trained in European academies. They had been preceded by several waves of Western antiquarians already from the seventeenth century, but such earlier travelers had no official role in the country.[1] In the 1830s, archaeology in Greece became a state-led project and Western standards of preservation became the law of the land through the introduction of legislation about the treatment of the local antiquities.[2]

The first person that Otto and his regency appointed as "Ephor [Εφορος]," that is, "Overseer" of Athenian antiquities—the highest official of the Greek Archaeological Service (founded in 1833)—was the Bavarian antiquarian Ludwig Ross. Two years later, however, Ross resigned and was replaced by a local. This was his close collaborator Kyriakos Pittakis, who occupied the position of Ephor General of Athenian antiquities[3]—and oversaw the country's most important archaeological sites and reserves—for almost three decades, until his death in 1863. Pittakis formed some of the first archaeological collections in the Acropolis and other ancient monuments in Athens, and also helped create a print discourse around them.[4] But he was not bereft of controversy. In his attempt to protect the antiquities of Athens, he often employed unorthodox methods of handling and storage, and this infuriated his peers.

Pittakis's life spanned a historic period of transition for Greece: Born in Athens in 1798, he grew up during the last decades of Ottoman rule. He fought in the Greek War of Independence (1821–1829), and after the establishment of the Greek state during the 1830s he quickly climbed the ranks of state archaeology. This becomes more striking if we consider that Pittakis was not the most academically qualified archaeologist in Athens during the 1830s. He had some education in philology, history, and archaeology,[5] but compared to his European

Future Anterior
Volume XXII, Numbers 1–2
Summer / Winter 2025

and German peers (and to his predecessor Ludwig Ross) Pittakis lacked extensive and formal academic education. He had enjoyed the mentorship of Louis-François-Sébastien Fauvel, a French vice-consul who lived in Athens until the early 1820s and had amassed a great collection of antiquities in his home.[6] But his knowledge of the Antiquities of Athens stemmed primarily from the fact that he was a local and knew the city and its sites more intimately than his newly arrived peers in the 1830s.

Pittakis's passion for the protection of local antiquities was appreciated, but he was often seen as lacking scientific rigor.[7] In an 1864 obituary, one Greek author wrote euphemistically that there "might be compatriots that surpass the late Pittakis in archaeological knowledge or other education, [but] there is no one surpassing him in his zeal for the antiquities, his diligence, his faithfulness to his duties."[8] Another obituarist portrayed Pittakis as a sort of "noble savage" of archaeology, the last romantic in vulgar times, who heeded only to "the voice of [his] simple heart [την φωνήν της αγνής σου καρδίας]."[9] This romanticized but also patronizing portrayal of a man with more zeal than knowledge, which persists in recent accounts,[10] is founded on the numerous anecdotes about his unorthodox methods of handling the local antiquities, even before he even assumed the official role of Ephor. One recurring story takes place during the Greek Independence War of the 1820s, when the Greeks besieged the Athenian Acropolis (a fortress for the city's Ottoman governor and his guard). After days of battle the besieged were running out of ammunition. When Pittakis heard that the Ottoman guards were beginning to melt the lead joints of the Parthenon to make bullets, he rushed to convince his fellow Greek combatants to provide the enemy with lead so that the battle could continue but the monument would be left intact.[11] This story is a common trope in the many obituaries of Pittakis, but also in popular lore where the deed is attributed to unnamed Greek fighters. Whether or not this story of patriotic preservationism bears any truth, by the middle of the nineteenth century Pittakis appeared a believable personification of that myth.

Another, equally exaggerated, story about Pittakis's deeds was narrated by a Greek author in 1844. After the end of the Independence War, the besieged site of the Acropolis was covered by the rubble of Ottoman and ancient buildings. Soldiers from the European boats that were docked on the port of Piraeus were rumored to be to plundering the site of the Acropolis for ancient fragments—taking advantage of the interim security vacuum as the Ottoman guard was departing. In his attempt to protect the Erechtheion, Pittakis purportedly did the following: "He covered [the entire temple] with stones, from top to bottom, and shaped the whole thing like a pile of rocks; wherever he found sculptural, architectural or epigraphic fragments, he placed them upside-down so that they were not visible, noting the exact place where he had left them. After the Turks left [. . .] he brought together all the ancient relics and formed . . . the first archaeological collection on the Acropolis."[12] Given the size and prominent position of the Erechteion, it is hard to believe that one could simply hide the temple by covering it with rocks. However, the fictitious story provides reliable evidence of how Pittakis was mythicized already during his lifetime, as the ultimate protector of the antiquities, whether against the "Turks," or against looting Westerners. The possibility that Pittakis did all this already before acquiring any position of power, and through tricks and contrivances, makes him heroic and yet approachable. Seen as a toiling, zealous, and cunning patriot, Pittakis was the folk hero of an emerging Greek archaeology.

Precious Rubble

When Pittakis became Ephor of Athenian antiquities in 1836, the site of the Acropolis was still covered by heaps of rubble and fragments of buildings from different periods, from the ancient to Byzantine, Frankish, and Ottoman (Figure 1). The exact provenance of each of these fragments was not always easy to determine. Many of them came from buildings in other locations and had been reused as spolia perhaps more than once. But the frequent instances of looting—such as the case of Lord Elgin, who managed to extract half of the Parthenon frieze to London between 1801 and 1805—made the safeguarding of all these fragments an urgent task. Pittakis left no stone unturned. He collected and stored fragments for almost three decades. This transformation of the Acropolis into a visitable archaeological site brought on radically new standards of security. An English traveler who visited the Acropolis in 1835 protested: "So very properly strict and jealous are the guardians of the works, that if a stranger stoops to pick up a piece of marble, even for cursory examination, he finds all eyes upon him; and I doubt whether he would be allowed to remove even a pebble from the sacred soil."[13] This was in tune with Pittakis's own advocacy for strict safety measures, which included exerting pressure on the municipality of Athens to hire special guards for the Parthenon and to install lamps that would allow better supervision of the site at night.[14]

The main aim of clearing the Acropolis site was the reinstatement of the Parthenon and other ancient monuments to their original form—an archaeological paragon of the Greek nation-building project, which prioritized classical monuments over later works and additions.[15] When Pittakis and his peers found fragments that they could identify as parts of a specific ancient building, they would try to reconstruct it. For fragments whose provenance could not be identified, Pittakis resorted to more unorthodox methods. Many of these were documented in a series of articles published in the Athenian newspaper *Aeon* [Αιών] in 1844, as a reportage on the "condition of the relics of our forefathers."[16] The unnamed Greek author of this series toured the Acropolis and other ancient sites with Pittakis, and made praiseful remarks about how he had dealt with the situation at hand. In lack of a proper building for the storage and display of antiquities, he reported that the Ephor had formed "archaeological collections" in four different places: on the Acropolis, in the Temple of Hephaestus in Theseion, in the Tower of the Winds, and in the Library of Hadrian.[17] Pittakis used ancient buildings that stood in good shape as enclosures for the storage and display of antiquities.

In two of these "collections," in the Temple of Hephaestus and the Library of Hadrian, he resorted to rather makeshift means for the display of the ancient fragments. He placed the epigraphs and the reliefs within wooden frames and "tightened these together with metal joints . . . , plaster and other materials."[18] As for larger sculptural and architectural relics, Pittakis "nailed [them] together . . . and tied them onto stone bases with nails and lead."[19] According to the reporter, these unorthodox methods were justified by the lack of proper museum spaces and the threat of looting. By being nailed and plastered together in wooden frames, "these precious fragments and relics are well secured [and] can be seen and studied easily."[20] According to the author, Pittakis's assemblies of ancient fragments appeared "as ancient tableaus [πίνακες] within the picture gallery [πινακοθήκη] of the Theseion and the [Library] of Hadrian."[21] Despite its applauding tone, the article evidences that Pittakis's "tableaus," in their attempt to protect these antiquities, would have actually harmed them.[22] Reconstruction of these fragments was not possible, but their provenance was documented. All of them were marked with "red, indelible numbers" that referred the visitor to a catalog of the collection, which provided information about "where [each piece] was found, how it was obtained, what monument it belongs to, what material it is made from."[23] A manuscript of this catalog, titled "Museum of Antiquities [Μουσείον Αρχαιοτήτων]" and dated to 1843, is held in the archives of the National Archaeological Museum in Athens.[24]

Although intended as temporary arrangements, Pittakis's tableaus stayed in place for at least two decades: Two photographs taken by Félix Bonfils in the 1860s show some of these panels in the Propylaea (Figure 2, in the background) and in the inside of another ancient construction, labeled as "le Pynacoteque" (Figure 3)—this was either the Temple of

Figure 2. Félix Bonfils, Some of Pittakis's "tableaus," photographed in the Propylaea in the late 1860s. Courtesy of Beaux-Arts de Paris, Dist. GrandPalaisRmn / image INHA.

Figure 3. Félix Bonfils, *Fragments de sculptures dans le Pynacothèque.* Pittakis's tableaus, possibly in the Temple of Theseion or the Library of Hadrian. Courtesy of Beaux-Arts de Paris, Dist. GrandPalaisRmn / image INHA.

Theseion or the Library of Hadrian. In these rare visual documents of Pittakis's displays, the tableaus appear to be simple constructions made with cheap materials and with an emphasis on security rather than aesthetics. The fragments are crammed together without any apparent classification. It appears as if the priority was to fit as many pieces as possible—some have even been rotated to fit in better, like in a game of Tetris—and to not leave wide, fragile plaster joints between them. In the photograph, loose fragments are piled on the foot of these tableaus, indicating a need for more.

Building with Spolia

These "tableaus" in Theseion and the Library of Hadrian were some of the more discrete spolia works of Pittakis. As the reportage of 1844 revealed, many of the bigger stones found in the excavations of the Acropolis were "piled up and built together in a row [δια κτισίματος εισί στιβαγμένοι κατά σειράν]" along the perimetric wall of the site.[25] This monumental construction, which in 1844 appears to have occupied about half of the perimeter of the Acropolis plateau,[26] eventually became known as "the Wall of Theseion," presumably because many of its pieces came from there. Like the "tableaus," this wall of spolia was a biproduct of the lack of proper storage space.[27] As other scholars have pointed out, this was simultaneously a display device and an anti-theft system.[28] In other words, it was an assemblage of spolia as protection against spoliation. Its overall form seems to have resulted from a pragmatic consideration. To clear the Acropolis plateau from the rubble, Pittakis moved the fragments along its perimeter and piled them on top of each other. Still, the wall must have been a dominant presence, possibly even visible from the city below.

This peculiar wall of spolia captured the attention of Félix Bonfils, who made four photographs of different parts (Figures 4–6). According to Andrew Szegedy-Maszak, even though photography was still a developing art, an archaeological canon was beginning to acquire solid form. Among photographers there was already "a consensus about which monuments were significant," as well as "a canonical set of points of view from which those monuments were to be photographed."[29] Bonfils's photographs from his trip to Greece, published in an album in 1870,[30] do abide to this canon. But his choice to photograph the wall of Pittakis and to publish the picture—perhaps the only one to do so—was a radical gesture driven by fascination for this eccentric work, which was most likely presented to him without explanation as Bonfils photographed the wall a few years after the death of its maker. As Yannis Hamilakis points out, Bonfils had not witnessed the earlier controversies and debates stirred by Pittakis's works, such

Figure 4. Félix Bonfils, a part of Pittakis's spolia-wall on the Acropolis, late 1860s. Handwritten caption: "Mur construit avec des débris." Courtesy of Gallica BnF.

Figure 5. Félix Bonfils, Pittakis's wall, detail. Courtesy of Ministère de la Culture, Médiathèque du patrimoine et de la photographie, Dist. GrandPalaisRmn / Félix Bonfils.

Figure 6. Félix Bonfils, Pittakis's wall, detail. Courtesy of Ministère de la Culture, Médiathèque du patrimoine et de la photographie, Dist. GrandPalaisRmn / Félix Bonfils.

as when the then prime minister Ioannis Kolettis wrote a letter to the king to protest that the Ephor contemplated repairing the marble walls of the Parthenon with mud bricks.[31] Athens of the late 1860s was a rapidly modernizing city. But as Hamilakis demonstrates, Bonfils "was not interested in what Athens was becoming but in what it had been."[32] To maintain this image of antiquity, he photographed primarily ancient works, and from angles that obscured the modern buildings that surrounded them.[33] In this sense, Pittakis's wall of ancient spolia was a convenient topic. But whether Bonfils was aware of it or not, the assembly of ancient fragments he photographed was a modern and in fact very recent work.

By the time Bonfils photographed it, the wall of Pittakis had been growing for more than twenty years. In some of the pictures, it looks like more than three or four meters high (see again Figure 4). Unlike the heavily plastered and nailed "tableaus," this was a dry stone wall construction, at times quite tight and precise in its assembly of fragments from different buildings—whoever built this had built walls before. The lower layers are solidly constructed and indicate some basic taxonomic order. We see many cornices and capitals together in one part, a large collection of relief slabs in another. The author of the newspaper reportage of 1844 also hinted to a basic taxonomic order when observing that Pittakis put "in one place all the Ionic capitals, all the Corinthian ones in a different place, and all the relics from constructions of the middle-ages [in a third place]."[34] Unlike the smaller "tableaus," this wall was—as far as we know—not accompanied by a numbered catalog that would have informed the visitor about the provenance of each of its pieces, or its overall taxonomic order. Looking at Bonfils's pictures, the wall looks like it started as a pragmatic ordering and stacking of archaeological finds but evolved into a more conscious aesthetic exercise. In the upper layers, Pittakis and his accomplices used small columns to form irregular arched openings and other picturesque, playful details [see again Figure 6]. But again, no written clues survive to explain the aesthetic aspirations of these complicated assemblies of ancient fragments.

While the wall remained in place for more than twenty years after the death of Pittakis, his obituarists never made anything but indirect and obscure references to it. One wrote that for Pittakis the antiquities were "more than piles of silent stones, they acquired a voice and spoke to his mind and to his heart."[35] Such romantic hyperboles thrive in obituaries, but in the case of Pittakis they are particularly ambiguous. They read like praises of his zeal, and at the same time like subtle hints to his quirks. By most accounts, Pittakis was a man who "worshipped . . . even the smallest crumbs of any ancient monument."[36] He was portrayed as a benign ghost that haunted the ancient site with his constant presence. Visitors "were almost certain to meet this infatigable guardian of the antiquities, either crouched over an epigraph . . . , or climbed up on a frieze, or picking up from the ground and meticulously storing the smallest fragments that bore the traces of an ancient chisel."[37]

Pittakis himself hardly mentioned the wall in his writings, let alone explain its logic and merits.[38] His one reference in a footnote of an article about epigraphs in 1853 was rather defensive: "I have been obliged to take this measure due to the extraction and theft of [such ancient pieces]. . . . If I had left all the little pieces of epigraphs or whatever other objects in place, would they be preserved? would they still be visible? Not at all. . . . Every relic which is not possible to be destroyed, and which contributes to the ancient topography, I have left in its place; but every relic that may be stolen, or cut off, I keep wherever there is hope of [its] salvation [ελπίς σωτηρίας]."[39] This short reference is indicative of Pittakis's pragmatic concerns. The wall was of course never "designed." It was assembled, in a process that would have necessitated spontaneous decisions and changes as different fragments surfaced from nearby excavations. The result is playful but also incohesive. Pittakis's writings often demonstrate a similar lack of overarching structure. His publications on epigraphs were extensive, serial arrays of ancient inscriptions. They read like accumulations of data without narrative and often without clear conclusions.[40] What mattered to him was the survival, collection, and display of facts, through which the reader could deduct their own conclusions. His wall of spolia on the Acropolis is congenial to his writing, an obsessive piling of material facts awaiting interpretation. His wall was only a temporary purgatory for all these unidentified building fragments. Their eventual "salvation" would arrive through the establishment of their historic and architectural provenance by later generations of scholars.

New Taxonomies and the End of Spolia Archaeology

After standing on the Acropolis for at least four decades, and continuously growing for at least the first half of that period, Pittakis's wall was dismantled in 1888. The lack of storage and display space for antiquities in Athens that had justified its construction in the late 1830s was mended. A museum for the antiquities of the Acropolis on the site itself was completed in 1874, based on an 1844 proposal by Pittakis.[41] The larger Archaeological Museum of Athens would be completed in 1889.[42] The decision to take down the wall was made by Pittakis's successor Panagiotis Kavvadias.[43] In a laconic announcement in the gazette of the Archaeological Society of Athens in 1888, Kavvadias referred to the wall as "built-together ancient stones [εντετοιχισμένοι αρχαίοι λίθοι]," which contained various "architectural parts, byzantine ornaments, etc." These fragments were extracted, divided "according to their kind and value [διακριθέντες κατ'είδος και σπουδαιότητα]," and eventually sent to different museums and collections.[44]

Kavvadias's dismantling of the wall was an erasure of the last traces of Pittakis from the ancient site to which he had devoted his life. But it was also a vindication of his hope for the eventual "salvation" of all the seemingly insignificant or unclassifiable building fragments that he had piled together over the years. Kavvadias's fleeting reference to "byzantine decorations" is an important detail. When Pittakis became Ephor of Athens in the 1830s, Greek archaeology was exclusively focused on classical remains and placed little value on later relics. For a large part of the nineteenth century, the byzantine monuments of Athens and its periphery were not systematically studied or protected.[45] This changed with the foundation of the Christian Archaeological Society (1884) and the establishment of the first collections of Byzantine art at the end of the nineteenth century. In 1915, about two hundred pieces from Pittakis's wall[46] became part of the collection of the newly founded Byzantine Museum of Athens.[47] In this context, researchers could work to establish the historic provenance of these architectural fragments. But Pittakis's wall and Bonfis's photographs of it remained an important point of reference. In a volume published by the Byzantine Museum in 2006, the provenance of a number of medieval sculpted marble pieces is listed as "Collection of Theseion" (i.e., the collection formed after Pittakis's so-called "Wall of Theseion" was dismantled), or even simply as "Depicted in Bonfils' photograph[s]."[48]

The dismantling of Pittakis's wall could be seen as a symbolic moment in the history of the Athenian landscape. It signaled the end of a centuries-long era of spolia and palimpsests, with Pittakis as its unwitting last hero. What followed was the establishment of a modern, state-led and academic archaeological project that sought to reestablish a historical order, to reconstruct monuments in their "original" form, and to order art according to new historic taxonomies (Classical, Hellenistic, Byzantine, Venetian, Ottoman).[49] An earlier decisive moment of this project was in 1834, when the Bavarian government of Greece issued a Royal Decree "about the discovery, conservation and use of the antiquities"—effectively the first archaeological legislation of modern Greece.[50] Its opening article (no. 61) declared, somewhat vaguely, that "all antiquities within Greece, [are] the works of the forefathers of the Greek people, [and thus] considered as national property [κτήμα εθνικόν] of all Greeks."[51] But the following article clarified that "all ruins and other ancient objects that are found on national soil [επί εθνικής γης] . . . are property of the State [ιδιοκτησία του Κράτους]."[52] The following articles listed some exceptions, but the overall position was clear: The Greeks could boast about the works of their forefathers, but ultimately these belonged to the state.

As the legislators clarified, this included the ruins of entire buildings and statues, but also any "volume of carved marble" or other fragment and object that might be of ancient origin.[53] Whoever discovered such objects in their property had to report them immediately to the authorities.[54] The decree also forbid a series of practices, from removing and reusing pieces of ruins, to more specific and unusual things. It was, for example, forbidden "to construct limekilns in the [vicinity] of Greek relics," as well as "to use temples and other Greek buildings, tombs and sarcophagi, or other ancient objects that might survive on one's private land . . . for any practical purpose [προς οικονομικόν τινα σκοπόν], particularly as houses, as storage for crops, as mangers, as watering troughs, etc."[55] In their urge to list in detail any potential violation, the legislators described practices that were common before the 1830s, and to some extent persisted in later years.

Before the advent of Western state archaeology in the 1830s, the people of Athens (and of the Ottoman world in general) had their own ways of relating to the material remains of the past. They transformed and reused ancient structures in situ, and built ancient spolia into the walls of houses and churches. Such common practices of reuse were fueled by material pragmatism—why cut new stone blocks if they are readily available in nearby ruins? But they also stemmed from a set of religious and magical beliefs. People believed that certain ancient structures were enchanted, and that fragments extracted from them were apotropaic. If built over the threshold of a house, or as a cornerstone, they protected those within from evil and disease.[56] Certain ancient columns in Athens were believed to heal fever and other illnesses. People venerated them and placed votives on them and even built small chapels around them.[57] And there were numerous folk tales about how certain ancient ruins were built by superhuman giants, or how certain statues were people who had once turned into stone.[58] Yannis Hamilakis describes such popular practices and beliefs as "indigenous archaeology," whereas Benjamin Anderson refers to "local interpreters" of antiquities.[59]

This local culture might have been obscure for the German, English, and French archaeologists who arrived in Athens with King Otto. It was certainly familiar to Pittakis who had grown up in late-Ottoman Athens, and whose life spanned a period of tremendous historical and cultural transition for Greece. As Ephor of Athenian antiquities, he was charged with implementing laws against spolia, but he occasionally sympathized with such vernacular practices. In an article about epigraphs published in 1854, Pittakis explained the material and architectural circumstances in which he had found these primary sources. He started out with discussing the inscriptions built into the walls of Athenian medieval churches, and then referred to more recent examples of spoliation: "Among the local population . . . there has always existed a love for the preservation of our forefathers' relics, which people would build . . . most of all over the doors of houses with the aim of preserving them. In many recent constructions, we have observed, with our own eyes, fragments of antiquities built with a lot of caution and care into the walls. . . . In some places these relics were surrounded by plain soil [i.e., without any use of mortar], so as to remain intact."[60] By the time Pittakis was writing this, such acts of spoliation were illegal. But this did not prevent him from romanticizing them for the purposes of nation building. Using the word "relics [λείψανα]," which signifies material remains of buildings but also bodily remains of humans (both in English and in Greek), Pittakis likened these vernacular practices of spoliation to a respectful burial of the "forefathers" of the Greeks. In other words, he presented activities that the law of 1834 deemed illegal as acts of patriotic preservation. This was a myth that would be nurtured by later generations of Greek national-romantics.[61] But it is also indicative of the way that Pittakis understood and justified his own spolia works, and of how he tried to compromise various inherent contradictions of post-Ottoman Greece. In a way, he lived between two archaeologies: the indigenous archaeology of his Greek compatriots and the Western archaeology of his German peers. His briefly lived spolia works point to a temporary compromise between the two, before the latter took over completely. But they also make us wonder about the multiple provenances of architectural fragments in a place like Athens: Does a carved marble fragment belong in the museum whose name fits the date of its carving? Or on the site where it was last used and found? And does it come from an ancient construction whose other pieces have been destroyed or reused beyond recognition? Or from the walls of the Ottoman house or the Byzantine church where it was rebuilt in order to be displayed? The example of Pittakis helps us resist the temptation of giving a categoric answer.

Biography

Nikos Magouliotis is a lecturer at the Institute for the History & Theory of Architecture of ETH Zurich. His research focuses on vernacular architecture and subaltern perspectives, as well as on the overlaps of architecture with archaeology and ethnography in the east Mediterranean and in central Europe. Magouliotis has published articles in *San Rocco, ARCH+, Architectural Histories, Future Anterior, The Journal of Architecture, Architecture Beyond Europe,* and *OASE.*

Notes

[1] Some of them had diplomatic titles of foreign states, while others had "firmans" issued by the Ottoman authorities that allowed them to survey and excavate specific sites. A detailed account of such negotiations between Ottoman authorities and Western travelers is given by Edhem Eldem, "From Blissful Indifference to Anguished Concern: Ottoman Perceptions of Antiquities, 1799–1869," in *Scramble for the Past. A Story of Archaeology in the Ottoman Empire, 1753–1914*, ed. Zainab Bahrani, Zeynep Çelik, and Edhem Eldem (Salt, 2011), 281–329.

[2] This paper owes a lot to recent critical histories of archaeology in Greece, such as Yannis Hamilakis, *The Nation and its Ruins—Antiquity, Archaeology and National Imagination in Greece* (Oxford University Press, 2007); and Angeliki Kokkou, *Η Μέριμνα για τις Αρχαιότητες στην Ελλάδα και τα Πρώτα Μουσεία* (Kapon Editions, 2009).

[3] In 1836, Pittakis was actually given the title of "Ephor of the Public Central Museum of Antiquities [Εφορος του Δημοσίου Κεντρικού μουσείου των αρχαιοτήτων]" and would acquire the title of "General Ephor" of Athenian antiquities only in 1843. Kokkou, *Η Μέριμνα για τις Αρχαιότητες*, 83, 89. In essence, however, he was already in charge of most ancient sites and had a key role within the Greek Archaeological service since the 1830s.

[4] Pittakis initiated the foundation, in 1837, of the Archaeological Society at Athens (Εν Αθήναις Αρχαιολογική Εταιρεία) and began publishing its official journal, the "Archeological Gazette [Αρχαιολογική Εφημερίς]," providing a crucial medium for the development of a local discourse on archaeology and antiquities. Additional details on Pittakis's life and work can be found in Kokkou, *Η Μέριμνα για τις Αρχαιότητες*, 85–89; Eirini Psarra, "Ο μορφωμένος Ludwig Ross και ο αυτοδίδακτος Κυριάκος Σ. Πιττακης," in *Ιστορίες επί χάρτου—Μορφές και θέματα της Αρχαιολογίας στην Ελλάδα του 19ου αιώνα*, ed. Elena Koundouri and Stavroula Masouridi (Διεύθυνση Εθνικού Αρχείου Μνημείων—Αρχείο Υπηρεσιών των Αρχαιοτήτων, 2013), 16–21; Chrysanthi Tsouli, "Κυριάκος Πιττάκης: ο αγνός πατριώτης, ο άοκνος αρχαιοφύλακας, ο άγρυπνος φρουρός," in *Δι' αυτά πολεμήσαμεν—Αρχαιότητες και Ελληνική Επανάσταση*, ed. Maria Lagogianni-Geograkarakou and Thodoris Koutsogiannis (Ταμείο Αρχαιολογικών Πόρων και Απαλλοτριώσεων, 2019), 266–75.

[5] Kokkou, *Η Μέριμνα για τις Αρχαιότητες*, 86–89.

[6] Kokkou, 85. A detailed account of Fauvel's activities in Greece can be found in Alessia Zambon, *Aux origines de l'archéologie en Grèce. Fauvel et sa méthode* (L'Art et l'essai, 2014).

[7] Kokkou, *Η Μέριμνα για τις Αρχαιότητες*, 90–92.

[8] Various authors, *Λόγοι επικήδειοι εις τον Γενικόν Έφορον των Αρχαιοτήτων Κυριάκον Πιττάκην . . .* (D. Ath. Mavrommatis, 1864), 7.

[9] Various, *Λόγοι επικήδειοι*, 16.

[10] Eirini Psarra recently described Pittakis as a man "without specialized archaeological knowledge" but filled with a "true love for the antiquities" (Psarra, "Ο μορφωμένος Ludwig Ross," 17).

[11] Various, *Λόγοι επικήδειοι*, 6.

[12] Anonymous, "Η κατάστασις των προγονικών λειψάνων," *Αιών* 591 (17/01/1845).

[13] Edward Giffard, quoted in Yannis Hamilakis, "Monumental Visions: Bonfils, Classical Antiquity and Nineteenth-Century Athenian Society," *History of Photography* 25, no. 1 (2001): 7.

[14] Anonymous, "Η κατάστασις των προγονικών λειψάνων," *Αιών* 573 (01/11/1844).

[15] Hamilakis, *The Nation and Its Ruins*, 57–123.

[16] Anonymous, "Η κατάστασις των προγονικών λειψάνων," *Αιών* 569 (18/10/1844), 571 (25/10/1844), 573 (01/11/1844), 575 (08/11/1844), 578 (22/11/1844), 588 (06/01/1845), 591 (17/01/1845).

[17] Anonymous, "Η κατάστασις των προγονικών λειψάνων," 569. The last of these ancient sites is referred to in the text as the "Stoa of Hadrian [Στοά του Αδριανού]." The anonymous author is hereby referring to the site now known as the Library of Hadrian, which was often referred to as a "Stoa" even in later years, for example in M. A. Sisson, "The Stoa of Hadrian at Athens," *Papers of the British School at Rome*, vol. 11 (1929), 50–72. I am grateful to Prof. Samantha Martin and Sylvie Dumont for their help in clarifying this.

[18] Anonymous, "Η κατάστασις των προγονικών λειψάνων," 569.

[19] Anonymous.

[20] Anonymous.

[21] Anonymous.

[22] Some pages later, the reporter explains that these bricolages were actually Pittakis's response to the criticism of fellow archaeologists about earlier and even more extreme acts, such as the former storage of ancient statue fragments in two damp, vertical water-wells at the Acropolis, out of reach for study (Anonymous, "Η κατάστασις των προγονικών λειψάνων," 591).

[23] Anonymous, "Η κατάστασις των προγονικών λειψάνων," 569.
[24] Chrysanthi Tsouli, "Έλληνες και αρχαιότητες τα πρώτα χρόνια μετά τη δημιουργία του ελληνικού κράτους: μαρτυρίες αρχειακών υπηρεσιακών εγγράφων και παλαιών ευρετηρίων," in *Δι' αυτά πολεμήσαμεν—Αρχαιότητες και Ελληνική Επανάσταση*, ed. Maria Lagogianni-Geograkarakou and Thodoris Koutsogiannis (Ταμείο Αρχαιολογικών Πόρων και Απαλλοτριώσεων, 2019), 262–63.
[25] Tsouli, "Έλληνες," 588.
[26] According to the reportage of 1844, the wall began from the Propylaea and stretched, on the northern side, until the northeast end of the Erechtheion, and on the south, until the southeast corner of the Parthenon (Anonymous, "Η κατάστασις των προγονικών λειψάνων," 588).
[27] Kokkou, *Η Μέριμνα για τις Αρχαιότητες*, 154–56.
[28] Olga Gratziou and Anastasia Lazaridou, *Από τη Χριστιανική Συλλογή στο Βυζαντινό Μουσείο (1884–1930)—Κατάλογος Έκθεσης* (Greek Ministry of Culture—Fund of Archaeological Proceeds, 2006), 280; and Kokkou, *Η Μέριμνα για τις Αρχαιότητες*, 169–70.
[29] Andrew Szegedy-Maszak, "Felix Bonfils and the Traveller's Trail Through Athens," *History of Photography* 25, no. 1 (2001): 14.
[30] The whole album from his trip to Greece is available at https://gallica.bnf.fr/ark:/12148/btv1b84471636.
[31] Hamilakis, "Monumental Visions," 9.
[32] Hamilakis, 5.
[33] Hamilakis, 9–10.
[34] Anonymous, "Η κατάστασις των προγονικών λειψάνων," 569.
[35] Various, *Λόγοι επικήδειοι*, 4–5.
[36] Various, 15.
[37] Various, 12.
[38] I have not been able to locate a published text in which Pittakis himself explains the construction of the wall or defends its existence. The catalog titled "Μουσείον Αρχαιοτήτων" that Chrysanthi Tsouli has found in the archives of the National Archaeological Museum (see again Tsouli, "Έλληνες και αρχαιότητες τα πρώτα χρόνια," 262–63) appears to be more a list of the different pieces of the wall (as well as of the other collections that Pittakis formed in the mid-nineteenth century) rather than an explanation of the logic by which they were assembled together, or the aesthetic intent behind it.
[39] Kyriakos Pittakis, [Untitled publication of Epigraphic findings in 1853], *Εφημερίς Αρχαιολογική* 35 (August-September-October 1853), reprinted in *Εφημερίς Αρχαιολογική—Περίοδος Πρώτη 1837–1860—Μέρος Τρίτον*, vol. 8–9 (Η Εν Αθήναις Αρχαιολογική Εταιρεία, 1990), 952–53n1.
[40] See for example Pittakis's first major publication, an extensive collection of epigraphs found in tiny fragments of ancient marble that he had found scattered all over the city: *L'ancienne Athènes, ou La description des antiquités d'Athènes et de ses environs* . . . (M. E. Antoniades / M. K. Nicolaides, 1835) and Pittakis [Untitled publication in 1853].
[41] Kokkou, *Η Μέριμνα για τις Αρχαιότητες*, 195–201.
[42] Kokkou, 242–50. Archaeological materials had started to be transported to the museum already before its official completion in 1889. For the history of this museum in general, see Kokkou, 201–58.
[43] Gratziou and Lazaridou, *Από τη Χριστιανική Συλλογή*, 280.
[44] Panagiotis Kavvadias, *Δελτίον Αρχαιολογικόν, εκδιδόμενον υπό του Γενικού Εφόρου των Αρχαιοτήτων και Μουσείων—Τόμος Δ'* (S. K. Vlastos, 1888), 176.
[45] For more on this: Eleni-Anna Chlepa, *Τα βυζαντινά μνημεία στη νεότερη Ελλάδα. Ιδεολογία και πρακτική των αποκαταστάσεων: 1833–1939* (Kapon Editions, 2011), 31–41; Nikos Magouliotis, "French Architects and 'églises grecques': The Discovery of Byzantine Architecture in Greece, 1820s–1840s," *The Journal of Architecture* 25, no. 8 (2020): 1028–54. https://doi.org/10.1080/13602365.2020.1849355.
[46] This estimation is taken from Gratziou and Lazaridou, *Από τη Χριστιανική Συλλογή*, 280.
[47] Gratziou and Lazaridou, 276–86.
[48] Gratziou and Lazaridou, 280–86. See also Tsouli, "Κυριάκος Πιττάκης: ο αγνός πατριώτης," 269–75, where the history and provenance of a series ancient pieces of sculpture is discussed in relation to the wall of Pittakis, of which they were once a part.
[49] Two rare exceptions of this were the author Pericles Yannopoulos, whose texts at the dawn of the twentieth century celebrated the landscape of Attica as a "crumbled world [τριμμένος κόσμος]," and his keen follower Dimitris Pikionis, whose mosaic pathways on the hill of Philopappos made extensive use of modern spolia in picturesque arrangements. (Nikos Magouliotis, "Ο Περικλής Γιαννόπουλος και η νεοελληνική αρχιτεκτονική," in *Τα τετράδια του Μοντέρνου 7: Το μοντέρνο βλέμμα*

στην 'ελληνική' φύση, ed. Amalia Kotsaki and Kostas Tsiambaos [Futura, 2020], 39–54.) As far as I know, neither of the two ever made explicit references to Pittakis, and it is not clear if they were even aware of his wall of spolia. Yannopoulos was born in 1869 (he was nineteen when the work got demolished), and Pikionis in 1887 (one year before its demolition). Still, their work (written in the case of the former, both written and built for the latter) appears to follow on Pittakis's legacy in a more deliberately aestheticized manner.

50 "Νόμος (10/22 Μαΐου 1834): Περί των επιστημονικών και τεχνολογικών συλλογών, περί ανακαλύψεως και διατηρήσεως των αρχαιοτήτων και της χρήσεως αυτών," *Εφημερίς της Κυβερνήσεως του Βασιλείου της Ελλάδος* 22 (1834): Section Γ', 171–90. See also Kokkou, *Η Μέριμνα για τις Αρχαιότητες;* and Daphne Voudouri, "The Legal Protection of Antiquities in Greece and National Identity," in *Ancient Monuments and Modern Identities: A critical history of archaeology in 19th and 20th century Greece*, ed. Sofia Voutsaki and Paul Cartledge (Routledge, 2017), 78–79.

51 "Νόμος (10/22 Μαΐου 1834)," 184, article 61.

52 "Νόμος," 184, article 62.

53 "Νόμος," 190, article 110.

54 "Νόμος," 184, article 65.

55 "Νόμος," 187, article 85.

56 Hamilakis, *The Nation and Its Ruins*, 64–74. See also Vangelis Zissis, *Η Μαγική Τοπογραφία των Αθηνών: Οι προλήψεις, οι δεισιδαιμονίες και οι παράδοξες ιστορίες της μεσαιωνικής πόλης* (Mundus, 2017); Dimitrios Kambouroglou, *Αι Παλαιαί Αθήναι* (Dionysios Notis Karavias Bookstore, 1990).

57 Ioannis Svoronos, "Ασκληπιακά μνημεία και κιονολατρεία εν Αθήναις," *Αρχαιολογική Εφημερίς* (1917), issue no. 1–2, 78–104.

58 Ioannis Kakridis, *Οι Αρχαίοι Έλληνες στη Νεοελληνική Λαϊκή Παράδοση* (National Bank of Greece Cultural Foundation, 1997).

59 Hamilakis, "Indigenous Archaeologies in Ottoman Greece," in *Scramble for the Past. A Story of Archaeology in the Ottoman Empire, 1753–1914*, ed. Zainab Bahrani, Zeynep Çelik, and Edhem Eldem (Salt, 2011), 49–69. Benjamin Anderson, "'An Alternative Discourse': Local Interpreters of Antiquities in the Ottoman Empire," *Journal of Field Archaeology* 40, no. 4 (2015): 450–60. I am editing a special collection of papers on this topic for *Architectural Histories*, under the working title "Indigenous Archaeologies, Vernacular Classicisms" (forthcoming, 2025).

60 Kyriakos Pittakis, [Untitled publication of Epigraphic findings in 1854], *Εφημερίς Αρχαιολογική* 38 (June-July-August-September 1854), reprinted in *Εφημερίς Αρχαιολογική—Περίοδος Πρώτη 1837–1860—Μέρος Τέταρτον*, vol. 10–11 (Η Εν Αθήναις Αρχαιολογική Εταιρεία, 1990), 1204–5n1.

61 In his book of stories of old Athens (*Αι Παλαιαί Αθήναι*) in 1922, Dimitrios Kambouroglou made a similarly national-romantic description of popular practices of spoliation. The book opened with a didactic dialogue between two fictional protagonists. One of them began by saying that "when the Turks conquered Constantinople . . . Greece was cut in pieces." This notion of the "piece [κομμάτι]" was used by Kambouroglou in a poetically ambiguous manner, signifying both geographical regions (pieces of what was once Greek territory) and fragments of antiquities (pieces of monuments used as spolia). Through the voice of his protagonist, Kambouroglou explained: "Every piece [of Greece], whether it was a city, a village or an island, tried to hide its own Greece, its own piece [of ancient matter and history]; and they did not keep this piece as a whole, but they cut it into little pieces and each hid one of these pieces in their home, until the time comes for all these little pieces [of the territory and of the monuments] to unite again and for the nation to become united and whole again . . . . [But until then], to protect each little piece, [the people] wrapped it tenderly and beautifully in beliefs, in customs, in traditions, in lore, in fairy-tales, in songs, in sayings . . ." (Kambouroglou, *Αι Παλαιαί Αθήναι*, 18–19). In this passage, Kambouroglou expanded the idea of spoliation as patriotic preservation to a vision of national reunification and related irredentist Greek narratives.

Figure 1. Installation by Carlo Scarpa, Picture Gallery, Museo Correr, Venice. The easel and the frame supporting two *Portraits of a Young Man* (one attributed to Marco Basaiti, the other by an anonymous artist) were designed by Carlo Scarpa and produced by Officina Zanon and Saverio Anfodillo. Photo: Paolo Monti, 1961. Gelatin silver print, contact proof from 10 × 12 cm film negative, b/w. Courtesy of BEIC Digital Library.

Flavia Crisciotti

Provenance on Display
"Carlo Scarpa (1906–1978), An Easel"

On December 12, 2016, an easel designed by Italian architect Carlo Scarpa (1906–1978) appeared at the Christie's *The Collection of Chiara and Francesco Carraro* sale in New York. At least thirty of these easels were produced between 1957 and 1964 for two public institutions, the Museo Correr in Venice and the Castelvecchio Museum in Verona.[1] While museum acquisitions normally terminate an object's life in the art market, Scarpa's easels are in the unusual position of having been created for museums, before entering into the art market. This movement raises questions: How did an object made for a museum come to reside in the private collection of the art collecting couple, Chiara and Francesco Carraro? How did it end up at the Christie's auction in New York? Perhaps most importantly: How can the easels' authorship be best described?

Before the Scarpa easels entered the art market, few would have questioned their provenance. Placed in the very interiors they were tailored for, the easels demonstrated the curatorial inventiveness of Carlo Scarpa while serving their intended function of displaying paintings of the Venetian Renaissance. But unlike the artworks they supported in the galleries, the easels lacked labels to document their provenance and authorship (after all, they were simply museum furnishings). As they began to circulate outside of museums, their provenance became a critical issue. The entry of the easel for the Christie's auction in 2016, for instance, describes neither its place of origin nor a previous collector but identifies the artisans who crafted it:

> **Provenance:**
> Studio Zanon, Venice;
> Acquired from the above by the present owner.[2]

The catalog for a similar easel offered at Christie's *Thinking Italian Art and Design Evening Sale* in London on October 22, 2020, also mentions another name: Falegnameria Anfodillo, a Venetian joinery with whom Scarpa collaborated for over three decades.[3] In marketing the objects, the auction house simplifies the conditions of production—allowing Scarpa's name to linger over the lots without clarifying exactly when they were crafted or exactly who played which role in their creation.

This essay seeks to explore this account by looking directly at

Future Anterior
Volume XXII, Numbers 1–2
Summer / Winter 2025

the provenance of the easels, switching the focus from Carlo Scarpa to the artisans who produced the object, and from the preoccupation with Scarpa's drawings to the easels themselves. Weaving together their seemingly distinct makers hints at a process of creation that may be more mediated than what is the case for a typical artwork offered in auction.

The appearance of Scarpa's easels at auction underscores their capacity to unsettle conventional boundaries between museum object and market commodity. This capacity to disrupt was evident from the outset. Already in the 1960s, the easels surprised visitors entering the neoclassical palace in Piazza San Marco, Venice. Only after threading through the crowded square, after accessing the Museo Correr through the ceremonial marble staircase, after passing through a sequence of rooms in the Napoleonic Wing, after reaching the picture gallery in the Procuratie Nuove, would they encounter the easels (Figure 1). One can imagine that the gleam of Empire-style salons, their mirrors, and the towering seventeenth-century cabinet would suddenly have felt distant. Distinctively modern easels, with minimal brass fittings and tall and slender wooden feet, supported Renaissance paintings at eye level and invited a measured examination. Standing face-to-face with these works by Venetian artists such as Giovanni Bellini and Vittore Carpaccio, one would have been struck not by grandeur but by proximity. The displays allowed for a certain degree of informality. For a moment, Italy's most celebrated painters were within reach.

The easel reappears in the Castelvecchio museum, Verona. Throughout his career, Scarpa searched for site-specific solutions and tailored his mounting mechanisms to the artworks on display. It is therefore surprising that Scarpa repurposed the very same easel designed for the Museo Correr in his remodeling of Castelvecchio (1958–1974), as remarked by Alba Di Lieto, longtime curator of the Carlo Scarpa Archive in Verona.[4] The easels resurfaced in several auctions between 2016 and 2020: as lot #25 in *The Collection of Chiara and Francesco Carraro* (Christie's New York, December 12, 2016), as lot #60 in *Thinking Italian Design* (Christie's London, October 17, 2018), as lot #101 in *Masterpieces of Italian Design* (Christie's London/March 6, 2019), as lot #162 in *Thinking Italian Art and Design Evening Sale* (Christie's London/October 22, 2020); and finally as lot #361 in *Important Design* (Sotheby's New York/December 10, 2020).

Positioning the Author

By depicting the easels on a monochrome backdrop, the auction catalogues present unforeseen, unfamiliar, decontextualized views of the objects. Like the easels isolated in auction photographs, Scarpa too occupies an isolated place in architectural history. He did never quite fit into any "movement," as acknowledged by the committee awarding Scarpa the Olivetti Prize for Architecture in 1956.[5] The accompanying report described him as "a solitary poet" who contributed to the Rationalist and postwar Organic movements, yet ultimately followed a different, more lyrical path.[6] This vision of Scarpa as a solitary figure is also found in two articles written over the next year by Bruno Zevi.[7] Scarpa's status had changed little by the early 1980s, when Manfredo Tafuri wrote: "Even those who lauded the high quality of Scarpa's arrangements in the sixties and more recently seem to have felt an instinctive need to enclose them in a kind of historical showcase, emphasizing (perhaps unwittingly) their isolation. Perhaps no other contemporary Italian architect is near to becoming a 'myth'—and hence impervious to analysis, like every authentic myth, and attracting all the anecdotes and gossip designed to foster a mythology."[8] More recently, Scarpa has been resituated within broader narratives of collaboration, by scholars such as Elena Tinacci and Renzo Zorzi.[9] Scarpa had strong ties to the Venetian cultural scene when he began remodeling the Museo Correr in 1957—the project in which his signature easel emerged. At the time, Scarpa was teaching *Disegno* at the Istituto Universitario di Architettura di Venezia (IUAV), where he was exposed to a radical rethinking of Italian architectural education. The IUAV dean, Giuseppe Samonà, was keen to reshape the curriculum by bringing to Venice a generation of leading architects and theorists, all associated with the world of Italian architectural periodicals. Among them were Luigi Piccinato, Franco Albini, Giovanni Astengo, Ignazio Gardella, as well as Bruno Zevi and Lodovico Belgiojoso. As for several Italian architects, it was the progressive entrepreneur Adriano Olivetti who ultimately boosted Scarpa's career.[10] The architect's international success derived from the way that the Olivetti-affiliated magazines *Metron, Comunità, SeleArte,* and *Zodiac* documented his work. The 1956 Olivetti Prize for Architecture paved the way for Scarpa's commission for the design of the Olivetti showroom in Piazza San Marco.

Regardless of a lack of evidence, the myth of Scarpa's persona has remained forceful. This is clear in the disputes, debates, and anecdotes surrounding his drawings, whose vast quantity and complexity only fuel the myth. Scarpa was a compulsive draftsman who generated approximately twenty thousand drawings—an output further expanded by materials retained by collaborators, craftsmen, clients or their heirs, and public and private institutions.[11] Scarpa's drawings are also difficult to interpret. As Orietta Lanzarini emphasized, Scarpa made his freehand sketches for himself.[12] Sketching was his primary vehicle for exploring ideas, and he repeatedly reworked a repertoire of elements and shapes throughout the development of his designs. His ideas often evolved in parallel across simultaneous commissions, with motifs reappearing in altered sizes in response to site-specific constraints and functional requirements. Each sketch can thus be seen as both a fully developed scheme and a fleeting trace within an ongoing and fluid process.

The difficulty of interpreting Scarpa's oeuvre becomes clear when examining a drawing for the easel (Figure 2). Here, the small study in the top-left corner represents a display panel similar to an earlier project for Palazzo Abatellis in Palermo (1953–54). The sketch in the lower left of the sheet instead shows the easel reduced to its structural diagram. Its shape resembles the model used by the Dutch abstract artist Piet Mondrian to display his work to visitors—a design that Scarpa knew well. Scarpa had installed it in the 1956 exhibition *Piet Mondrian,* at the Galleria Nazionale d'Arte Moderna in Rome (Figure 3).[13] The easel in the exhibition likely belonged to Mondrian.[14] The Mondrian show is a missing link between Scarpa's precedent display panels and the first appearance of the easel. An elevational sketch at the center of the sheet finalizes, with greater care and attention to detail, the ideas that had appeared only in rudimentary form in the smaller studies. It represents one among an indeterminate number of existing easels.[15] Yet the several, overlapping freehand sketches must have raised doubts for the first archivist, who discretely noted in the upper right corner: "Correr?"

Comparing Scarpa's final plans and elevations with the actual easel reveals no differences in dimensions or connection points (Figures 4 and 5). He pursued the idea down to the most minute technical detail. From the unusual height of 260 centimeters to the diameters of the fastenings, nothing was left to chance. Refined round pegs bound together straight wooden sections. Where the feet meet the T-shaped iron base, they extend and unfurl into clamps as if to evoke metal woodworking tools. Perhaps most surprising is how these details reveal the easel's function. At the intersection of the central vertical post and the rear wooden foot, a flat, metal bracket creates a 120-degree angle. Precisely at the vertex, Scarpa leaves a small gap, as if a bolt had been removed, and accentuates this absence with a small brass washer.[16] It is a minor yet significant gesture that suggests that the easel was meant to stand freely in space, each of its sides demanded to be seen. Another detail is telling: The feet are adjustable but lack wheels—perhaps to protect the integrity of the historic floors in Museo Correr and Castelvecchio, while preserving the careful calibration of the display.

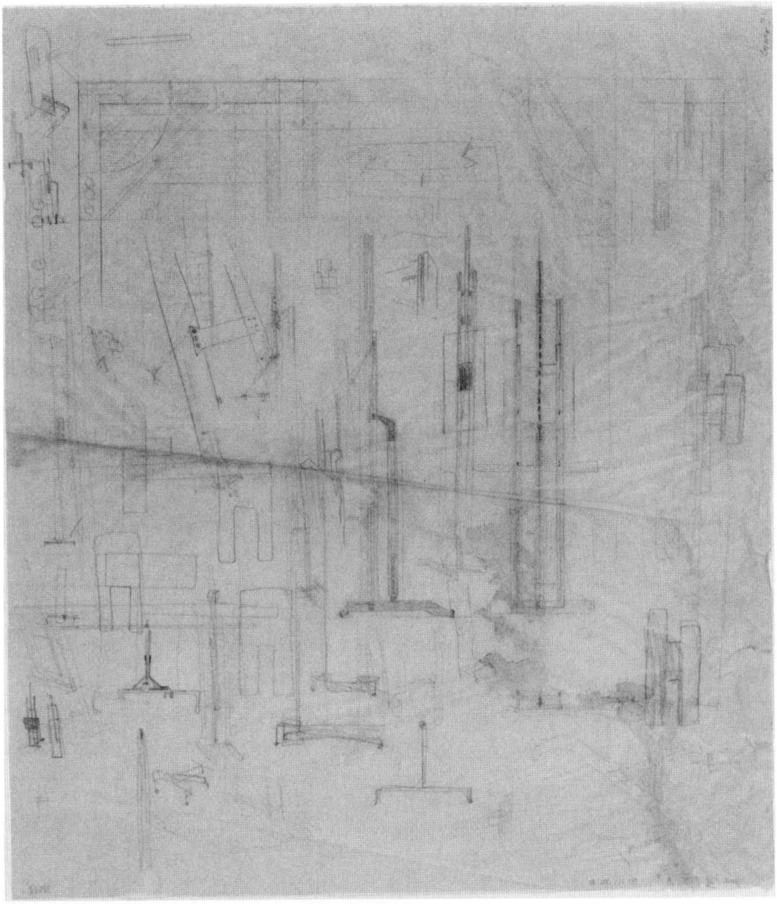

Figure 2. Carlo Scarpa, Sketch for the easel designed for the Museo Correr, Venice. Courtesy of MAXXI Museo nazionale delle arti del XXI secolo, Rome. MAXXI Architettura Collection.

Figure 3. The easel supporting *Broadway Boogie Woogie* in the 1956 *Piet Mondrian* exhibition at the Galleria Nazionale d'Arte Moderna in Rome, curated by museum director Palma Bucarelli and designed by Carlo Scarpa. Displayed next to Arnold Newman's 1942 photograph of Mondrian in his New York studio, where presumably the same easel was used to display works intended for sale.

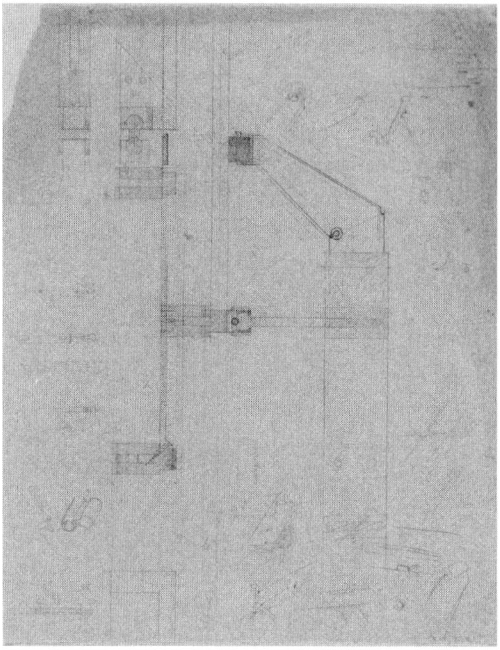

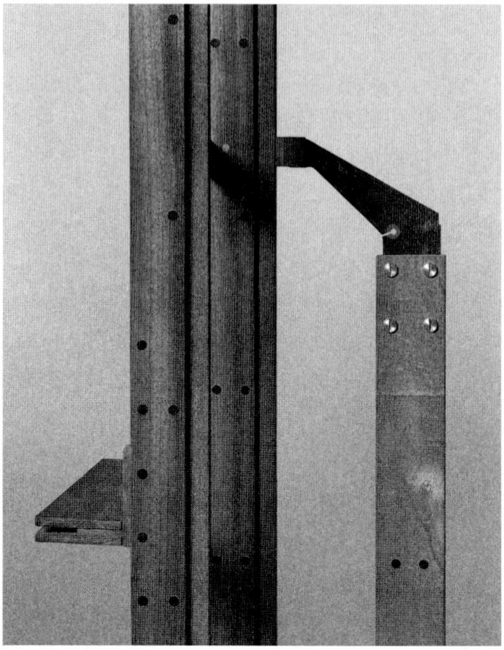

Figure 4 (*left*). Carlo Scarpa, Technical drawing for the Museo Correr easel, Venice, displaying the precise brass joinery details. Courtesy of MAXXI Museo nazionale delle arti del XXI secolo, Rome. MAXXI Architettura Collection.

Figure 5 (*right*). Details of joinery and bolts on the easel. Lot #101, from Christie's catalog *Masterpieces of Design and Photography* (London, 2019).

Re-dating the Easel

Who produced the easel and when? One answer is that they were crafted in steel, brass, and hardwood, and that the easel was manufactured by the Officina Zanon blacksmiths and Saverio Anfodillo, cabinetmaker, both based in Venice's Cannaregio district, at the heart of the historic Jewish Ghetto.[17] The fact that the two workshops stood next door to one another was convenient for Scarpa, since he could oversee every stage of production from a single location. Scarpa promoted and worked with these two Venice craftsmen, and the names Officina Zanon and Anfodillo were mentioned in the issue of the 1960 *Bollettino dei Musei Civici Veneziani,* which was entirely devoted to the remodeling of the Museo Correr.[18] The artisans' visibility was further solidified through their appearance in a 1972 television interview. Here, Gino Zanon and his sons Paolo and Francesco, together with Saverio Anfodillo provided personal insights into their working relationship with Carlo Scarpa or "Il Professore," as they often referred to him. Within this context, "Il Professore" denoted not only Scarpa's actual role as a professor at the IUAV University in Venice but also reflected a tone of deference and admiration conveying a professional hierarchy that depended upon the conventions of the day. But the emphasis on "Il Professore" overshadowed the artisans' agency. It gave the impression that they were mere executors while further fueling Scarpa's legend as the sole author of his works.

An interview from 2010 reveals a different relationship. The craftsmen were significant in the creation of the easel, as Francesco Zanon recalled: "If he (*Il Professore*) wanted something that was technically unfeasible, we would make suggestions, and he would follow us, adapting to our proposals—which at times helped simplify the work without altering the final result."[19] Scarpa "entrusted himself to the hands of craftsmen, debating at length with them and almost placing their work on equal footing with his own design practice," argues art historian Giuseppe Mazzariol. Craftsmen were for him "essential repositories of knowledge, on the same plane as the *monumenta* of the past or books."[20] From this perspective, different specialists, such as the blacksmiths or the joiners, contributed to the completion of a single easel, revealing a new record of ownership.

But when was the easel made? There is no doubt that the first stage of production took place between 1957 and 1960, when Scarpa was rearranging the painting section of the Museo Correr. It is also clear that the Zanons and Anfodillo were requested to produce another series of easels sometime between 1958 and 1964 as part of the remodeling of Castelvecchio in Verona overseen by Scarpa. The production of the easels did not stop after Scarpa's death in 1978 and this is when the timeline becomes murky. "At some point, friends of *Il Professore* began commissioning easels from us," says Francesco Zanon, now eighty-three.[21] Apparently, these requests did not come out of a desire for profit but arose from an improvised collective fascination with Scarpa's legacy—a tribute to the architect from an elite, erudite market.

Among those "friends" were the collectors Chiara and Francesco Carraro who purchased one of Scarpa's easel for the double-height *salone* of their apartment near Palazzo Grassi in Venice.[22] The Carraros likely came into direct contact with the Zanon workshop through the architect Gilda D'Agaro, a former collaborator of Scarpa, who had renovated their house in the late 1970s. The easel was among the fifty-two pieces of their collection that were sold at Christie's New York in 2016, and the first Scarpa easel to be offered in auction. Francesco Zanon recalls that the Carraros displayed the easel without any artwork, as a Scarpa-designed object in its own right.[23]

It is difficult to establish how many easels were produced after 1978. Francesco Zanon estimates around forty. One easel continues to inhabit the space of its production at the Officina Zanon. A photograph from 2011 shows the two brothers, Francesco and Paolo Zanon, standing proudly beside one of the easels still preserved in the workshop, a testament to their craftsmanship (Figure 6). The Officina Zanon keeps this object alive alongside other Scarpa-designed objects such as the geometric sculpture *Crescita*. During a visit to the Zanon workshop, I was allowed a glimpse into certain easels' details that are, rather astonishingly, more elegantly resolved than those of the 1960 models held at the Museo Correr.

Figure 6. Francesco and Paolo Zanon with the easel still present in their workshop. Courtesy of Officina Zanon.

A shortcoming of the earlier editions was their inability to fix the paintings to the structure. This meant that even the lightest vibration, like the passing of a visitor, posed a risk to the artworks. The Zanon brothers devised a discreet yet effective solution: integrating two metal pegs into the bottom canvas holder, and an S-shaped hook on the back of the stretcher to further stabilize the painting. While these technical improvements might seem minor, they speak of the level of care and ingenuity applied by the Zanons—qualities that, of late, have led the Italian cultural heritage authority (Soprintendenza) to entrust them the restoration of the entrance door of the Olivetti showroom.[24] The Museo Correr and Castelvecchio museum turned to the Zanons when new easels were needed to accommodate an ever-growing art collection.[25]

An image illustrating the Anfodillo workshop encourages us to consider a very different story (Figure 7). Taken by the Italian photographer Guido Guidi shortly after the carpentry closed in 1996, the photograph shows four easels stacked

Figure 7. Anfodillo workshop. Photo: Guido Guidi, c. 1996. The Italian photographer Guidi began documenting Carlo Scarpa's Brion Tomb in San Vito di Altivole in 1996, commissioned by the Canadian Centre for Architecture in Montréal. He continued documenting Scarpa's work through the Centro Internazionale di Studi di Architettura Andrea Palladio (CISA), Vicenza. Courtesy of Guido Guidi/CISA Palladio.

together—crowded, inert, almost lifeless—a striking visual metaphor for the suspended state of these objects when they are no longer in use and when their makers have ceased their craft. Today, only two workshops in Venice are able to produce and restore these easels. In addition to the Officina Zanon, there is the Falegnameria Augusto Capovilla, another joinery with which Scarpa collaborated and to which Zanon turned after Anfodillo's closure. Now the Capovilla features the easel among its signature pieces on its website.[26]

A comparison of the easels from the Museo Correr and Castelvecchio with their post-1978 counterparts makes their differences clear. The first were crafted from Sucupira and Brazilian rosewood, dense, richly grained hardwoods while later versions, though produced with the same care and rigor, have typically been realized in teak and iroko. Looking at the offered lots at auction more carefully, we see differences between their dimensions and materials. Lot #25 at Christie's New York 2016 is in walnut. Lot #60 at Christie's London 2018, lot #101 at Christie's London 2019, and lot #361 at Sotheby's New York 2020 are in teak. Lot #162 at Christie's London 2020 is in iroko. Lot #101 measures 282 centimeters in height and is approximately 20 centimeters taller than the other easels. These variations were due to changing availabilities and sourcing constraints. But if one looks beyond their material distinctions, the posthumously produced easels also challenge conventional notions of authenticity.[27] On the one hand, they were neither realized under Scarpa's supervision or by his collaborators during the architect's lifetime. On the other hand, the post-1978 easels were created by the very same artisans who crafted them originally, using the same techniques, tools and sensibilities. These posthumous easels would appear, then, to have a considerably stronger claim to authenticity than certain collaborative industrial prototypes that were developed by Carlo Scarpa and Sandro Bagnoli, such as the *Ultrarazionale* furniture collection.[28]

Labeling

Is it reasonable to suppose that the easel is an artwork? Carlo Scarpa has long been regarded as an artist. Scarpa graduated from the Art Academy in Venice in 1926, the same year the Istituto Universitario di Architettura was inaugurated; yet he struggled throughout his career to gain recognition as an architect. In 1955, he was accused of practicing architecture without a formal degree, which is why, when receiving the 1956 Olivetti Prize for Architecture, Zevi praised him as "one of Italy's best artists."[29] IUAV eventually awarded Scarpa an honorary degree in architecture in 1978, just before an accident in Japan ended his life. In this light, the pre-1978 easels might be considered the product of an educated artist.

The production, sale, and transformation of the easels into private art commodities happened after Scarpa's death. When Francesco and Paolo Zanon felt the need to mark the easels with Scarpa's signature and their company logo for a brief period in the 1990s, they affirmed the easels' status as salable items. Even though the practice was promptly discontinued following objections from the architect's son, Tobia Scarpa, the Zanon brothers inadvertently recast the easel within the conventions of an art auction.[30] In 2014, the traveling exhibition *Carol Bove/Carlo Scarpa* further crystalized the easel as work of art. In the show of the American artist Carol Bove, visitors had the opportunity to draw tenacious associations and savor the easel's formal qualities, finding the charms in its refined details without a painting on it.

Less than two years later, and benefiting from the international visibility generated by the *Carol Bove/Carlo Scarpa* exhibition, one easel sold at Christie's New York for $187,500. With an estimate of $10,000 to $15,000, the sale was a success.[31] The auction catalog underscored the inclusion of the piece in Bove's exhibition, thickening its provenance and celebrity, in an attempt to market it to contemporary art clients as well as to enthusiasts of modern architecture. A discourse of artistry and rarity helped fuel the desire for Scarpa's design pieces. When a

Scarpa easel appeared as lot #361 at Sotheby's New York 2020 *Important Design* auction, the sale catalog described it as an exceptional example from a "limited edition of approximately twenty easels . . . bearing the artist's signature."[32]

Apart from its aesthetic qualities, Scarpa's easel also provides a striking material record of the development of Italian museography during the decade following World War II. In particular, it shows how interventions modified, adapted, and modernized ancient buildings through aesthetics.[33] In Italy, approximately three hundred museums were renovated between 1945 and 1970.[34] The architects who designed these interiors were not in charge of the whole restoration work, and so their contributions have been dismissed as "interpretative," for valuing the original building more than the later additions.[35] One of the few to have reached a level of interest comparable to Scarpa's Correr is Palazzo Bianco, redesigned by Franco Albini, whose work is, so far, less sought-after at auction.

In an effort to reframe the easel in architectural terms, the installation *Art on display. Formas de expor 1949–69* inserted a Scarpa easel in two new contexts, at the Calouste Gulbenkian Museum in Lisbon and at Het Nieuwe Instituut in Rotterdam.[36] Two easels on loan from the Correr Museum were showcased together with coeval art mounting mechanisms that were designed by prominent architects such as Franco Albini, Aldo van Eyck, Lina Bo Bardi, and Alison and Peter Smithson. The emphasis on the method of presentation over the artworks on display reflects how the art market redefined the easels, by embedding them within a broader system of value and meaning related to exhibition design and curatorial intent. No longer anchored in the intended architectural envelope, the easel was reimagined in a spirit of flexibility and performativity as an object for display.

Displaying Provenance

Let us redirect our attention to the myth of Scarpa with which we began. Firsthand experience shows the extent to which the Museo Correr and Castelvecchio sustain the cult of Scarpa. Photographic documentation of Scarpa's original installation such as room no. 38 at the Museo Correr reveals a gesture of authenticity—an easel placed in a room conceived ad hoc with blockboard panels, a carpeted floor that muffled the visitor's footsteps, and artworks fully framed by the architecture itself. That stands at odds with what I encountered in May 2025. The room had undergone a series of material substitutions: The carpet had been replaced, the walls repainted, a new lighting system installed. St. Sebastian by Vittore Carpaccio was absent; *Two Venetian Ladies,* also by Carpaccio, had been reframed. Even the finer details had shifted: Labels were removed or

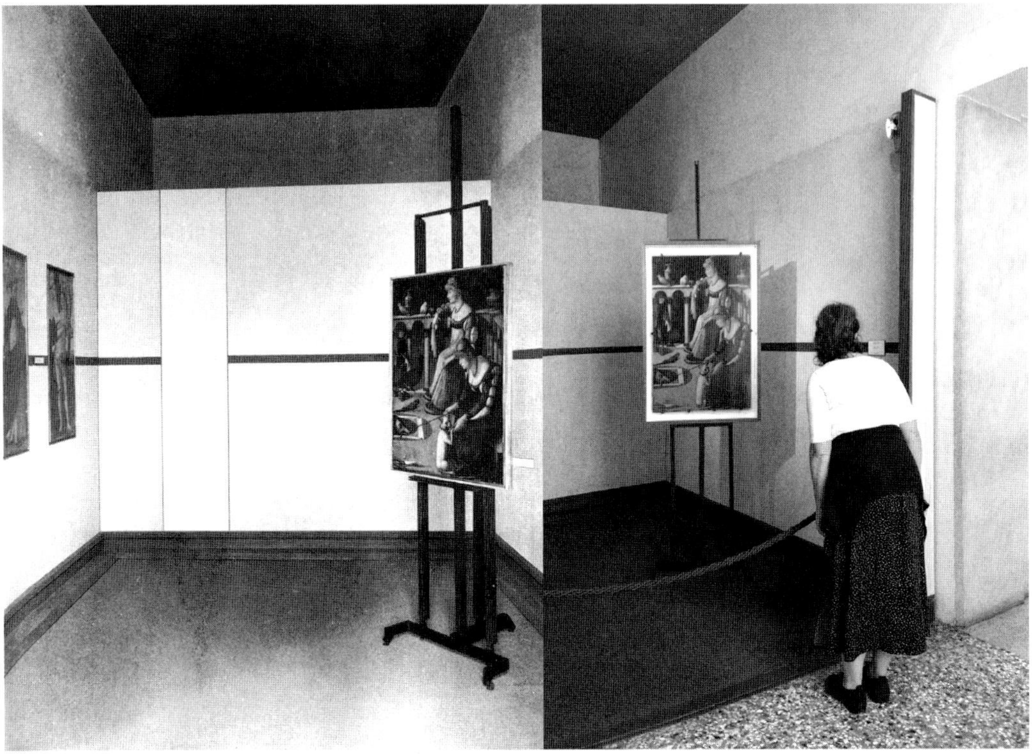

Figure 8. Comparison between the original installation of room no. 38 at the Museo Correr, Venice, and its condition as documented by the author in May 2025.

repositioned, the easel itself had been rotated, and a rope barrier had been installed restricting visitors' proximity to the artworks (Figure 8).[37] To maintain an illusion of integrity and authenticity, the museum remains silent about the repairs.[38] In an attempt to preserve the moment of Scarpa's creation, room no. 38 ceased to be distinctly different from the existing, and began, in a kind of reversal, to become a period room.[39] Yet this preservation of the "original Scarpa" has not stopped the easel from developing a life of its own. Today, Scarpa's easel is a first feature to be spotted upon entering the neoclassical palace in Piazza San Marco.[40] At least for the entire duration of exhibition *Il Correr di Scarpa 1953–1960,* ending in October 2025, its elevation to a pedestal in the *Sala delle Quattro Porte* supports Tafuri's Scarpa mythology and contributes to the reception history of these small museum objects.[41]

Yet, in a quiet and telling shift, the easel's label now acknowledges its makers: "Falegnameria Capovilla, Fabbri Zanon." For the first time, the easel's provenance is made visible in the realm of a museum. The timing of this revelation follows a string of high-profile auction sales and coincides with the exhibition *Carlo Scarpa and the Officina Zanon. The Materials of the Project* at the Palazzina Masieri (May 3–July 25, 2025).[42]

Through the auction catalogs, the easels unfold the selective and incomplete story of a circulating art-historical object. Their provenance is marked by multiple hands: Carlo Scarpa, who designed them; the Officina Zanon, who fabricated the metal fittings; the Anfodillo and Capovilla workshops, who executed the joinery; the collectors Chiara and Francesco Carraro, who treated the easel as an artwork. Later, exhibitions reframed these frame-works, and museums contributed to their preservation as iconic objects. Each actor leaves a mark of provenance in the evolving life of the easel, be it a signature, a physical alteration, or a simple label.

Biography
Flavia Crisciotti is a Walter Benjamin Fellow and postdoctoral researcher in the international research project *Provenance Projected: Architecture Past and Future in the Era of Circularity,* at the Oslo School of Architecture and Design. She completed her PhD at the Technische Universität München in 2024, specializing in the history of twentieth-century architecture and museography. Her current research investigates the afterlives of museum furnishings in postwar Italy, with a focus on authorship, authenticity, and conservation. She studied architecture at Sapienza Università di Roma.

Notes

[1] The number of existing easels is difficult to determine. During my site visit to the Museo Correr in May 2025, I counted fifteen easels on display. According to information kindly provided by the responsible of the Carlo Scarpa Archive at the Castelvecchio Museum, Ketty Bertolaso, that institution currently preserves seventeen easels, two of which were reconstructed more recently. One additional easel, supporting *The Presentation of Christ in the Temple* by Giovanni Bellini, is located in the galleries of the Fondazione Querini Stampalia (although Scarpa's intervention at that site, undertaken between 1961 and 1963, was limited to the ground floor, portico, and garden). Another edition is housed in the Palazzetto Aldo Businaro in Monselice, now home to the Museo delle Rarità di Carlo Scarpa. To this provisional count—approximately thirty-five—should be added the easels presumably held in storage.

[2] Sale catalogue, *The Collection of Chiara and Francesco Carraro,* December 12, 2016 (London: Christie's): https://www.christies.com/en/lot/lot-6033260 (accessed April 10, 2025).

[3] Sale catalogue, *Thinking Italian Art and Design Evening Sale,* October 22, 2020 (London: Christie's): https://www.christies.com/en/lot/lot-6285707 (accessed April 10, 2025).

[4] Alba Di Lieto, *I disegni di Carlo Scarpa per Castelvecchio* (Regione del Veneto; Marsilio, 2006), 80. The easel was first introduced in the 1958 temporary exhibition *Da Altichiero a Pisanello* at the Castelvecchio Museum, and later retained in the permanent installation of the museum.

[5] Report by the Jury: 2nd Olivetti National Prize for Architecture and Urban Planning, brochure printed by *Ing. C. Olivetti & Co., S.p.A.–Ivrea,* 1956. MAXXI Archive Rome.

[6] Report by the Jury.

[7] Bruno Zevi, "Premi Olivetti. Scarpa e Quaroni, due scommesse sul futuro," *L'Espresso,* December 23, 1956; Bruno Zevi, "I premi nazionali di architettura e urbanistica a Carlo Scarpa e Ludovico Quaroni," *L'Architettura. Cronache e storia,* no. 15 (January 1957): 628.

[8] Manfredo Tafuri, "Carlo Scarpa and Italian Architecture," in *Carlo Scarpa: The Complete Works,* ed. Francesco Dal Co and Giuseppe Mazzariol (Electa/Rizzoli, 1985), 72.

[9] Elena Tinacci, *Mia memore et devota gratitudine: Carlo Scarpa e Olivetti, 1956–1978* (Edizioni di Comunità, 2018); Renzo Zorzi, "Per una storia dei rapporti tra Carlo Scarpa e Olivetti," in *Carlo Scarpa: Mostre e Musei 1944–1976, Case e Paesaggi 1972–1978,* eds. Guido Beltramini, Kurt W. Forster, and Paola Marini (Electa, 2000), 27–40.

[10] Bruno Zevi's intercession was crucial in the professional relationship between Carlo Scarpa and Adriano Olivetti.

[11] The largest collection of Carlo Scarpa's drawings is held at MAXXI in Rome and the State Archives in Treviso. The corpus has been inventoried and partially digitized, either as individual items or grouped by project. Documentary materials related to the restoration of Palazzo Abatellis in Palermo, the Museo di Castelvecchio in Verona, and the Fondazione Querini Stampalia in Venice are cataloged and preserved at the respective institutions. The Brion Tomb drawings, conserved in San Vito d'Altivole, have been cataloged under the supervision of Vitale Zanchettin.

[12] Orietta Lanzarini, "Carlo Scarpa e il disegno," in *CDP. Codici del Disegno di Progetto. Appunti di studio,* ed. Luca Cipriani, *DISEGNARECON* 2, no. 3 (2009), https://doi.org/10.6092/issn.1828-5961/1683.

[13] The exhibition was curated by Palma Bucarelli, director of the Galleria Nazionale d'Arte Moderna in Rome, and designed by Carlo Scarpa.

[14] This hypothesis has been advanced through visual comparison between archival photographs of Scarpa's installation and historical images of Mondrian's studio, most notably the portrait by Arnold Newman showing Piet Mondrian leaning on his easel in New York, January 17, 1942.

[15] See note 1.

[16] This minute detail recalls Kenneth Frampton's account of Scarpa's design of L-shaped steel brackets in his buildings: "Scarpa drilled a small hole at the crossing point so that the saw would change tone when it hit the intersection and thus produce a clean cut with no overrun." He then inserted "a small brass washer at the point of intersection" in order "to finish this productive detail." Kenneth Frampton, *Studies in Tectonic Culture: The Poetics of Construction in Nineteenth and Twentieth Century Architecture* (MIT Press, 1995), 308–9. The detail had been reinterpreted by the designer and Scarpa's son, Tobia, in the *Biagio* lamp (1968).

[17] Richard Murphy, *Carlo Scarpa and the Castelvecchio* (Butterworth Architecture, 1990), 135.

[18] The names of the artisans are explicitly cited in G. Mariacher, "L'allestimento della Quadreria Correr," *Bollettino dei Musei Civici Veneziani* 2 (1960): 14.

[19] *Un'ora con Carlo Scarpa,* directed by Maurizio Cascavilla and curated by Gastone Favero (RAI Radiotelevisione Italiana, 1972). The documentary was first broadcast on November 11, 1972, on RAI, Italy's national public broadcasting network. For an analysis and full transcription, see Orietta Lanzarini, "Fermare la complessità. La videobiografia *Un'ora con Carlo Scarpa* (1972)," in *Costruire il dispositivo storico: Tra fonti e strumenti,* ed. Jasenka Gudelj and Paola Nicolin (Mondadori, 2006), 247–73.

[20] Francesco Dal Co and Giuseppe Mazzariol, eds., *Carlo Scarpa: The Complete Works* (Electa/Rizzoli, 1985), 19.

[21] Francesco Zanon, interviewed by the author in January 2025.

[22] Gilda D'Agaro had likely been recommended to Francesco Carraro by Licisco Magagnato, then director of the Museo di Castelvecchio in Verona.

[23] Francesco Zanon, interviewed by the author in May 2025.

[24] The iconic entrance door of the Olivetti showroom in Piazza San Marco—designed by Carlo Scarpa as part of the overall interior in 1958—was dismantled in 2022 and restored in 2024 by the Officina Zanon. The showroom had been significantly altered in 1984 to accommodate a souvenir shop. Officially recognized as a site of historical and artistic interest, the space was placed under legal protection by decree on March 17, 1997. This led to a fruitful collaboration between the Soprintendenza and the building's owner, Assicurazioni Generali, with the shared goal of restoring the structure and securing public access. For the restoration details, see "Il restauro del cancello scarpiano del Negozio Olivetti a Venezia," Fondo Ambiente Italiano, https://fondoambiente.it/news/il-restauro-del-cancello-scarpiano-del-negozio-olivetti-a-venezia (accessed December 2024).

[25] The Castelvecchio museum holds two easels produced after 1978. For the Museo Correr, no definitive data are available. However, a photograph taken by Guido Guidi in the Anfodillo workshop, bearing the note "4 cavalletti x Correr," suggests that four easels were commissioned by the institution from the artisans around 1996.

[26] See *Falegnameria Capovilla* official website, https://www.falegnameriacapovilla.it/attivita/carlo-scarpa/ (accessed December 2024).

[27] "Authentic," in *The Shorter Oxford English Dictionary,* Vol. 1 (Clarendon Press, 2002), 153.

[28] Carlo Scarpa and Sandro Bagnoli, *Il design per Dino Gavina* (Silvana Editoriale, 2014).

[29] Report by the Jury: 2nd Olivetti National Prize for Architecture and Urban Planning, 1956.

[30] Francesco Zanon, interviewed by the author in January 2025.

[31] "Most recently the American contemporary artist Carol Bove exhibited Scarpa's easels, a sculpture (a variant of lot 26) and vitrines alongside her new body of work in the exhibition *Carol Bove/Carlo Scarpa,* curated by the Henry Moore Institute in Leeds, England and Museion, Bolzano." *Francesco and Chiara Carraro: A Passion for Italian Art* (London: Christie's, October 2016), lot 25, https://www.christies.com/en/lot/lot-6033260 (accessed December 2024).

[32] https://www.sothebys.com/en/buy/auction/2020/important-design-6/easel (accessed December 2024).

[33] In 1950s Italy, the conversion of historic *palazzi* into museums was a widespread phenomenon, often coinciding with the restoration of buildings damaged during World War II. The architects responsible for these museum transformations were frequently distinct from those charged with the restoration. For further discussion of the phenomenon, see Patricia Falguières, "Politics for the White Cube: The Italian

Way," trans. Natalie Dupêcher, *Grey Room*, no. 64 (Summer 2016): 6–39; Maria Cecilia Mazzi, *Musei anni '50: Spazio, forma, funzione* (Edifir, 2009); and Paolo Morello, "La museografia del dopoguerra. Opere e modelli storiografici," in *Storia dell'architettura italiana. Il secondo Novecento*, ed. Francesco Dal Co (Electa, 1997), 392–417.

[34] Raffaella Fontanarossa, *La capostipite di sé: una donna alla guida dei musei. Caterina Marcenaro a Genova 1948–'71* (Cartograf, 2015), 150.

[35] Marco Mulazzani, "Lo spazio interno come spazio architettato," in Antonella Huber, *Il museo italiano: la trasformazione di spazi storici in spazi espositivi. Attualità dell'esperienza museografica degli anni '50* (Edizioni Lybra Immagine, 1997), 73.

[36] A precedent for the display of the easel outside the Italian context is the exhibition *Carlo Scarpa, Architect: Intervening with History* at the Canadian Centre for Architecture in Montréal (May 26–October 31, 1999). For the exhibition catalogs, see Lisa Le Feuvre et al., *Carol Bove / Carlo Scarpa* (Leeds: Henry Moore Institute; Bolzano: Museion; Deurle: Museum Dhondt-Dhaenens, 2015) and Penelope Curtis and Dirk van den Heuvel, eds., *Art on Display 1949–69 = Formas de Expor 1949–69* (Lisbon: Museu Calouste Gulbenkian, 2019).

[37] The *St. Sebastian* by Vittore Carpaccio was officially returned to the Strossmayer Gallery in Zagreb following the 1961 bilateral agreement between Yugoslavia and Italy, concluding restitution negotiations that had begun during World War II. Although the niche created for the *St. Sebastian* remains empty, it seems unlikely that the audience would understand the story.

[38] Reflecting on the legacy of museum masters like Scarpa, Lanzarini asks, "What remains then, in today's museums, of the masters of postwar museography and their lessons? My answer, as a scholar who has studied these issues for over two decades, is: nothing." Orietta Lanzarini, "Reputations. Carlo Scarpa," *The Architectural Review*, no. 1501 (May 2023): 36–38.

[39] My thanks to Jorge Otero-Pailos, with whom the idea of room no. 38 as a period room emerged in Turin, May 2025.

[40] The easels are no longer confined to the picture gallery on the second floor; they are also in the Napoleonic Wing.

[41] *Il Correr di Carlo Scarpa 1953–1960*, exhibition curated by Chiara Squarcina and Andrea Bellieni, Museo Correr, Venice, Sala delle Quattro Porte, May 1–October 19, 2025.

[42] The exhibition *Carlo Scarpa e l'Officina Zanon. I materiali del Progetto* at the Museo Correr, Venice, Palazzina Masieri (May 3–July 25, 2025) was curated by Maria Bonaiti and Marko Pogacnik. See Maria Bonaiti and Marko Pogacnik, eds., *Carlo Scarpa e l'Officina Zanon. I materiali del Progetto* (Venice: Quaderni IUAV, Ricerche IUAV at Work, April 2025).

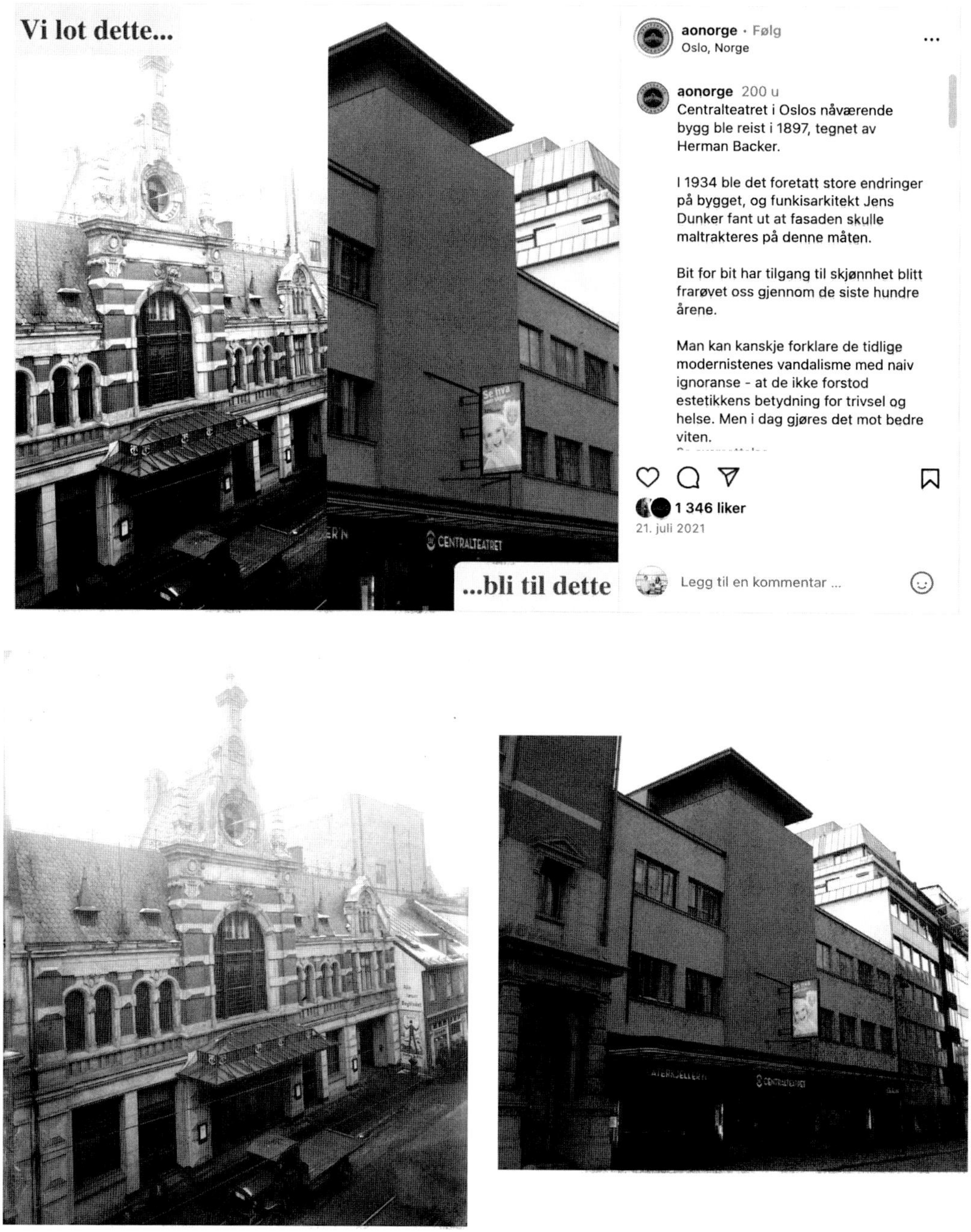

Figure 1. *Top*: Instagram post, July 21, 2021, by *Foreningen Arkitekturopprøret Norge* (Architectural Rebellion) shows Centralteatret viewed from Akersgata. *Lower left*: The original nineteenth-century facade, photographed between 1924 and 1926. Photo: Narve Skarpmoen, The National Library of Norway, Nasjonalbiblioteket. *Lower right*: The renovated modernist facade, 2009. Photo: GAD.

Amandine Kastler and
Erlend Skjeseth

Anachronic Hybrids

Cuts into Architectural Time

Sometime in 2021, while scrolling aimlessly through social media updates provided by the all-seeing algorithm, a peculiar post appeared. The diptych showed two very different images of the same theater building in downtown Oslo. Although the superimposed text made it abundantly clear, it took a moment to comprehend that this was in fact the same building. The first photograph showed a "classical" facade in black and white, a typical urban building in Oslo from the mid-nineteenth century with deep reliefs, moldings, and plaster ornaments. The second full-color photograph depicted a facade from the 1930s, with large surfaces of multicolored rendered wall, curving baldachins, and a stone veneer base. A fluorescent sign in a particularly 1930s pink font stacked vertically read: "Centralteatret" (The Central Theatre). At first glance, this appeared as a fine example of pared-back and sober modernism. However, a superimposed text aimed to convince the reader that this was a not just a scene for dramatic performances but the scene of a crime. It read: "*How could we let this* (exhibit 1: 'Classical' façade from 1880), *turn into this* (exhibit 2: Modernist façade from 1935)?"[1]

This bombastic antimodernist call to arms was asking rhetorically how we, as a society, have allowed for the degradation of our built environment since the emergence of modernism. The popular appeal of the argument, authored by "Foreningen Arkitekturopprøret Norge" (Architectural Rebellion, Norway) was evident in the comments, most of which were indignant toward the perceived vandalism. One commentator suggested that it was time for a publicly funded action to remove the modernist facades of these buildings and restore them to their original splendor. The superimposed text, and the many comments below, represented a group of people aggrieved by a nearly century-old renovation. One could take this cultural phenomenon as yet another representation of polarized online rage-bait meme culture: a particular brand of populist reductivism that has altered the political landscape around us. Yet this example also tells us something about how the complex provenance of a building sometimes fails to be cherished by the public. What some (and in this case maybe many) see as a historical error that needs rectifying might instead be a pluralistic fragment.

Future Anterior
Volume XXII, Numbers 1–2
Summer / Winter 2025

Centralteatret is as a cornucopia of architectural elements, a literal section through history where beauty lies in the adjacency of time and the durability of a *cadavre exquis*. The hybrid form of this exquisite cadaver, produced by the theater's centuries-long evolution can be likened to the Dadaist game, an analogy also used by Marvin Trachtenberg to describe the "morphogenesis" typical of medieval to Renaissance construction. During this era, the extended duration of building projects, some spanning generations, brought in new architects, patrons, and styles. These changing conditions frequently caused structures to be altered during their realization.[2] The changes over time at Centralteatret reflect this pre-Renaissance mindset that proceeded the notion of a singularly authored architecture. Centralteatret is a hybrid containing multiplicities that converge at a razor-sharp edge in the buildup of its walls. If we are to take the stance in the outraged social media post seriously and symptomatically, then an appreciation of the chaotic and redundant seems to be under threat.

This essay attempts to understand how architectural provenance might lead to a better cultivation of existing buildings and how provenance might be an active driver in making new ones. To aid this endeavor, we analyze the existing Centralteatret and unpack strategies employed in built fragments of contemporary architecture. The set of buildings discussed are perhaps incomparable in program, history, location, and situation, yet they are linked by shared sensibilities shaped over time by the circumstances of their creation.

Learning from Centralteatret

Let us first return to the crime scene in downtown Oslo. What the author of the indignant social media post failed to appreciate is what happens when you step off the street into the building and beyond the surface of the century-old modernist facade. Entering through the shallow veneer of the interwar, modernist facade, the bones of a nineteenth-century building are revealed. Visitors enter through a narrow entrance, followed by a truncated lobby. Less than half a meter in, an older interior unfolds, of many times and temporalities. This sequence moves the visitor from a twenty-first-century city outside, through a 1930s shallow portal, draped across a historicist interior from the late nineteenth century. The effect is dumbfounding but not without precedent. There are numerous examples of the facade of a building being severed from its interior. Casa Cogollo in Vincenza, a fifteenth-century Quattrocento house, supposedly had its facade remodeled by Andrea Palladio[3],while the medieval structure of Santa Maria Novella in Florence was given a new representational front, designed by Leon Battista Alberti and completed in 1470.

Further into Centralteateret, the vestibule bottlenecks into a classically structured theater hall that seats approximately three hundred sixty people. A semicircular mezzanine sits above, a pronounced proscenium arch frames the stage, active and obsolete infrastructure collides. Spill-out spaces, originally designed to provide axillary functions to the theater-like bars and vestibules, now provide sequences of classically proportioned rooms interspersed with archaic cables, curtains, furniture, and acting paraphernalia accrued over the years. Among this sequence of rooms is the colonnaded *Søylehallen* (Hall of Columns) from 1802, designed by the architect Hans Jørgen Rawert, where Oslo patricians once played amateur theater, and from which the modern transformations of Centralteateret grew. Around 1760, before Søylehallen appeared, the theater most likely consisted of a stand-alone pavilion replacing an older *orangerie,* also used for private amateur theater, set in a private pleasure park just outside the city border of what was then called Christiania. The area is still called *Grensen* (The Border) today, even though it has long since been engulfed by the city. Then again in 1826, the structure is extended, likely based on designs by the same architect. With the exemption of the truly classical Søylehallen, much of Rawert's designs and other additions disappeared when the buildings were sold as building materials in a demolition auction in April 1890, including the presumably first skylight in Oslo, designed by the city architect Georg Andreas Bull, who had transformed the theater into an exhibition hall in 1872.[4] We have yet to find inflammatory material on social media decrying this act. Just a few years after this demolition, the hyper-historicist front much adored by the Instagrammers a decade later as a "classical" feature is erected, designed by architect Herman Major Backer, who in 1882 had designed virtually the same facade for the popular bierstube Olympen in Grønlandsleiret in Oslo, which still exists. The history of this building, and its constantly changing name and function, makes a complex series of transactions in the market, with countless owners and subletters across three centuries. Soon after the 1890 demolition, the second in the history of the property, a new building was in place, with interiors designed by Henrik Bull, a major Norwegian art nouveau architect. Yet this iteration of the theater was but a blip on its long trajectory. In 1934, a new facade by the modernist architect and preservationist Jens Dunker was realized. Then, in the 1960s, when the Norwegian Broadcaster (NRK) used the theater for their first television transmissions, parts of the gallery were sliced up and removed to make way for filming equipment. This cut was patched when NRK left the building and is not visible today.

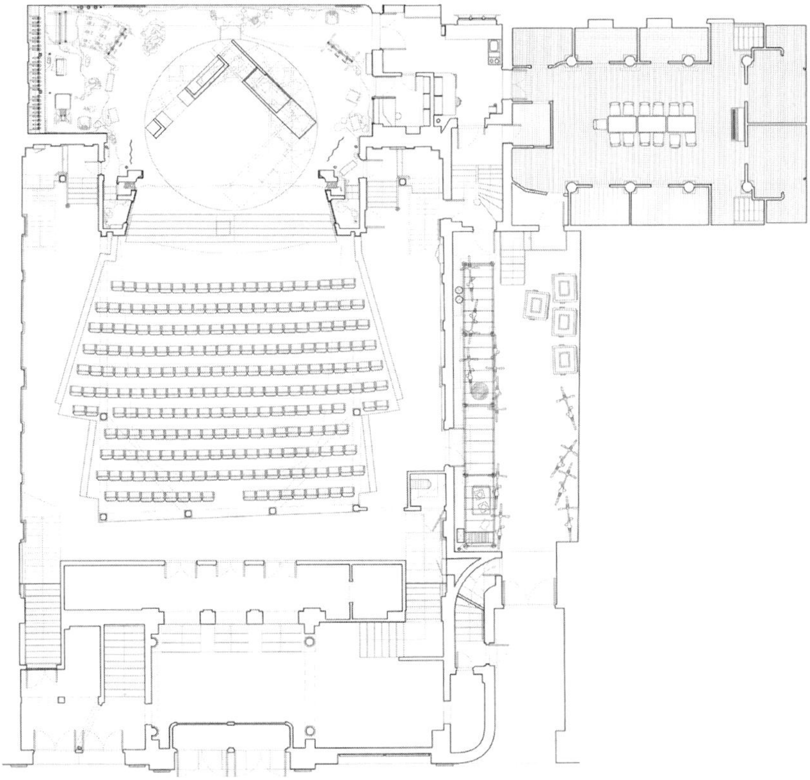

Figure 2. Plan of Centralteatret, showing Søylehallen (the column hall) to the right, secondary rooms, service courtyard, main stage, theater hall, vestibule, and entrance lobby. The drawing is part of a survey produced collectively by students from the *Transformation in Practice: Centralteatret* studio at the Oslo School of Architecture and Design (AHO), 2022.

The long and complex provenance of Centralteateret served as the subject of the design studio *Transformation in Practice: Centralteateret* at the Oslo School of Architecture in 2022.[5] The studio presented the theater as a machine for illusion and storytelling, where architecture worked to signify and symbolize, flatter, and seduce. Seventeen students studied the spaces and components of the building for ways to improve its existing conditions. The speculative projects devised surgical approaches to allow for continued use of the theater without erasing the many layers of history evident in all its messiness.[6] Centralteateret is a rarity in the Norwegian context, with its near undisturbed historical patina a contrast to the interiors of many cultural buildings, where an influx of wealth and investment has seen renovations erase all signs of original surfaces. In analyzing Centralteateret it became clear that any intervention in its delicate fabric needed to be in tune with the building's complex provenance, but whether that rich history will be considered in future architectural projects remains to be seen.

The pluralities at Centralteateret are common in buildings of a certain age and ought to be embraced, and perhaps even cultivated, in future examples of reuse and transformation. Mari Lending depicts Centralteateret as "a three-dimensional palimpsest across centuries."[7] Perhaps this layered building shaped by a series of historical "glitches" can be best understood as an *anachronic hybrid,* to borrow a term introduced

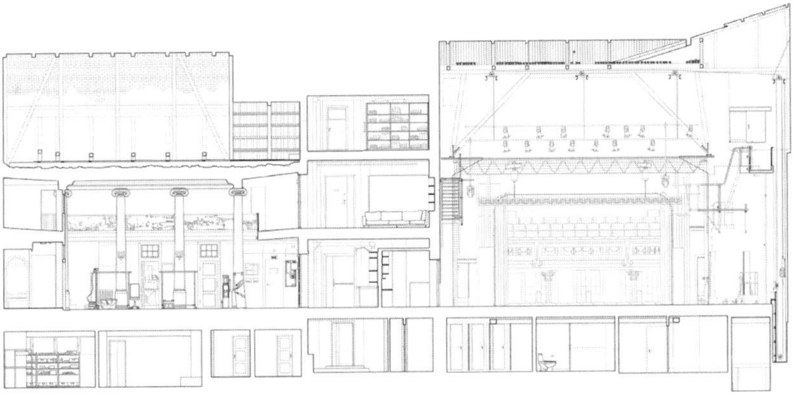

Figure 3. Section of Centralteatret; *from left to right*: Søylehallen, secondary rooms, and main stage. The drawing is part of a survey produced collectively by students from the *Centralteatret* studio, AHO, 2022.

Figure 4. Artifact model showing interconnected fragments of Centralteatret by Siebe Jansegers and Emilia Lindgren. Produced as part of the *Centralteatret* studio, AHO, 2022.

in the book *Anachronic Renaissance,* when discussing works of art that linger outside easily chronological placements. Alexander Nagel and Christopher Wood's definition of *anachronic* in art and architecture offers a way of understanding, communicating, and even celebrating a nonlinear reading of history that is necessary to appreciate multilayered situations like the one found at Centralteateret:

> To many that double postponement came to seem troublesome, calling for correction, compensation, or, at the very least, explanation. The work of art when it is late, when it repeats, when it hesitates, when it remembers, but also

when it projects a future or an ideal, is "anachronic." We introduce this term as an alternative to "anachronistic," a judgmental term that carries with it the historicist assumption that every event and every object has its proper location within objective and linear time. From a historicist point of view, an artifact that has been unmoored from its secure anchorage in linear time and has drifted into an alien historical context is an "anachronism."[8]

Centralteateret is a survivor of societal changes—a robust hybrid that offers insight into the changing field of architecture, as the reuse of existing structures becomes a central part of the discipline. Its current condition is not the result of a dispute between "modernism" and "classism" but emerges from a choir of authors who have shaped the building into an anachronic hybrid over centuries. Its modernist mask must be understood as part of a long tradition of cuts in architectural time that have, for good and bad, changed the trajectory of buildings through appropriations and misappropriations. Perhaps it is better to embrace this beautiful mess rather than clean it up and flatten its history?

Weaving a Red Thread

An appreciation of this complexity and a desire to embed it into contemporary practice has been central to our work since we founded Kastler Skjeseth Architects in 2015. Our work has predominantly focused on the transformation of existing buildings and places through surgical interventions in the building fabric of protected pieces of heritage. Many of the formal strategies employed in our extensions and transformations of historic houses stemmed from close encounters with vernacular buildings, drawing from their morphology and subsequent public perception. Questions of how to translate the accidental into the devised reappear throughout our portfolio.

This interest was not formed in a vacuum but emerged over the last decade alongside a zeitgeist in architectural practices of a similar mindset and generation around Europe. In 2023, *Rotterdam Ripresa,* which, in the words of the editor Marius Grootveld, "adopted an alternative method" of imagining cities of the future.[9] Through twelve collaged images, adapted iteratively by several groups of relatively young European practices, the publication challenged the neoliberal ways in which cities often develop. The collages produced offer visions of "fragmentary interventions" that suggest a form of urbanism created by "diluted rather than distilled" authorship.[10] Grootveld defines this movement as *the weaving generation*—a group of practices that find "existing common threads and weave them together'" rather than creating something original in isolation, highlighting an approach to design that "lies in enriching the existing fabric; building upon anecdotes from history, incident, and context."[11] In Ireland, a scene of architects emerged in the midst of the financial boom of the early noughties. These offices worked primarily with domestic assignments for private clients, often involving intricate alterations to their existing homes. One of its central architects, Andrew Clancy, writes about the "plurality of critical practice" when describing the contingencies informing contemporary architecture.[12] Contingencies are the many circumstances that inform a building project, from the client's brief and personality to statutory guidelines, to the competencies of the builder, and the provenance of an existing structure.

As Jeremy Till rightly points out, from the first sketch to the handover to the contractor, to the client's move-in and the building's subsequent use, "architecture is never alone."[13] Even an initial drawing, he argues, is "conditioned by previous experience and present expectations."[14] In practice, when altering an existing situation, the contingencies of the past, present, and future inevitably come into play. To understand how provenance informs architecture, we must examine the conditions that underlie its making. This means going beyond surface readings to trace a *red thread*—a continuous line of meaning that ties new interventions to their inherited context.

Hearth Surgery

Our practice began with the transformation of Norwegian vernacular buildings and a recurring strategy in these early projects was our use of the vernacular hearth. As in many cold climates, the fireplace had been a driving force in the development of the domestic plan in Norway since the medieval period. The technology of the hearth, the cast-iron woodstove, and the invention of the chimney all acted as catalysts to the evolution of the plan. This central element served many purposes: It provided structural support and heat, as well as areas to cook, gather, store, and sleep. Today, as Sébastien Marot points out, these tasks have been divided among various household devices, making what once was a necessary object into "a nostalgic luxury, redundant but cherished."[15] Considering its loss of function, Marot suggests that the fireplace might be the first architectural element to become extinct. However, in reuse projects where an obsolete hearth is already in place, it is precisely its provenance, combined with its redundancy, that makes it a potent catalyst for transformation. The hearth might be a linchpin between the past and the future of a building.

In our office, references to vernacular hearths gather alongside multifunctional hearths designed by modernist architects. The Swedish architect Gunnar Asplund used the

Figure 5. Three Hearths by Kastler Skjeseth Architects, 2017–23. *From left to right*: Renovation of a nineteenth-century agricultural building, renovation of a nineteenth-century manor house, renovation of an eighteenth-century storehouse. Photo, *left and right*: Erlend Skjeseth. Photo, *middle*: Ole Brodersen.

hearth in his summer house in Stennäs from 1937 to negotiate a kink in the plan and change of height in the interior. As in the vernacular house, Asplund's oversized rounded hearth, "large enough to sit within," serves as both a heat source and a step, mediating internal changes in level and orientation to better situate the house within its surrounding landscape.[16] Irish designer Eileen Gray, who was accustomed to the compact living quarters of luxury trains and boats, designed a series of bespoke multifunctional furniture pieces for the house E-1027, completed in 1929.[17] She later designed one of these as a fireplace inside her own house at Tempe à Pailla, above Menton in southeastern France. The modest black square hearth, built in 1934, forms part of an intricate constellation of "paired functions," connecting column, chimney, windowsill, mantel, guardrail, bench, stair, and storage into a single spatial composition.[18] The interior of Robert Venturi's 1962 Vanna Venturi House in Chestnut Hill, Philadelphia, is also centered around a central core, but this house presents an unusual twist. The fireplace is compacted next to a stair, and both vertical elements contort to accommodate the other. Venturi often experimented with scale in domestic interiors, making certain elements "too big," such as the oversized fireplace and the height of the mantel compared to the size of the room.[19]

Our early projects often exploited the energy of the hearth as a spatial and symbolic element. Necessary repairs to inimitable features became an opportunity not only to reproduce what once existed but also to translate it into something new. Added elements would be grandfathered in—compact and technical plug-ins could incorporate functions such as rainwater drainage, structural support, thermal windows, bathrooms, stairs, and fireplaces.[20] These buildings combine different elements, types, and systems to create a new, integrated whole. Similar to Centralteatret with its transplanted facade, they are no longer straightforwardly classifiable, neither vernacular nor high architecture. Charles Holland explains this tension succinctly: "As soon as we go near the vernacular, we kill it.

But in so doing, we make something else."[21] Remodeling the hearth creates "something else" out of the building it is situated in—surgical cuts merge the new with the existing, forming anachronic hybrids that maintain continuity with the past while enabling contemporary use, ultimately creating new value from within the original fabric of the building.

Columns, Plinths, and Drip-Boards

In the last few years, the office of Kastler Skjeseth has grappled with how to evolve our approaches.[22] An ensemble of renovated and newly built structures on the south coast of Norway completed in the summer of 2025 shows how provenance might act as a catalyst for architectural design at a larger scale. Situated on the southern Norwegian coastline that faces the westerly shores of Denmark, this complex of buildings grew out of a set of briefs in which the restoration and extension of an institutional building erected in 1925 is central.

The existing building is exemplary of late Nordic classicism with a sober expression and strict symmetry in its facade. Although its features are more civic than domestic in scale, the building borrows many traits from the *Sørlandshus,* a vernacular timber house type that still dominates the villages along Norway's southern coast. The structure was originally built to house retired sailors from a region historically associated to Norway's commercial fleet, a fleet that was the third largest in the world at the outset of World War II. The south coast was for centuries the main sea faring region of Norway, whether through timber export, herring booms, or whaling, with close ties to continental Europe. This region had its golden era channeling Norwegian timber to the continent in the nineteenth century but as the emphasis changed, from agriculture, industry, and forestry to heritage management and leisure, so too did the requirements of this building.

Several defining characteristics of the Sørlandshus have served as springboards for the design of our new additions. First, the capacity to absorb and translate international influences into a local building culture—by appropriating, or perhaps misappropriating, elements of continental stone architecture and reinterpreting them in timber, a more readily available material. Second, their tectonic composition: timber structures made from overlapping wooden elements that serve technical, aesthetic, and symbolic functions. Third, the all-encompassing white paint applied to the exterior cladding—or at least, this is how it was perceived in the nineteenth century. This "pristine" white surface was once an exclusive feature reserved for the wealthiest but later became an industrial product and has remained a constant presence along the coastline ever since.[23]

The south-facing extension to the existing building previously housing the retirement home is centered on the front facade, with two additional extensions, serving as fire escapes, located at each gable end. Taking cues from the existing pared-back classicism, the additions both recreate and distort some of the formal effects of overlapping timber elements. As a formal "binding agent," a concave motif recurs across several new architectural elements, including columns, paneling, railings, and corner boxes. The provenance of the fluted white column, its concave form originally a timber element translated into stone, is referenced to integrate new infrastructure into the building.

The use of overlapping sections of timber to create corner boxes is an important building technique in Norwegian traditional architecture, designed to hide the notched log nodes and protect their end grain. Corner boxes often appear as pilasters on the facade, sometimes topped with a small plinth and capitol. In our extension, which is built from studwork, the corner box has lost some of its original purpose. Instead, it has been scaled up to serve a new contemporary function, as a vertical shaft housing storage, gutters, and other technical infrastructure. Clad in concave seven-inch timber panels, the fluting continues the corner boxes' long-standing aspiration to be perceived as a column.

The south-facing extension sits adjacent to two white concrete fire escapes required for the building to meet contemporary fire codes. From a distance, all three extensions appear as fluted and paneled white surfaces, echoing the traditional timber architecture's details. Only upon closer inspection does the concrete, chosen for its fire resistance, reveal itself. The holes from the formwork fixing provide the first hint that all is not as it initially seems. The monolithic plasticity of the white concrete, composed of crushed marble, resonates with the thick layer of white paint that binds the timber elements of the main house. This material translation sets up an interplay between tectonic earnestness and ornamental relief, continuing the *principles* that shaped the local vernacular.

The Provenance of Spatial Arrangement and Expression.

The compulsion of the local vernacular to merge continental ideas with local materiality formed the backdrop to the formation of a new pavilion adjacent to the former retirement home. The pavilion, best classified as a type of bathhouse, is subservient in silhouette to the protected main building. In the early twentieth century, public bathhouses in Scandinavia were erected as part of a government drive to improve public health after the rapid urbanization during the Industrial Revolution. The expression of this typology was often civic in appearance, frequently in

Figure 6 (*above*). The former retirement home with three contemporary additions: central extension, white concrete fire escape, and the colonnade of the pavilion. Photo: Max Creasy, 2025.

Figure 7 (*right*). White concrete fire escape. Photo: Max Creasy, 2025.

Figure 8. The back facade of the pavilion extending from the former retirement home. Photo: Max Creasy, 2025.

the form of a pared-back classicism. The pool house as a type was itself often a hybrid, somewhere between domestic and public in character. While most of these public pools and their adjacent buildings along the Norwegian coast have been lost, many are retained and active in Sweden, and these examples formed a precedent for the expression of this building.[24]

The new bathhouse pavilion in question features two quite distinct and contrasting facades, forming a clear front and back of house. The adjacent former retirement home from 1925 has one foot in the neoclassical and the other in modernism, and the pavilion continues this duality, creating a Janus-like face. The south-facing front facade is dominated by six oversized columns that form a distinct symmetrical colonnade while the back facade draws from the latter part of the interwar period, translating the "*byggmesterfunkis*" of the time, and channeling facade compositions employed by architects such as Joseph Frank and Thilo Schoder, the latter a German architect who emigrated to Norway in 1932 and worked primarily on the Norwegian south coast, blending continental impulses with the local building culture.[25]

The plan of the pavilion is organized into two distinct zones that correspond with its external expression. This subdivision between formal, square spaces at the front and more compact service areas at the back is a spatial arrangement that can be observed in the development of the Norwegian domestic plan. Over time, these houses established a clear demarcation between representational square rooms and secondary service spaces. This division can be traced back to Georgian architecture in Great Britain during the mid-nineteenth century. Reaching further back in time, the ideals of Palladian architecture informed the local vernacular on the south coast of Norway through the formation of "Den Mandalske Stueform" according to the pioneering Norwegian sociologist Eilert Sundt.[26] In the present project, these spatial sequences were adapted to fit the project brief, with compressed secondary spaces supporting more formal, unprogrammed rooms.

The architect Ryan Kennihan writes about the need to situate architecture inside a specific building culture, locating it "within a web of interconnected and coinciding patterns of past and present."[27] Traditional timber buildings along the southern coast of Norway could be described as porous amalgamations of fleeting external impulses realized in local materials. The pavilion attempts to create a resonance with these characteristics, defined by mimicry and assimilation—by translation and *inflections*. An inflection, as described by Robert Venturi, is when architectural elements, by orienting themselves toward external references, establish their own internal coherence. Inflected parts, he suggests, are more integrated with the whole precisely because they distinguish themselves while implying continuity. This "art of the fragment" allows individual parts to suggest meanings and relationships that extend beyond their immediate form.[28] In the case of the pavilion, the aim was to continue to filter and translate these principles, allowing for the provenance of the local building culture to become an active driver in the formation of its expression, tectonics, and spatial sequencing.

Don't Look Back in Anger

An archaeologist once told us that he had employed an architecture student to survey and draw up a complex and irregular excavation of a medieval wall fragment but found to his horror that the student made all the lines on the page perfectly perpendicular and straight—in essence drawing an idealized and abstract assumption of what was there but not the thing itself. Over the last decade, through practice and teaching, we have been exploring how to look at something in detail, and draw out particularities through architectural means, cultivating them as part of a design practice—surveys and drawings that capture a building past and present condition and models that imagine and design its future potential.[29] Borrowing from the fields of art history and archaeology, provenance offers a potential lens through which to understand buildings not as static artifacts but as layered entities shaped by time, memory, distortion, and reinterpretation.

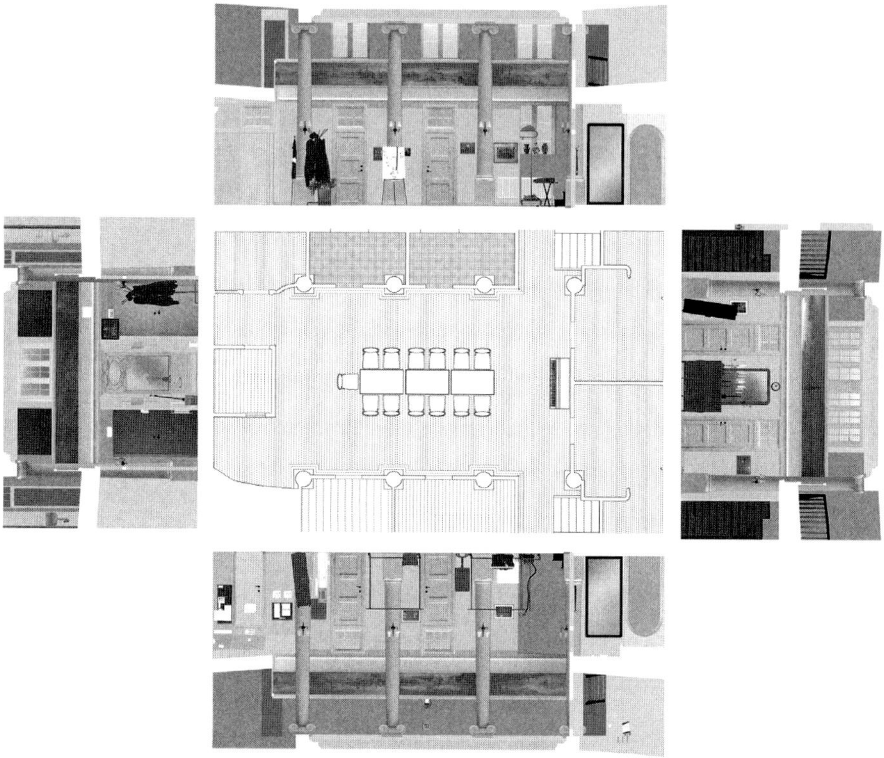

Figure 9. Unfolded elevation of Søylehallen by Åsne Storli and Charlotte Mellbye. Produced as part of the *Centralteatret* studio, AHO, 2022.

When working with these complexities, the *undesigned* offers hints at a way forward: vernacular forms, accidental moments, and hybrid architecture that resist purity or perfection. These fragments, when handled with care, can form the foundation of a "difficult whole," as Venturi suggested—a composition that avoids pastiche by remaining deeply connected to its past while also looking toward the future.[30] This is an architecture that embraces ambiguity and contradiction, accommodating the disorder of reality rather than forcing it into a sanitized vision. However, the production of architecture is contingent on so many checks, balances, and outside influences that we have frequently asked ourselves if this compulsion to appropriate the casual and undesigned is even possible in built work. Simultaneously, the pitfalls of this approach are many and obvious, risking romanticism and sheer formal conservatism or becoming subject to the shortcomings of late postmodernism with its acerbic aftertastes.

The expanses of capital-driven developments that have mushroomed across most European cities have fed a populist disdain for much of the architectural production of the last century. Yet as the existing built environment continues to be reshaped amid these reactionary currents, the potential lies not in a return to classicism or a rejection of modernism—as was suggested by the antagonist in the story of Centralteatret—but rather in seeking an alternative path: one that honors provenance in architecture as a living, evolving force, with the capacity to frame radical transformation. It is worth returning to the words of Nagel and Wood, who describe art and architecture as "the possibility of a conversation across time, a conversation more meaningful than the present's merely forensic reconstruction of the past."[31]

As we learned from the reaction to the cuts in time that define Centralteateret, fragments requiring multiple readings are too often unappreciated as a growing proclivity for the binary takes hold. The ambiguous characters in our built environment might prove uncomfortable for those with an urge to "clean up" and seek to rationalize the world into chronological constraints and essentialist narratives. In such cases, the responsibility to communicate the value and inherent potential of an architecture that resists easy classification falls to those who can appreciate its mercurial qualities. As the future is shaping up to be made of fragments of the past tied together by the technology of tomorrow, we as a profession should be hopeful that the inherent skillsets of architects to synthesize elements and trades into a coherent whole will find a renewed cultural relevance.

Biographies

Amandine Kastler studied at the Architectural Association in London, graduating with Honours in 2010. She is a founding partner of Kastler Skjeseth Architects, with previous experience from OMA/AMO in Rotterdam and at David Chipperfield Architects in London. Kastler is an associate professor in the Architecture Institute at the Oslo School of Architecture and Design (AHO), where she co-leads the Transformation in Practice course series. She has also taught at the Oslo National Academy of the Arts (KHiO) and the AA in London, where she previously co-led a design unit and now co-directs the MA/PG Diploma in Conservation and Reuse.

Erlend Skjeseth is the managing director of Kastler Skjeseth Architects. He graduated from the Architectural Association in London in 2010 after studying art history at the University of Oslo. He has led numerous transformation projects as project architect and coordinator, with previous experience at David Chipperfield Architects, AOC in London, and Jarmund Vigsnæs in Oslo. Skjeseth is an assistant professor of transformation at the Oslo School of Architecture and Design and has taught at Oslo National Academy of the Arts (KHIO) and the AA in London. He is a deputy member of Oslo's Council for City Architecture.

Notes

1 https://www.instagram.com/p/CRlrGiJgHI8/.

2 Marvin Trachtenberg, *Building in Time: From Giotto to Alberti and Modern Oblivion* (Yale University Press, 2010), XIV, 67.

3 James S. Ackerman, *Palladio* (Penguin Books, 1966), 85. Casa Cogollo is widely attributed to Andrea Palladio. However, the attribution is contested. Ackerman highlights this in his book and notes that in his opinion it is not by Palladio.

4 See Mari Lending, "Photography," in *Provenance in Architecture. A Dictionary of Terms*, ed. Uwe Fleckner and Mari Lending (Hatje Cantz, 2025), 142–143.

5 *Transformation in Practice: Centralteateret* ran in the autumn semester of 2022 for master students of Architecture at the Oslo School of Architecture and Design (AHO) and was taught by Benjamin Sjøberg, Alena Rieger, and Erlend Skjeseth. The studio's output was a series of interventions, provocations, and extensions that balanced the need to preserve the existing condition with the building's potential for future use. The studio was aided by a seminar taught by Mari Lending and

Thomas McQuillan that performed a deep dive into the archives of this misunderstood building and provided much of the research on its history.

[6] *Transformation in Practice: Centralteateret* students: Pernille Marie Boye Ahlgren, Timofey Aleksandrov, Alexandra Kyttari Djupesland Andrea Cristina Herraiz, Siebe Jansegers, Apollo Karmatskiy, Anatole Lefevre, Jiahong Lin, Emilia Lindgren, Frida Matschullat, Charlotte Elisabeth Mellbye, Rita Oliveira Bastos Serra, Rakel Emilie Emhjellen Paulsen, Ysabela Louise Ariem Ramirez, Åsne Storli, Mirte Wambacq, Hanna Elise Jozefiak.

[7] Lending, "Photography," 142.

[8] Alexander Nagel and Christopher Wood, *Anachronic Renaissance* (Zone Books, 2010), 13.

[9] Marius Grootveld, "Future Fragments of the Neoliberal City," in *Rotterdam Ripresa: Future Fragments for the Neoliberal City*, ed. Marius Grootveld (Architectura & Natura and Lemon Press, 2023), 7–8.

[10] Grootveld, *Rotterdam Ripresa*, 7–8.

[11] "A weaving generation" was shown at DAM Frankfurt in 2016 and XX MUHKA in 2017: https://veldwerk.cargo.site/A-Weaving-Generation. While *A Weaving Generation* was specifically aimed at a selection of emerging practices in Flanders and the Netherlands, *Rotterdam Ripresa* broadened the reach of the moniker to a selection of practices across Europe.

[12] Andrew Clancy, "Critical Practice: Can Architecture Be Critical?" *Architectural Review* (July/August 2020): 27.

[13] Jeremy Till, *Architecture Depends* (MIT Press, 2009), 45–46.

[14] Till, *Architecture Depends*, 46.

[15] Sébastien Marot, "Fireplaces," in Rem Koolhaas, *Elements of Architecture* (Taschen, 2018), 3.

[16] Malcolm Woollen, *Erik Gunnar Asplund: Landscapes and Buildings* (Routledge/Taylor & Francis Group, 2018), 155.

[17] Caroline Constant, *Eileen Gray* (Phaidon Press, 2000), 95–107.

[18] Constant, *Eileen Gray*, 152–53.

[19] Robert Venturi, *Complexity and Contradiction in Architecture* (The Museum of Modern Art, 1966), 118–19.

[20] See Amandine Kastler, "Renovation," in *Provenance in Architecture*, 167–169.

[21] Charles Holland, "Outrage: The Vernacular Can Lead to a Toxic, Reactionary Culture," *The Architectural Review*, no. 1466 (November 2019): 106–7.

[22] Kastler Skjeseth Architects was founded in 2015 by Amandine Kastler and Erlend Skjeseth. The small team of architects working on the projects referred to in this text include Benjamin Sjøberg and Louis Gervais.

[23] See Erlend Skjeseth, "Pristine," in *Provenance in Architecture*, 152–154.

[24] See Helena Lind, *Kallbadhus* (Byggförlaget, 2004).

[25] Frank Falch and Nina Stokset Nilsen, eds., *Thilo Schoder. Tysk arkitekt i Norge 1932–1979* (Sørlandets Kunstmuseum, 2002).

[26] Ulf Hamran, *I Sørlandshuset: Hus, interiør og inventar 1650–1920* (Huitfeldt Forlag, 1985).

[27] Ryan Kennihan, "Architecture and Resonance: A 501 Word Case for Communicative Architecture," in *Resilience and Joy*, ed. Amelia Brandão Costa and Rodrigo da Costa Lima (Indexnewspaper, 2020), 211.

[28] Venturi, *Complexity and Contradiction*, 88–90.

[29] *Transformation in Practice (TIP)* is a master's-level studio and seminar course at the Oslo School of Architecture and Design. Established in 2017, it is led by Amandine Kastler and Erlend Skjeseth and forms part of the *Provenance Projected* research project, directed by Mari Lending. See: https://provenanceprojected.no/teaching/transformation-in-practice.

[30] Venturi, *Complexity and Contradiction*, 88–105.

[31] Nagel and Wood, *Anachronic Renaissance*, 18.

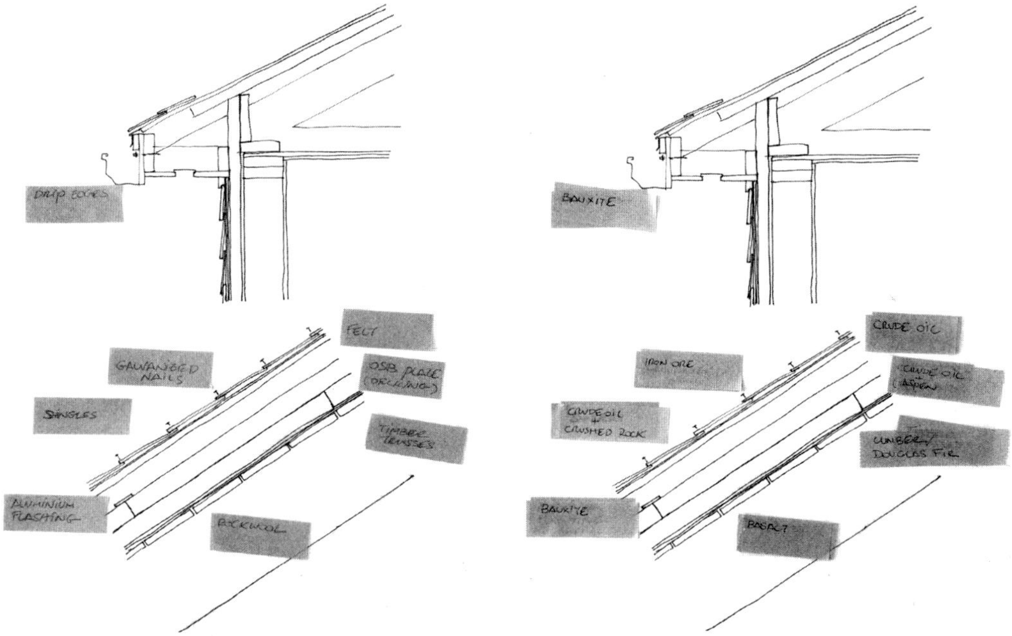

Figure 1. Charlotte Malterre-Barthes, *Evidence of Extraction*, 2025. Courtesy of Charlotte Malterre-Barthes.

Charlotte Malterre-Barthes

Details as Evidence
Architectural Extractivism and the Politics of Provenance

> We see the details of form as innocuous and seldom give them a second thought.
>
> —Langdon Winner, "Do Artifacts Have Politics?" (1980)

Visiting the Musée du Quai Branly (Jean Nouvel, 2005) in Paris, designed to host largely art and artifacts from former French colonies, the friend I was perusing the rooms with concluded that the building was decent but that the details were *degeulasses* (gross).[1] My architect friend meant that the finishing of the building's small-scale arrangements was poorly executed. It was not the architecture's function and use, nor what its details were made of, that was at fault, but how these materials were assembled. When I visited the Walt Disney Hall in Los Angeles (Frank Gehry, 2003) to research its maintenance protocols and see how it had aged, another architect friend recommended me to "check the impressive detail of how the slates are hung."[2] Architects often look to details as a sign of building quality. Details are obsessed over, whether one marvels at how a colleague solved a corner or how a detail was poorly executed.

What remains conspicuously absent from these conversations is the material provenance of the building details: the conditions of their extraction, installation, maintenance, and the norms and legal frameworks that define them. Instead, our focus is often on their aesthetic render or technical capability, in accordance with their structural purposes, sealing properties, or economic efficiency, and perhaps on how skilled those who designed and assembled these elements were. Take the architecture magazine *Detail*. It has a large following, a run of thirty-five thousand copies per issue, and devotes its content to "building details in architecture . . . documented with beautiful photographs and comparable drawings at a scale of 1:20."[3] Understanding how one has reached a visually pleasing solution is a technical accomplishment associated with design and constructive craft. It speaks to a culture of approval in architecture that values the technical resolution of a detail over the social or ecological lives of the materials used to accomplish it.

In his 1980 essay "Do Artifacts Have Politics?" Langdon Winner identified how neutral components bear political meaning and embody the "material conditions under which we produce and make products circulate."[4] While architectural

Future Anterior
Volume XXII, Numbers 1–2
Summer / Winter 2025

details are not his explicit focus, Winner's critique holds true to them. He provides a framework for arguing that seemingly innocent components of our built environment can encode systemic violence and exploitation. Even though architectural details are now often standardized components or industrial ready-mades, the prestige of the beautiful detail remains. But there is a paradox in fetishizing details as markers of architectural mastery, with little regard for *how* they are made or what they demand materially. What if our fascination with details shifted from their aesthetic appeal to the material conditions of their production?

This essay argues that architectural details function as records of the extractive processes underpinning architecture.[5] Every joint, connection, and assembly embodies and visualizes resource extraction, processing protocols, labor conditions, and socioecological impacts. By critically examining details, I build upon the concept of "architectural extractivism" as a framework for understanding how the exploitation of materials, labor, and cultures shapes our built environment.[6] Using architectural extractivism as a lens for understanding these relationships means positioning all types of extraction as foundational aspects of construction. While extractivism as a concept originated in 1990s South American scholarship about the mining industry and its devastating impacts, its application to architecture represents an emerging and largely uncharted terrain of research—one that has become urgent given accelerating climate change and mounting concerns about its social and material impacts. By attending to details as evidence, we can develop new modes of critical practice that reconsider the connections between minute technical decisions and large-scale environmental and social impact. This is a call for the discipline to pay attention to its reliance on and compliance with destructive industries and then to move toward post-extractive protocols and systems for life that are regenerative rather than extractive, as called for by voices from various realms such as Arturo Escobar, Paula Serafini, or Alton Kreinak.[7] The architectural detail represents a scale of accountability between the material fact of extraction and the larger political economy.

Anatomy of a Standard Roof Detail: Evidence of Extraction

One could begin with the exceptional detailing of architectural masterpieces since these occupy much of the disciplinary spotlight. Yet politicizing architectural details and tracing their material provenance requires a reorientation—one that begins with a standard detail, since the replicated assemblies of ordinary detailing constitute much of the built environment at scale. What is at stake is not just the celebration of prestigious details but a deeper understanding of the ordinary ones. The banal roof assemblage in a suburban, North American home is replicated across millions of buildings, making its environmental and social footprint exponentially more significant than the minutiae of architectural icons.

A wooden truss or rafter framework provides structural support for the roof. They are commonly made from dimensional lumber sourced from regions such as Pacific Northwest forests. These beams exist thanks to enduring and ongoing deforestation practices including the clear-cutting of old-growth forests, the displacement of Indigenous communities, and the disruption of complex ecosystems. Further investigation into material histories like those documented in James Farmer's story of Californian logging, reveals that architectural details embody the matter, territories, and entire legal frameworks that enable their existence.[8] As argued by Jane Bennet, these wooden beams are active characters in material stories, with their own geological and biological agency.[9] These beams are not simply technical objects that support suburban living; they are living archives of forest ecologies, weather patterns, soil conditions, and tree species that have sometimes grown over centuries before being harvested, transformed, and installed. This material vitality continues even after the tree is transformed into lumber—expanding, contracting, and responding to humidity and temperature changes with cracks and changes in color that transgress the permanence of the drawn detail.

When the material provenance of a beam is traced, it evidences a broader and more complex host of relations, mechanisms, and infrastructures of power. The beam can be directly traced to forest harvesting facilitating mechanisms following a chronological chain of events, starting from the dispossession of Indigenous territories through genocidal violence and colonial land tenure systems. The compendium of federal laws and regulations that govern forest practices on federal lands in the United States, such as the National Forest Management Act, includes state environmental regulations that determine which forests may or may not be exploited and where wood can be harvested, facilitating timber extraction. Thus, the beam can be seen as condensing centuries of industrial legislation that has prioritized extraction over preservation. Critical examination of nearly any architectural element will similarly expose the legal frameworks that made extraction permissible.

Decking, typically plywood or Oriented Strand Board (OSB), is laid over this framework. OSB is made by bonding together wood strands (i.e., aspen, poplar) with a waterproof, formaldehyde-based adhesive (such as synthetic resin) and pyrethroid termiticides into the wood under the application of heat and pressure.[10] The OSB industry has cultivated a virtuous image, portraying the misleading narrative of an efficient product that utilizes forestry waste. However, logging residues today have been reduced to less than 10 percent, which means regular logging occurs to feed the demand of OSB.[11]

A petroleum-based, asphalt-saturated felt underlay—commonly produced by companies such as Tarco, Mid-States Asphalt, GMC, Fontana Paper Mills—is then applied to the OSB as a moisture barrier. The felt connects directly to asphalt manufacturing industry, including producers like Owens Corning's Trumbull™ division, which sources materials from major oil companies such as ExxonMobil. In turn, these oil companies rely on extensive networks of crude oil extraction: from offshore drilling platforms like the Baldpate oil rig in the Gulf of Mexico to fracking operations in towns such as Penn, Pennsylvania, where XTO Energy (an ExxonMobil subsidiary) remains active. The contaminating effects of such sites is well documented, yet the enrollment of new extraction projects is still happening—despite resistance by local communities.[12]

Shingles, the visible component on the top of the roof, are made from a fiberglass mat, coated with asphalt and ceramic granules. They are installed in overlapping rows, from the bottom edge of the roof to its top, to ensure water runoff. Asphalt is connected to broader geopolitics of oil extraction: from destabilized Middle East countries to Alberta's tar sands, where Indigenous land rights are routinely violated.[13] The ceramic granules contain crushed rock colored with mineral oxides mined through extensive pit operations that permanently alter landscapes and deplete aquifers.[14]

Galvanized nails fix the shingles to the structure. In North America, most nails are manufactured in one of the petrochemical plants in the so-called "Cancer Alley," a 137-kilometer-long corridor along the Mississippi River. The manufacturing corridor continues a long history of exploitation and extraction along the river. Before the chemical plants, this land was occupied by plantations worked by enslaved people. These sites later became home to disenfranchised African American communities directly suffering from the pollution caused by these industries. This connection between building materials and environmental racism is documented in the work of Kathryn Yusoff and Imani Jacqueline Brown, who trace how extractive landscapes disproportionately burden communities of color with toxic legacies of industrial production.[15]

Flashing of aluminum or galvanized steel is used to seal joints and penetrations, such as chimneys and vents, to prevent leaks and ingressions. Flashing embodies the energy-intensive processes of metal mining, smelting, and manufacturing. Aluminum production alone ranks among the most power-hungry industrial processes, often powered by coal plants or hydroelectric dams that have flooded Indigenous territories.[16]

The roof is finished with ridge cap shingles. Drip edges of metal strips run along the eaves to guide water away from the fascia. Fascia boards and soffits made of wood, aluminum, or vinyl complete the edges, providing ventilation and protection against the elements. These too are made through resource extraction, chemical processing, and global shipping networks, all before the first raindrop has fallen on the finished roof.

The assemblage of this roof detail relies on labor arranged in hierarchies of value, risk, and reward. Roofing labor operates through a stratified system in which contractors and supervisors manage projects, skilled roofers handle specialized tasks, and often legally undocumented workers under precarious labor conditions perform the most dangerous jobs with minimal protection. Assembling a detail on a roof requires operating at heights—a work with disproportionate casualties.[17] The physical toll includes fall risks, exposure to extreme temperatures, repetitive motion injuries, toxic material inhalation, and long-term health impacts rarely documented or compensated.[18] This extraction of value from workers' bodies remains as invisible in architectural detailing as the ecological devastation embedded in the materials themselves.

Rather than treating the materials in an ordinary roof detail as incidental or neutral, this quick investigation centers its material origins. The mundanity of the mass-produced detail often belies the global networks of exploitation it represents. The careful execution of this detail to ensure durability, weather resistance, and aesthetic appeal simultaneously obscures its material pedigrees, labor extraction, and the harm embedded in each component. This scale is typically only discussed in the event of a failure, but in centering material origins, the detail becomes an artifact of the extraction and destruction that lays in its wake.

Vanishing Act

Has the architectural profession developed a value system that relies on the aesthetics of concealing? A seamless joint, a flush transition, a concealed fixing mechanism—these are some hallmarks of architectural sophistication. The disappearance of the detail is what Edward Ford might categorize as "abstract" detailing.[19] The mark of a "good" detail is where material connections are purposely subordinated. A detail that calls attention to itself through its visibility is often deemed less successful than one that disappears into the overall composition: *degeulasse.* Ford's examination of the detail in his respected 2011 book *The Architectural Detail* remains distant from the profound questions of the political economy of the detail—namely its material origins, production, and value generation. The book, according to Mark Burry, values formal abstraction over material reality.[20] Burry calls for us to examine the detail through its production and construction, arguing that "to detail effectively is to understand not only what the building 'is,' but how it will be made."[21] This critique begins to draw a connection between aesthetics and production, though it still stops short of confronting the extractive nature of architectural detailing.

Let us nevertheless return briefly to iconic details with Mies Van der Rohe's onyx wall in his Barcelona Pavilion (1929)—the stuff of architects' wet dreams. A smooth surface with symmetrically arranged patterns, described by Robin Evans as "most exotic, improbable and expensive."[22] According to Mies, the choice of the onyx was inspired by a visit to a marble show room in Hamburg: "I found an onyx block of a certain size and since I only had the possibility of this block, I made the pavilion twice that height and then we developed the plan."[23] If one takes this post-rationalized explanation at face value, then it is not the raw stone that is central to the architecture, but an already processed object with defined dimensions and conditions.

Evans's critique of Mies's onyx wall reinforces rather than challenges the distance between architectural discourse and the extraction processes on which they depend. While he offers an admirative litany of the wall's effects, describing how "panels of blue, yellow and red on a white ground would turn into panels of dark green verd-antique marble; filigreed grey-green Tinian marble; and grotesquely varicose orange onyx doré, on a ground of creamy, pock-marked travertine," his attention remains fixed on the object's visual properties and makes no mention of its provenance—that the onyx stone was mined in the Atlas Mountains of what was then the French colony of Morocco, not to mention the labor force mobilized to cut, transport, and secure it into place.[24] By focusing on the wall's formal "paradoxical symmetries" and aesthetic qualities, Evans perpetuates the very erasure he seems positioned to critique. His analysis reproduces the problem of architectural discourse's distancing from the violent realities of material production.

The extractive reality of the material was not of interest to Mies, nor to those admiring the building afterward—including Evans himself. This scholarly omission reveals how even critical architectural discourse fails to account for the colonial context and exploitative labor that enabled such "exotic" materials to appear in European modernist projects. Evans's critique stops short of examining how the wall's very "improbability" stems from networks of imperial extraction that made Moroccan stone available for a German architect's temporary pavilion in Barcelona. Those who visit or read about Mies's onyx wall rarely understand this violence, materialized by the stone's origin.

Well-designed details often conceal their extractive geneses. The concealment represents what Peggy Deamer identifies as architecture's refusal to acknowledge its position within networks of production and labor. In "Details: The Subject of the Object," Deamer argues that architectural details exist at the intersection of design intent and construction reality, where the abstract labor of design confronts the material labor of building.[25] To paraphrase Jennifer Bloomer, the details reveal architecture as an archive of material and labor.[26] An argument can be made that patterns of concealment emerge across architectural history. Modernist architecture is revealing: Its rejection of ornament in favor of the "honest" expression of materials ironically obscures the extraction processes necessary to produce these. This perpetuated the illusion of architectural autonomy—our view of the building as a self-contained object rather than a node, or even a propeller, within global networks of resource extraction and labor exploitation. By presenting materials as abstract and smooth, modernist detailing participated in the broader cultural project of separating consumption from production, and matter from its sources.

In *Detailing Worlds* (2021), architecture historian Eric Bellin breaks down the disciplinary concept of the detail into its various aspects of construction. In his attempt to write the history of detail, Bellin comes closer to addressing the political economy of architectural production. Still, he stops short of a full examination of the extractive nature of detailing.[27] Perhaps simply exposing the hidden detail is a first step in uncovering the networks of extraction and production that make every building possible. When Andrés Jaque exhibited the contents of the Barcelona Pavilion's basement in the installation "Phantom: Mies as Rendered Society," he revealed the maintenance infrastructure usually kept out of sight and the social relations that maintain the building's pristine appearance.[28] The cleaning supplies, replacement marble tiles, and maintenance tools exposed the ongoing labor required to sustain the building's apparent timelessness—a small but significant step toward making visible what architecture often conceals.

The Leak Reveals the Failure of the Detail

In his 1983 essay "The Tell-the-Tale Detail," architect Marco Frascari is dithyrambic about how essential this scale is. He writes that "careful detailing is the most important means of avoiding building failure, on both dimensions of the architectural profession—the ethical and the aesthetic. The art of detailing is really the joining of materials, elements, components, and building parts in a functional and aesthetic manner."[29] Yet this is Frascari's only mention of ethics. Architects have long been aware of our contribution to capitalism's accumulation enterprise and the harms of building: namely, a contribution of 40 percent of global CO_2 emissions yearly, including 9 percent just for the materials used in the construction of buildings. Still, this number excludes the often unaccounted-for harms, such as the ecological and social damage produced through mining, deforestation, displacement, and gentrification. Perhaps our apathy toward the ethics of the detail is simply a reflection of the attitudes of the architecture and construction industries, more generally—namely carelessness and negligence.

Nothing is as revealing of an architectural detail than its failure. What is more embarrassing than a leak, which sometimes exposes technical inadequacy, material malfunction, or the hubris of architectural control? Architect Katherine Shonfield paved the way for this discussion in her seminal contribution "Why Does Your Flat Leak?"[30] Shonfield breaks down the Greater London Council's GLC Good Practice Details through language and medium, by showing how leaks expose the failure of critical joinery details, speaking not only about the detail but giving it a voice. Describing the job of the mastic joint, she anthropomorphizes it: "In this way, someone whose role should be incidental, merely a means of introducing two others, becomes overwhelmingly decisive. In his role as a flexible mastic joint, the host is subjected to an intolerable level of stress trying to keep two panels together. He does the constructional equivalent of retiring to the kitchen and getting drunk."[31] With this riotous feminist metaphor, Shonfield tackles what is at stake in designing joinery and construction details: control and liability.

Shonfield's argument on the impossibility of control—through real impermeability—points to the fallacy that architects can design the world down to its tiniest detail. Architectural theorist Francesca Hughes shares this perspective and in *The Architecture of Error* alerts us to the absurdity of architectural control. The architect's dream of retaining command over the construction process is simply that, yet nothing turns out as planned on a construction site.[32] Shonfield and Frascari agree that the most challenging details are joints that deal with a fundamental task of architecture: keeping moisture out of the building.

We might begin by scrutinizing iconic buildings that are also famous for their failures, from the leaks of Villa Savoye (Le Corbusier, 1929) to the Ray and Maria Stata Center (Frank Gehry, 2004) and on to standardized details and everyday solutions. These technical failures represent a collapse of our aesthetic ambitions and material realities. Water finds its way into a building through the detail, just as extraction, labor exploitation, and environmental harm can find their way into even the most aesthetically refined building. The architect's failure to keep water out parallels the discipline's failure to keep the messy realities of production out of its pristine discourse. A history of failed details would reveal its politics, addressing unacknowledged realities in the production of spaces (something akin to Howard Zinn's *A People's History of the United States* (1980), but for the architectural detail).[33] Better yet, more in-depth knowledge on the political economy of construction details might shift how we design them: Our awareness of power structures, material cultures, normative systems, and value generation, as well as flaws and successes in assembly and materials performance, should change how we source materials, connect them, and replace them.

Toward Post-extractive Details

If the task is to "politicize" details within past and present buildings, then how can accounting for the extractive aspects of a detail's materials and arrangements become part of architectural practice? In revealing how components are combined, produced, and sourced, designers can direct the production of architecture toward less damaging processes. It is urgent that the still prevailing view of architectural details as a neutral, strictly performative entity for building assembly, as described by Ford, is challenged.[34] Kenneth Frampton offers another path forward in his investigations of tectonics, arguing that architectural details can be evidence of nonalienating forms of labor and craft. His tectonic approach positions the detail as a site where material intelligence can resist the abstracting forces of capitalist production. However, like Evans's critique of Mies's onyx wall, Frampton's nostalgia for craft traditions stops short of addressing the violent extraction that underpins even the most carefully crafted detail.[35] A new approach to the architectural detail, drawing on critical perspectives from ecofeminist, queer, and other radical counterpoints, would speak for unheard voices—humans and more—behind the production of these spaces.

What would a post-extractive roof detail look like? Such a brief is not calling for a greenwashed solution but for a fundamental reconsideration of the materials we use, how they are sourced, who installs them, and how they might eventually be disassembled. This is not abstract speculation but an urgent practical challenge for contemporary architecture. But such a shift also requires new forms of documentation and representation, such as a reinvention of the technical drawing and its norms. Today, technical detail drawings show materials in abstract form: Hatched and checkered patterns denote layers of polystyrene foam, asphalt, or concrete without any required thought toward their origins or impacts. Conventional architectural drawings neutralize the chains of extraction that precede

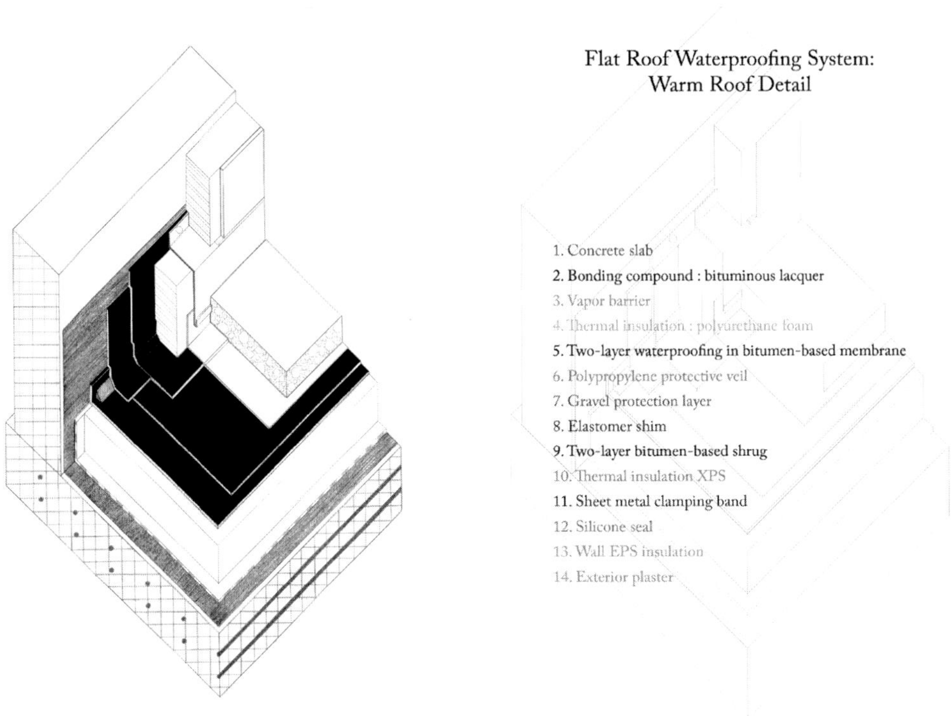

Figure 2. Lydia Genecand and Raul Hansra Sartorius, RIOT Design Studio 'Halt Extraction,' Episode 02: 'Normatted Matter,' EPFL; *Dear Modernism, It's Still Leaking* Inside, 2025. Courtesy of Genecand- Hansra Sartorius.

it. But what if architectural detailing included more than its typical descriptions of dimensions and material specifications? What if it included material provenance information, labor, and the impacts of its specified materials' extraction? What if plans for the standard roof detail included annotations about the source of its lumber, the labor conditions of its harvesting, or how much heat and carbon its insulation panels have emitted through production and transportation

An accountable detailing practice that is more dependable than current metrics (such as the Life Cycle Assessment/ LCA) could infuse technical drawings with provenance data and construction documents that would convey how each material layer carries its full extractive context: the emissions generated during manufacture, the communities displaced by resource extraction, the health impacts on installation workers, and the chemical persistence in soil and water.

As Shonfield revealed in her reading of the humble mastic joint, even the most mundane elements of construction embody relations of power and control. Her anthropomorphizing of the joint that was "subjected to an intolerable level of stress trying to keep two panels together," offers a method for giving voice to the silent aspects of architecture.[36] Similarly, our post-extractive detail might speak for the humans and more-than-humans involved in its creation and maintenance. This approach to detailing would require architects to extend our practices beyond ordinary standards of quality assessment. Instead, our methods could include the social and ecological contexts of materials and engage with questions such as: Where did this material come from? Whose land was it extracted from? Under what labor conditions? With what ecological consequences? There is a potential in rethinking the detail to bring together technical performance, aesthetic concerns, and ethical accountability in a single scale of design attention. By embedding provenance research directly into the practice of detailing, architects can transform a key site of professional knowledge into a tool for accountability.

Detail as Tools for Change

Every material in a building carries a direct extractive footprint (mining, harvesting, manufacturing) and an indirect one (digital tools for design, prospection technologies, labor systems, ecological impacts, and cultural displacement). This essay argues that the politics of provenance are most clearly revealed at the scale of the detail, where single and disparate components with complex histories assemble and converge. By reading details as evidence, we can trace these extractive relationships in both directions. Tracing backward reveals their origins in colonial land appropriation, labor exploitation, and environmental destruction. Tracing forward tracks their ongoing implications for maintenance workers, building occupants, and ecosystems. The evidence contained in the details challenges architecture's tendency to present itself as autonomous from these material realities. The most celebrated details—such as invisible joinery or perfect waterproofing solutions—achieve their apparent simplicity through a complex network of extraction and exploitation that remains conveniently out of frame. As architects, we admire the precision of a glass curtain wall meeting a stone floor with minimal visual interruption; yet we are not trained to see the global supply chains, resource depletion, and labor conditions that made such a junction possible. The aesthetic refinement of the detail distracts us from its material reality.

Failure of the detail is also an important moment of truth. When a leak exposes the hubris of control or when maintenance reveals the hidden labor that sustains architectural appearances, it tells us that architecture cannot keep its pristine discourse separate from the messy realities of its production. By attending to the detail as both a technical composition and as documentary evidence, architects can begin the work of repairing disciplinary aspirations with their material realities. This work has argued that architectural details function as material evidence that documents extractive relationships between humans, environments, and economies. It has also explored how applied, politicized processes to detailing might answer to past and present problems of construction in more accountable, post-extractive ways. To politicize architectural detailing is to question how a detail is brought into being. What materials is it assembled from? Which solutions does it answer to? And at what cost?

As a framework for critical practice, architectural extractivism provides a lens through which details can be understood as both technical achievements and political artifacts. The scale of accountability begins at the scale of the detail. It is the point where intent meets material reality, where abstract labor confronts physical labor, and where the most intimate decisions about material combinations unravel global systems of production and extraction. This recognition creates the possibility of a different kind of detail, one that does not conceal extraction but seeks to mitigate and account for it. It makes visible what architecture renders invisible: the accumulation of seemingly innocuous decisions that, when aggregated across millions of buildings, reveal the true scale of extractive violence.

Biography
Charlotte Malterre-Barthes is an architect, urban designer, and assistant professor at the Swiss Federal Institute of Technology-EPFL, where she leads the laboratory RIOT. Malterre-Barthes's interests relate to urgent aspects of contemporary urbanization, material extraction, climate emergency, and social justice. While assistant professor of Urban Design at Harvard University, she started the initiative "A Moratorium on New Construction," interrogating current development protocols (2025, Sternberg Press / MIT Press). Malterre-Barthes holds a PhD (ETH Zurich) on the political economy of commodities and the built environment and is a founding member of the Parity Group (Meret Oppenheim Prize 2023) and the Parity Front, activist networks dedicated to equality in architecture. She serves on the scientific board and is an ambassador for the initiative "House Europe," against demolitions.

Notes

[1] "Paris's Quai Branly Museum Hosts Final Show in France for Looted Benin Treasures," *France 24*, October 26, 2021, https://www.france24.com/en/africa/20211026-paris-s-quai-branly-museum-hosts-final-show-in-france-for-looted-benin-treasures (accessed June 13, 2025).

[2] Two percent of the 833 stainless steel slates had to be sanded off because of the reverberation causing heat to the neighboring buildings. Ten thousand tons of structural steel were used for the construction. See F. Gehry et al., *Symphony: Frank Gehry's Walt Disney Concert Hall* (Harry N. Abrams, 2003); Jamie Wetherbe, "Cleaners Make Walt Disney Concert Hall's Curves Sparkle," *Los Angeles Times*, September 20, 2013.

[3] "Review of Architecture and Construction Details," *Detail Magazine*, https://www.detail.de/de_en/detailshop-detail-magazin (accessed March 6, 2025).

[4] Langdon Winner, "Do Artifacts Have Politics?, *Daedalus* 109, no. 1 (Winter 1980): 121–36. Reprinted in Langdon Winner, *The Whale and the Reactor: A Search for Limits in an Age of High Technology* (University of Chicago Press, 2020), 30.

[5] I have addressed architectural details in Charlotte Malterre-Barthes, "The Devil Is in the Details- Who Is It That the World Belongs To?," in *Non-Extractive Architecture: On Designing without Depletion*, ed. Space Caviar (Sternberg Press, 2021); and Charlotte Malterre-Barthes, *A Moratorium on New Construction* (Sternberg Press, 2025).

[6] For more on architectural extractivism, see Charlotte Malterre-Barthes, "Architectural Extractivism in Times of Post-Accountability: A Restorative Approach," in *Abundance Not Capital: The Lively Architecture of Anupama Kundoo*, ed. Angelika Fitz and Elke Krasny (MIT Press, 2025).

[7] See Arturo Escobar, *Designs for the Pluriverse: Radical Interdependence, Autonomy, and the Making of Worlds* (Duke University Press, 2018); Paula Serafini, *Creating Worlds Otherwise: Art, Collective Action and (Post)Extractivism* (Vanderbilt University Press, 2022); and Ailton Krenak et al., *Life Is Not Useful* (Polity Press, 2023).

[8] Farmer, *Trees in Paradise.*
[9] See Jane Bennett, *Vibrant Matter: A Political Ecology of Things* (Duke University Press, 2010).
[10] E. Benetto et al., "Life Cycle Assessment of Oriented Strand Boards (Osb): From Process Innovation to Ecodesign," *Environmental Science & Technology* 43, no. 15 (2009).
[11] Yue-Sheng Hou et al., "Global Estimation of the Climate Change Impact of Logging Residue Utilization for Biofuels," *Forest Ecology and Management* 462 (2020).
[12] See Max Liboiron, *Pollution Is Colonialism* (Duke University Press, 2021).
[13] See Carola Hein, *Oil Spaces: Exploring the Global Petroleumscape* (Routledge, 2022); "Sanctions on Venezuela Mean More Expensive American Roads" Bloomberg, 2019: https://www.bloomberg.com/news/articles/2019-07-24/paved-in-black-gold-rains-and-sanctions-spawn-500-u-s-asphalt (accessed June 18, 2025).
[14] Nina I. Buravchuk et al., "Use of Technogenic Raw Materials in Ceramic Technology," *Open Ceramics* 18 (June 2024).
[15] Kathryn Yusoff, *A Billion Black Anthropocenes or None* (University of Minnesota Press, 2018); Nina Wexelblatt et al., "Round Table: Landscapes and Logics of Extractivism," *Thresholds* no. 49 (2021): 21–28; Imani Jacqueline Brown, "Black Ecologies: An Opening, an Offering," *MARCH International* (2021).
[16] Daphne Bakker et al., "Submerged Heritage," in *Thursday Night Live!,* ed. Ine Apapoe (Nieuwe Instituut, 2022). See Richard and Sally Price, *Rainforest Warriors: Human Rights on Trial* (University of Pennsylvania Press, 2011).
[17] Xuanwen Wang et al., "Fatal Falls from Roofs Among U.S. Construction Workers," *Journal of Safety Research* 44 (February 2013).
[18] Swarnabh Ghosh, "Toward a Critique of Labor-in-Construction," in *Non-Extractive Architecture: On Designing Without Depletion,* ed. Space Caviar (Sternberg Press, 2021); E. Boadu et al., "Work-Related Respiratory Health Conditions Among Construction Workers: A Systematic Narrative Review," *BMJ Open Respiratory Research* 10 (2023); A. Sussell et al, "Health Risk Behavior Profile of Construction Workers, 32 States, 2013–2016," *Journal of Occupational & Environmental Medicine* 67, no. 2 (May 2020).
[19] Edward R. Ford, *The Architectural Detail* (Princeton Architectural Press, 2011), 125.
[20] Mark Burry, "The Architectural Detail and the Fear of Commitment," *Architectural Design* 84, no. 4 (2014).
[21] Burry, "The Architectural Detail."
[22] Robin Evans, "Mies Van Der Rohe's Paradoxical Symmetries," *AA Files,* no. 19 (1990).
[23] Quoted from Dietrich Neumann, ed., *The Barcelona Pavilion by Mies Van Der Rohe: One Hundred Texts Since 1929* (Birkhäuser, 2021), 70.
[24] Evans, "Mies Van Der Rohe's Paradoxical Symmetries."
[25] Peggy Deamer, "Craft and Design; "Detail: The Subject of the Object," in *Architecture and Labor,* ed. Jane Rendell (Routledge, 2020), 8.
[26] Jennifer Bloomer, "Pale Houses, Silenced Shadows," *Assemblage,* no. 37 (1998).
[27] Eric Bellin, *Detailing Worlds: A Conceptual History of Architectural Detail* (Bloomsbury, 2025).
[28] Andrés Jaque, *Phantom: Mies as Rendered Society: Intervention in the Mies Van Der Rohe Pavilion* (Fundació Mies van der Rohe, 2013).
[29] Marco Frascari, "The Tell-the-Tale Detail," in *Semiotics 1981,* ed. John N. Deely and Margot D. Lenhart (Springer US, 1983).
[30] Katherine Shonfield, *Walls Have Feelings: Architecture, Film and the City* (Routledge, 2000).
[31] Shonfield, *Walls Have Feelings,* 14.
[32] Francesca Hughes, *The Architecture of Error: Matter, Measure, and the Misadventures of Precision* (MIT Press, 2014).
[33] Howard Zinn, *A People's History of the United States, 1492–2001* (HarperPerennial, 2005).
[34] Ford, *The Architectural Detail,* 125.
[35] Kenneth Frampton and John Cava, *Studies in Tectonic Culture: The Poetics of Construction in Nineteenth and Twentieth Century Architecture* (MIT Press, 1995).
[36] Shonfield, *Walls Have Feelings.*

Figure 1. A butterfly valve handled by Martin. They are devices used to regulate the flow of liquids or gases between a pipeline. Photo: Simon Mitchell, 2024.

Simon Mitchell

Partial Provenances

Staging Minor Matters Inside a Reuse Warehouse

What do a plumbing component, a wrought iron bracket, a stencil-spray-painted sheet of MDF, and a glass block all have in common? At first glance, very little, aside from the fact that they are all building components. More specifically, however, they are all fragments. That is to say they comprise a small part of a greater whole: partial constituents that when assembled with other partials form something larger. The reason I am able to choose and present this seemingly random and benign set of objects is that they have all been donated, acquired, or salvaged and are now held in storage. Only where they are stored and the reasons for their storing differ significantly. One of these items resides within the architecture collection of the prestigious Victoria & Albert Museum (V&A) in London, documented and classified within a rich institutional taxonomy. The other three objects sit on the shelves of a warehouse named Ombygg (Rebuild), a company in Oslo involved in the circulation and reuse of secondhand building materials and unused surplus. These objects had lives prior to their placement in storage: roles in which they fulfilled certain obligations—until they were no longer needed, at which point they became something else.

What these objects become once removed from their former environments depends on where they end up and the storages through which they are subsequently made legible. Within the conventions of cultural institutions like the V&A, provenance plays a key role in how architectural fragments are turned into artifacts: describing their origins and affiliations, and helping to reposition them within curated frameworks of value. In the context of Ombygg, a different mode of valuation and accumulation takes place. From the warehouse, building components are not gathered to preserve or construct the historical record. Instead, materials converge in arrangements that prioritize their future use and reentry into the construction market. They bring together the often overlooked, ordinary, and mass-produced components that sit beyond the scope of institutional collecting logics and the more precious fragments typically accessible in the making of an architectural history.

The contrast between the practices of the V&A and of Ombygg is not my central concern, but a prompt to think differently about the relationship between provenance and the understudied fragments of architecture that move within

Future Anterior
Volume XXII, Numbers 1–2
Summer / Winter 2025

circulations of reuse. Where architectural histories have traditionally been built around the coherence of complete buildings inside stable and progressive narratives—what historian Carlo Ginzburg might call a "high knowledge" kind of history—then the emerging field of architectural reuse presents a different view.[1] It shows how architecture is sustained by partial provenances: ongoing, fragmentary histories traced through the components and materials that quietly sustain the architectural whole.

What happens when we begin from the unsettled granularities and architectural in-betweens that underpin our histories of wholeness? What kinds of knowledge about architecture become possible? The aim here is not to reconstruct a total chain of ownership in the conventional sense of provenance. Rather, it is to begin—with an ethnographic orientation—in the reuse warehouse: a site I came to know through walking interviews, informal conversations, and work-based observations of warehouse staff and visitors. The warehouse is a place where the minor and residual parts of architecture await uncertain futures. It's a regime of acquisition that places much less value on where architectural fragments come from, and a lot more value on where they could end up.

An Ambiguous Object: Butterfly Valve

"What is it?"

"I'm not really sure what it is," says Martin, as he holds up a blue and weighty-looking instrument so we can both take a closer look. "It's plumbing equipment of some kind . . . It's outside our jurisdiction, but yeah, we take stuff like this too—even if we're not sure whether it will get sold."[2]

Martin, the general manager of Ombygg since its founding in 2022, describes the valve as a "funny example" of the kinds of things they receive. This is not to dismiss the peculiar object, but to illustrate the broad range of components acquired during pilot phase of their operations, which ran from 2023 to 2025. I point the big, nosey lens of my DSLR camera toward the blue and metal object and Martin readjusts slightly, turning his wrists and offering it as I press my finger down on the shutter button and the camera makes a *click*.

For a moment, our attention is focused solely on this unusual component (Figure 1). It is not something I would choose to focus on myself, not least because I don't know what it is. But in this moment, it is not me who has chosen it. It is Martin who pulls it from the bottom shelf of a unit he describes as full of "odd items."[3] Holding the plumbing equipment in his hands, he recollects: "It's probably a vent or a valve for a big solid tube so that you can actually open or unlock it." He points to a circular, black perimeter that looks like a plastic sealant with a muted metallic disk in the middle: "If there is a tube it would go in here." I've never seen an object like this before, and that alone sparks curiosity. Martin explains that it arrived as part of a larger delivery from AF Gruppen—a major Nordic construction and engineering company—following the completion of Oslo's new swimming pool Tøyenbadet, a building less than three kilometers away.[4]

As general manager, Martin's role has been to establish the operational and organizational structure of Ombygg. The finer details—tracking the technical specifications of each object, categorizing them, and setting prices—fall to the storage and sales managers. Still, an encounter with components like the plumbing valve is part of the joy of being here, walking through the warehouse. The warehouse brings into view the kinds of components rarely seen in everyday experiences of the city, yet here they're placed in plain sight. The uncertainty of where each object might next travel next carries a kind of tentativeness; decoupled from their former lives whether buildings, construction sites, or private storages, they are made visible and granted potential through their emplacement in the warehouse setting. And while the previous owners of each acquired component is formally recorded by Ombygg upon arrival, I only encounter them from a partial vantage point. It's through this walking, talking interview with Martin that we are able to reflect on specific objects in real time. Knowledge here unfolds gradually—through the shifting details that surface as we navigate and meander through a variety of architectural components.[5] Rather than working from a full picture, we're instead prompted by the serendipity of the objects encountered along the way.

The plumbing instrument isn't the first object photographed today, and it certainly won't be the last. Jawad, the sales manager, is also walking with Martin and me, and we are surrounded by stacks of building components: Blunted timber battens lay horizontally; rows of pristine windows stand tall like dominoes; a cluster of old ceramic toilets and wash hand basins are stored compactly on industrial shelving (Figure 2). The fragments and components around us would often otherwise find their way to municipal waste stations, but instead find their way here, under the roof of a large warehouse in Økern, a district in northeast Oslo.

Ombygg emerged from Resirqel, a reuse consultancy founded in 2013 to address the waste of reusable building materials and components.[6] Since its establishment, Ombygg has operated as a full-scale pilot project under what has been called "ideal terms": supported by both public and private stakeholders and, for now, somewhat insulated from the full pressures of the commercial market.[7] This initial phase of accumulation has been deliberately expansive, encompassing

Figure 2. Shelves of sanitary ware and plumbing equipment stacked compactly in the warehouse. Photo: Simon Mitchell, 2024.

everything from standardized components to more obscure components—a way of testing what materials might feasibly circulate within the wider construction economy. Following the pilot phase, their plan is to narrow the catalog to focus on high-demand products with "proven potential for resale," as the company transitions toward a more systematized and commercially scalable model.[8] Described as possibly Europe's largest reuse hub, it works at a scale that reflects growing institutional interest and commercial investment in circular construction.[9] The facility includes a vast 4,500m^2 sheltered warehouse, alongside 2,500m^2 of outdoor storage space, loaded with a wide range of once-utilized or surplus building materials. It is backed by some of Norway's largest public and private developers, and on any given day the warehouse is also used by a range of individuals, including carpenters, builders, artists, and those undertaking domestic renovation projects.[10]

Wandering the grounds, one witnesses familiar construction components, like bricks stacked on pallets (Figure 3) next to less familiar, sometimes kitschy objects, including a crude imitation of graffiti artist Banksy's famous *Kissing Coppers* stenciled onto a board of MDF (Figure 4). The composite of materials, assembled in sometimes unusual combinations, provides a distinctive and unpredictable cross-section of Oslo's contemporary built environment. While components are broadly grouped by type, the system is not strictly codified, differing from the tightly ordered spatial logics of archive or museum collections. Doors, windows, insulation, tiles and bricks, furniture, plumbing equipment, electrical units, and

Figure 3 (*above*). A stack of old and used bricks under spotlight in the warehouse. I learn from Martin that some goods like these are scrapped items on their way to being discarded. Photo: Simon Mitchell, 2025.

Figure 4 (*right*). A replica of Banksy's 2004 *Kissing Coppers,* found propped up against a shelf of insulation panels and next to an assortment of corrugated cable piping. Photo: Simon Mitchell, 2025.

ventilation systems are clustered into their own specific zones. But these are often punctuated by ambiguous and seemingly random objects from the city: supermarket shopping trolleys, a stack of skateboard decks, a basketball net, and a hanging punching bag. Such items seem adrift when witnessed in between and beside the far more categorical items typically associated with the world of architecture.[11] Yet in Ombygg, the odd coalesces with the ordinary inside the same logical ecosystem, and it makes for a different kind of architectural encounter.

The warehouse offers a partial view of Oslo and its environs, unfolded and made traceable through the slow and often awkward assembly of its leftover things. This is not a view composed of totalities or sweeping panoramas, like those found on postcards or experienced through tours of Oslo's iconic landmarks like the Opera House or the Rådhus (Oslo's city hall). Such experiences affirm a more resolved version of the city. Instead, from the warehouse, fragments and incompletes form the basis of the architectural experience. Dislodged from their former contexts and caught in between circulation, each piece patiently awaits new purpose.

But these materials don't just accumulate; they point to some minor parts of the city's operations, including routines of maintenance, the work of dismantling and gathering architectural components, and the quiet infrastructures of reuse. In light of the work of philosopher and anthropologist Bruno Latour, and psychologist-photographer Émilie Hermant, the warehouse can be thought of as an *oligopticon*. This concept describes a site of concentrated and partial vision, offering narrow but intense insight into the functioning of often invisible urban infrastructures. Unlike the panoramic or totalizing gaze of Jeremy Bentham's panopticon—so often employed as a framework through which to critique the governing forces of architecture and society—the oligopticon shows how urban life is coordinated through highly contained yet connectable sociomaterial networks. They are grounded and incomplete vantage points that, when assembled with other parts of the city, show a closer, more complex picture of urban life.[12] From the vantage point of the warehouse, what might otherwise be dismissed as unfortunate residues of construction practice act as provocations. They are small clues into the afterlives of buildings that evidence the mechanisms and networks through which the architectural past is able to remain and recirculate.

Low Knowledge and Loose Ends: Building Architectural History from Its Unknown Parts

Reuse has gained traction in response to the growing pressure to decarbonize construction and reimagine how to work with surplus and waste in the built environment. Of course, the repurposing of building materials is a centuries-old practice. But the scale of recent efforts reflects a changing historical landscape in which material recovery and recirculation are embedded in deeper questions and discourses about human-induced climate change. Yet, knowledge about the construction industry's hazardous effects on the habitability of the planet does not necessarily correspond with the changes required to make a meaningful difference in practice. As architect and architectural historian Lionel Devlieger states, many of the challenges facing the reuse sector today are legal, while the policies and procedures architects adhere to remain written in a linear and capitalist market economy.[13] In this regard, determining how such changes might be addressed is complex and often conflicting. While reuse practices may reframe the value of building components around adaptability or carbon reduction, they nonetheless operate within an overarching profit-driven political economy.

In its most cynical rendering, the reuse of building materials represents the latest chapter in the economization of the environmental crisis by continuing a fifty-year legacy of governance under the banner of "sustainability." Historians Cristophe Bonneuil and Jean-Baptiste Fressoz argue that from the 1970s onward, sustainability became central to "the fundamental ideological battle to circumvent mounting criticisms of the Western growth model."[14] Rather than confronting the structural causes of ecological breakdown, sustainability modeling often translates the environmental crisis into familiar economic terms—*extending* rather than dismantling logics of capitalistic extractivism.[15] Architects and researchers Tom Schoonjans and Michaël Ghyoot similarly warn that efforts to systemize reuse remain subsumed within linear, growth-oriented economic systems. Like the sustainability movement that preceded, "circular construction promises a radical new building system but risks appropriation by extractivist market forces."[16] Nonetheless, material reuse and circularity principles are advancing across multiple scales across Europe—through public, private, and policy-driven initiatives reshaping both design practices and regulatory infrastructures.[17]

Rather than surveying all the actors involved in building material reuse, this essay explores the epistemic and methodological possibilities that arise from following the materials themselves, as they move through and coproduce reuse circulations. Warehouses like Ombygg's offer one such grounded constellation of components: sites that should intrigue researchers and practitioners, or at the very least expose them to the random and often frighteningly wasteful abundance of loose architectural matter. This warehouse is far removed from the V&A's East Storehouse, which presents a curated, referential view of architectural fragments that are fixed within an organized historical system.[18] Ombygg, by contrast, invites attention to uncertainty: the excess, and the occasional ambiguity of what these objects are, where they came from, or how they might next be used. It stages architecture's unruly aftermath—caught in medias res—laying bare the debris of production that in its intimidating vastness is often not acknowledged. To borrow philosopher Timothy Morton's term, the warehouse is a site of "grey goo." It contains the residues of capitalist production where vital earthly materials are converted into "featureless chunks of stuff"—matter stripped of its ecological vitality, unable to return to the earth's natural life cycles.[19]

Working through such residues raises questions about how to make sense of objects whose pasts are fragmentary and whose futures remain unresolved. This difficulty becomes especially pronounced when building components or fragments are approached through historical narratives that aspire to the completeness of buildings, or that reproduce a triumphalist account of architecture as a marker of human progress. Through the development of microhistory, historian Carlo Ginzburg explores how canonic narratives about the past are bound up in epistemological assumptions that prioritize evidence produced through formal disciplinary methods over the "conjectural" and informal knowledges through which other historical forms and experiences take shape.[20] Formal, or *high* knowledges, often reproduce grand narratives of wholeness while invisibilizing the groups, materials, and practices that do not conform to its regimes of legibility. In articulating the methodological stakes of microhistory, Ginzburg contrasts high knowledge with *low knowledge* as a more experiential mode of historical engagement grounded in observations of the everyday, oral traditions, and even highly interpretive veins of evidence that might otherwise be overlooked. Far from being a lesser form of understanding, Ginzburg frames low knowledge as an alternative paradigm that foregrounds and legitimizes uncertain and partial strains of evidence.[21]

Drawing from traditions outside the historical discipline, including ethnography, this mode of inquiry values knowledge that emerges through proximity and observation, often inaccessible through conventional historical methods.[22] As Ginzburg writes, it is knowledge, "learnt not from books but from listening, from doing, from watching," that is richer than any written authority on the subject. Their strength lay in being "born of experience, of the concrete and individual," even if their subtleties could scarcely be put into words or formalized.[23] It's in this space that ethnographic practice can offer a different mode of historical attention; one attuned to the indeterminations that surface *through* material encounters.

Material fragments in the warehouse, when approached through this lens, become sites that hold the potential for architecture's renarration, through the constituent and contingent trajectories of its minor parts. Uncertainty becomes a generative condition of inquiry, particularly when materials defy stable categorization, when their origins are only partially known, or when their potential futures remain unsettled. It is "an ongoingly emergent and inevitable condition of moving forward into the unknown."[24] Such an ethnographic stance makes visible ambiguous—even awkward—objects like the blue plumbing valve, whose future use or status remains unresolved. Yet its material presence within an ethnographic narrative of provisional fragments invites a form of provenance-thinking grounded in *projection* rather than proof.

A Replicated Object: Banksy's *Kissing Coppers*

If the more typical objects of architectural reuse available in Ombygg's warehouse raise questions about afterlife—how materials persist, circulate, and find renewed purpose—then the encounter with Banksy's *Kissing Coppers* presents a different set of concerns: how value is assigned, what qualifies as collectible, and where the boundaries of architectural provenance are drawn. The replica is recognizable because its original, a Banksy artwork, has a well-documented trajectory from a pub wall in Brighton to an art auction in Miami.[25] Its cultural significance is already bound to a specific kind of provenance, one tied to the mechanisms of the art world, where value is closely tracked through authorship and authenticity. Historian Sophie Raux shows how provenance research emerged as a valuative mechanism within elite institutions, noting that "a prestigious provenance was already an essential tool used to increase the value of a work [of art], sometimes even more powerful than praising its intrinsic qualities."[26] Against this backdrop, the Banksy facsimile—now resting on shelves of insulation panels in a reuse warehouse—unsettles conventional expectations of both artistic and architectural value. It is materially unexceptional, aesthetically kitsch, and of course a reproduction. These qualities typically fall outside the purview of provenance research, where authenticity, originality, authorship, and ownership have been treated as core benchmarks in determining an object's value.

It also lacks a defined place in the warehouse's architectural taxonomy. Its placement is determined by spatial happenstance rather than classification or by preservation logics. Outliers like this challenge assumptions underpinning established provenance frameworks—especially in a setting like Ombygg, where the object is neither historically significant nor institutionally curated. Its provocation lies precisely in this: that despite resisting institutional criteria of value (like those used for original artworks), it is still acquired, stored, and circulated within a reuse economy. Its inclusion reflects a different set of judgments, oriented toward pragmatics and potential rather than cultural pedigree. This divergence prompts a rethinking of what architectural provenance might entail when approached through a lens of reuse and the criteria involved in selecting objects for continued life. Addressing this shift requires engaging with the historical context of provenance research and some institutional logics that underpin its practice.

A Historical Object: Wrought Iron Bracket

Provenance research has historically developed alongside the art market and has largely been reserved for objects housed within recognized institutions—museums, archives, and heritage bodies—where it aligns art and architectural fragments with predetermined historical narratives and frameworks of value. Historians Christian Fuhrmeister and Meike Hopp argue that provenance research has often operated within rigid institutional and bureaucratic structures, limiting its scope and critical potential. Instead of enabling new inquiry, it has frequently been treated as a "mechanistic" and "imposed duty" reinforcing institutional authority and reproducing hierarchies. Without systemic change they insist provenance research risks remaining a "patchwork, piecemeal process" siloed within specific institutions and disconnected from broader historical inquiry.[27]

Provenance research is a familiar cornerstone of acquisition practice in institutions like the V&A, whose online architecture collection includes thousands of fragments—many of which have gained greater physical proximity to audiences through the opening of the East Storehouse in May 2025. Some fragments are linked to known architects or commissions; others, like an eighteenth-century wrought iron bracket (accession number: CIRC.309–1910), are only loosely attributed—recorded simply as "England" (Figure 5).[28] A typical V&A catalog entry includes multiple signifiers that construct how a collected object is to be known: artist/maker, origin, object details, type, materials and techniques, physical description, dimensions, and accession number. Even when uncertain about the exact origin, an object is situated within a taxonomy of significance—preserved and stabilized by institutional classifications. In this case, this bracket's value is not granted by authorship; its attributions in that regard are vague. Rather, the object's renewed existence—historical and archival—emerges through its assimilation into a classificatory system, where provenance is shaped by institutional routines that render it legible. As STS scholars Geoffrey Bowker and Susan Leigh Star argue, classification

Figure 5. A photograph of a bracket from the Victoria & Albert architecture collection, not on display and described as "Wrought iron bracket with scrollwork." Courtesy of Victoria and Albert Museum, London.

systems—whether institutional, or everyday—shape what becomes visible and knowable. They state that "each standard and each category valorizes some point of view and silences another." Things become meaningful through their placement within authorized systems of ordering, which do not simply describe the world but participate in constructing it.[29]

This institutional framing of provenance, as a tool to stabilize meaning and reinforce historical authority, is not incidental. As historian Dominique Poulot has shown in his study of art and museums during the French Revolution, provenance research was enrolled as a museological practice that was inseparable from the political aims of the time. In reassembling collections like those at the Louvre, revolutionary curators were not just recovering ownership histories but constructing a republican narrative that recast cultural objects as public heritage. "Thinking about provenance under these conditions," Poulot writes, "meant constructing a specific form of knowledge linked to the process of musealization."[30] Provenance research was less about locating truth than about asserting legitimacy, determining what entered the museum, and on what terms.

Museum curators Tone Hansen and Ana María Bresciani argue that provenance research still functions as an institutional mechanism that fixes an object's meaning toward display. "In theory," they note, "the arrival of an object or artwork at the museum terminates this circulation. The museum is at once an asylum . . . and a final destination, given the perpetuity of the museum perspective."[31] Once an object enters a collection, its status becomes permanent. Where its past is described, and preserved, so too its future is determined, ringfencing its role in the world. In other words, provenance research is not only a form of historical inquiry but also a form of gatekeeping: It stabilizes value through origin, but in doing so, makes that value—and the role of the object—hard to unsettle.

Ombygg, by contrast, presents a collection governed by a different logic. It is not an archive of the exceptional nor historical, but a working infrastructure of reuse. The warehouse does not define or organize its holdings like that of a museum's collection of architectural fragments. As we move through the warehouse, Martin shares some of what guides their priorities on the ground: "We're interested in the amounts. That's where the value is for us. In volume."[32] It speaks to an operation of storing that privileges quantity and movement over holding and preserving objects for their historical significance. This effort reflects an ambition to scale up and attract larger industry players—including contractors and developers—by aligning with construction protocols such as providing product guarantees and meeting compliance standards.[33] Since the pilot phase began, recording provenance has been mandatory for all incoming materials, registered through a digital inventory system.[34] And while the integration of Ombygg's digital systems remains ongoing, it points toward a model of material organization that prioritizes each object's eventual resale over their permanent storage. But it also opens the space of provenance research to a whole new category of object—those that have typically been overlooked by institutional collections and historiographic traditions alike.

If the reuse warehouse is approached as a vestibule into traceable circulations, then the criteria for historical significance begins to shift beyond the conventional thresholds set by archival norms and disciplinary traditions witnessed at collecting institutions such as the V&A. Provenance and valuation need not hinge on traditional standards like aesthetic merit or historical pedigree. Instead, they could draw attention to the conditions of collection, the contexts of circulation, and the futures each material enables; especially given the materials in question—those in reuse—are often overlooked as historically relevant. The components found in Ombygg; the standardized, the mundane, and (like Banksy's facsimile) the kitschy, become newly legible under such a lens. This legibility not only raises questions about how everyday architectural materials are collected, stored, classified, and reused; it also expands the remit of what counts in the making of an architectural history. The historical trajectories of the mundane and still usable open the *possibility for provenance* to emerge as a critical and speculative lens—foregrounding how materials circulate and coproduce different settings and gain meaning through their potential futures and contextual afterlives.

A Multisited Object: Glass Block

Among us in the warehouse, boxes of unopened surplus leave clues to their provenances. Nearby, a cardboard box of translucent glass blocks reads: "GERRIX-GLASSTEINE MADE IN W.-GERMANY" (Figure 6). I shift my lens from the blue plumbing valve and Banksy's facsimile toward these West-German-made glass blocks some meters away. I like the look of them. They remind me of a host of prestigious architecture projects. The Maison de Verre in Paris with its glass block facade designed by architects Pierre Chareau and Bernard Bijvoet is one such example. Another is Villa Stenersen in Oslo, designed by architect Arne Korsmo and completed in 1939 for financier and art collector Rolf E. Stenersen. Once a private residence, it became a listed heritage building administered by the National Museum of Art, Architecture and Design in 2014.[35]

Visitors to Villa Stenersen would immediately notice the glass blocks forming the middle floor of its famous south-facing facade (Figure 7). Art and architectural historian Tim Benton analyzed the detailing of this facade, noting how Korsmo tested various block types, eventually selecting "Insulux" blocks from Owens-Illinois in the US. The 11¾-inch blocks were chosen for their appearance and insulation but also imposed a specific dimensional logic that Benton claims "may well have influenced the change of dimensions of the façade."[36] Korsmo had also considered Nevada glass tiles from Saint-Gobain in France—solid units with textured exteriors and hollowed interiors designed to diffuse light. Benton notes their "charisma," attributed not only to their use in the Maison de Verre but also to their appearance in several projects by Le Corbusier.[37] Despite their prestige, Korsmo rejected them due to their poor thermal performance in Nordic climates, and therefore opted for the Insulux blocks. With each bay of the facade measured in exact multiples of block width and joint spacing, the glass blocks likely determined the "curios dimension" of the 3.675-meter column intervals and the full 18.35-meter width.[38] It's a small but telling example of how an architectural fragment

Figure 6. Glass blocks from Düsseldorf-based company Gerresheimer Glas, the product is called Gerrix-Glassteine. Photo: Simon Mitchell, 2024.

Figure 7. The south-facing front facade of Korsmo's Villa Stenersen, including the 11¾-inch glass block replacements that have been installed along the third story. Photo: Simon Mitchell, 2025.

can quietly determine the resolution of the architectural whole. Though the glass block might appear—in isolation—a minor technical component, it defined aspects of the building's spatial organization. It linked Korsmo's need for thermally efficient construction to the constrained palette of standardized blocks available that ultimately informed the facade's proportions.

While Benton writes extensively on the details of the Insulux glass blocks that occupy the iconic south-facing front facade, he gives less attention to the smaller 5¾-inch glass blocks on the north-facing rear (Figure 8).[39] These smaller glass blocks form four distinct screens: two on the left-hand facade, lighting the service entrance and its stairwell, and two on the right-hand facade, a vertical screen illuminating the main staircase and a horizontal screen for the upstairs bathroom. The smaller blocks are also believed to be products of Insulux, labelled "Insulux 5¾"" on two of Korsmo's original elevation drawings.[40] Yet it is not entirely clear—based on the publicly accessible database of Oslo kommune's Planning and Building Agency (PBE)—whether the blocks on the rear facade are originals from 1939.[41] The larger glass blocks on the south-facing front facade are certainly not originals. What documents from the PBE's database do show is that the south facade was renovated and its glass blocks replaced twice, in 1995 and again between 2002 and 2005.[42]

Yet, on a visit to the Villa Stenersen what becomes obvious is how the glass blocks to the rear bear a striking resemblance to those found in Ombygg's warehouse. It's a likeness that urges deeper investigation, but perhaps of key concern here is how such attention only comes into view through exposure to an alternative "archival" vantage point—with an archaeology-like sensibility toward ordinary building materials. Encountering a half-opened box of Gerrix-Glassteine glass blocks at Ombygg unsettles what the official record at Villa Stenersen leaves ambiguous, and provokes questions that could help build a bigger picture: what is the history of the blocks to the rear? Why are they less discussed and less accounted for? What or where is their provenance? Where much of the villa's history—read through books, permits, drawings, and renovation files—documents and frames the front of the building into celebrity, the rear of the building persists only in scraps and partials. And while the point here is not to prove an exact match of two glass blocks across different architectural regimes (one of heritage preservation, and one of reuse), their tentative connection presents an entryway toward mapping and testing alternating trajectories of provenance.

Back in the warehouse, I ask Martin if he knows about the historical provenance of the glass blocks in front of us: "We only care that they came from a particular person or group on a specific date," he explains.[43] The glass blocks, in other words, carry uneven associative weight; their capacity to summon different contexts and meanings depends on who engages with them. What for me triggers a line of architectural-historical and archival inquiry, appears for Ombygg, as nothing more than a material unit donated by a retired bricklayer in Oslo, as Jawad

Figure 8. The north-facing rear of Villa Stenersen occupies little limelight in the building's history and features 5¾-inch glass blocks, believed to be from Insulux. Photo: Simon Mitchell, 2025.

recalls, "I think we got these from an older man . . . We call him the Danish guy." There is a pause. "Yeah, it was the Danish guy. He told us he didn't need all this stuff anymore. He said, 'I don't want to throw all this stuff away because for me it's value.' So he gave us maybe half a pallet of tiles, and other stuff like that. It was all the stuff he collected over his career. We just had to pay for the transport to get everything to our shop."[44] Martin and Jawad's account sketches the outline of a different regime—another investigative lead, but one grounded in the situational practices of reuse rather than in history books or archival records. The possibility of another tracing here arises through conversation, unfolding from encountering the glass blocks within a circulation of reuse. But it connects the glass blocks to another mise-en-scène; a former setting made by a retired tradesman and the micro-routines of his working life in Oslo.

Set apart from the educated "gaze" of the institution—one that connects the glass blocks to histories like that voiced by Benton—I am confronted with an alternative account: a gaze that brings into view the small-scale economies and incremental accumulations that mark the practices of a working life in construction.[45] It emerges from a patchwork of fragmentary traces and partial clues that surround us in the warehouse. The components we encounter, like the glass block, are by no means definitive records. Their meanings diverge and multiply, as seen in the differing interpretations of Martin, Jawad, and I. These objects are not secured to singular origins, nor are they contained within panoptical frameworks of meaning. The glass blocks in the warehouse activate the margins of Korsmo's architectural legacy while also building a periphery of the retired bricklayer's work. What differs is the degree to which the institutions of provenance—typically museums, collections, and archives—recognize, let alone prioritize, the possibility for one history to emerge over the other. This has lasting consequences on how the past is known, and for the kinds of presents and futures it enables.

Archivist Terry Cook writes that archivists exercise an invisible yet consequential agency through their archival practices. They determine what is preserved and what becomes accessible, thereby shaping the kinds of histories that can be assembled and remembered.[46] Like archives, reuse warehouses such as Ombygg quietly sort and redistribute fragments and materials; yet, unlike archives, they do so without necessarily aiming to preserve or monumentalize objects, nor to inventory or formally document provenance. Yet through their acts of sorting and valuation, they nonetheless coauthor the terms through which certain architectural pasts are retained and the extent to which their futures become possible. If we consider the ordinary and mass-produced objects in the warehouse as documentary evidence in circulations of reuse, questions emerge around what counts as worthy of attention and which histories such materials are able to sustain.

Provenance Made from Partials

There is no single way to frame an object; its meaning and status shift depending on the contexts and exchanges through which it travels over time.[47] Within the warehouse, fragments and components present open-ended possibilities rather than fixed meanings. They invite a different kind of attention—description, even—to the ways materials undo and redo architectures. My use of description draws from Latour's argument that description (or, more precisely, redescription) is central to ethnographic knowledge production. It provides a closer and more real account of how things unfold and acquire meaning in practice.[48] Describing such processes makes space for the in-between and hard-to-define actions and movements that matter in the making of knowledge and form, but are so often overlooked in traditional, "high-knowledge" historical methods. On this terrain, provenance becomes an invitation to follow things: even the most mundane objects, to witness and record the differing worlds they coproduce, the controversies they generate, and the circulatory paths they inscribe in contemporary reuse economies.

Questions are further raised about whose gaze matters in the making of an architectural provenance and how one might deal with the diverse and even conflicting ways an object accrues meaning and value through its various translations. As architectural historian Andrew Ballantyne writes, "a multiplicity of narratives intersect in any building, and it is important for our understanding of them to realize that any single narrative will be seen to be reductive if it is claimed as the only narrative that really matters. For buildings to be given their proper due as evidence, they need to be included in narratives that are constructed in ways that allow for multiple perspectives."[49] While Ballantyne writes about whole buildings, his emphasis on multiplicity applies just as urgently to the fragments that give them form. If architecture is to be understood as evidence, then that evidence often takes form through partial components whose histories are dispersed, layered, and continually reassembled. Extending Ballantyne's insight, we might say that the narrative richness of architecture does not disappear when buildings are dismantled—or even when they're never realized. Rather, it migrates, with altered force, into the circulatory lives of their constituent parts. To follow provenance through these circulations is to engage with overlapping, and sometimes contested, narratives. Each is shaped by the actors, settings, and exchanges that give them meaning. Fragments removed from their original (and often multiple) contexts carry histories still in formation. Their reuse unsettles the impulse—evident in places like the V&A—to stabilize meaning through classification. Instead, these materials invite more grounded and open-ended accounts of architectural history. Such accounts remain attentive to partiality and movement.

Within this setting, reuse warehouses like Ombygg function as sites of practice, where materials are not only stored but revalued, repositioned, and circulated toward new architectural possibilities. The warehouse offers a window onto infrastructural interchanges where building histories are continually negotiated. These sites make visible the passage of materials from one use to another, offering opportunities to trace their partial and fragmentary provenances. In doing so, they complicate the dominant, linear trajectory of industrial construction—from extraction to obsolescence, with little regard for reuse. As theorist Hélène Frichot succinctly puts it, "the progress of architecture is inextricably tied up with the production of waste."[50] Reuse warehouses thus serve as both material and historiographic junctures, where new circulations interrupt the cradle-to-grave logic of architectural production and offer a critical lens into the ecological and epistemic consequences of an architecture that moves, from one use to the next. But if reuse companies are beginning to unsettle architecture's waste-bound flows, an equally urgent task faces those who narrate it: practitioners, historians, theorists, and social scientists alike. The challenge is to reflect critically on how each discipline has been implicated—complicit even—in sustaining linear modes of production, especially by privileging narratives that uphold the completeness of buildings and the forward-bound, developmentalist narratives of progress. These narratives not only map onto but further construct the problematic logics of linear development and reinforce a wasteful version of historical progress.

The reuse of architectural materials and the infrastructures it requires is not an entirely technical process. The formation of these circulations offers to provenance thinking a different category of object and indeed alternative, traceable trajectories through which architecture can be explored and reconceptualized. As anthropologists Albena Yaneva and Latour remind us, "a building is not a static object but a moving *project*."[51] Architectural provenance, too, unfolds through the unfinished, the fragmented, and the still circulating—bound up in ongoing processes of reassembly and transformation. It is not simply a matter of staging or documenting overlooked things through former chains of ownership. Instead, provenance offers a pathway toward rethinking the scaffoldings through which architecture's pasts and futures are made, unmade, and made again.

Biography
Simon Mitchell is a postdoctoral researcher at the Oslo School of Architecture and Design. He holds a PhD in architecture from the University of Manchester, funded by the Arts and Humanities Research Council (2023). Working at the intersection of ethnography, archival theory, and architecture history, his current research focuses on the storage lives of architectural fragments. Originally trained in architecture, Simon has practiced across Europe and in Asia, tutored at the Manchester School of Architecture and the GEC Academy in Beijing, and published on behalf of the Bauhaus Dessau Foundation.

Notes

1 Carlo Ginzburg, "Morelli, Freud and Sherlock Holmes: Clues and Scientific Method," *History Workshop Journal,* no. 9 (1980): 5–36.

2 Interview with Martin, General Manager at Ombygg, Oslo, November 15, 2024. Conducted in person by the author. Informed consent was obtained.

3 Martin Eid, interview with author, November 15, 2024.

4 "About AF," *AF Gruppen,* accessed June 22, 2025, https://www.afgruppen.com/about-af/.

5 Tim Ingold and Jo Lee Vergunst, "Introduction," in *Ways of Walking: Ethnography and Practice on Foot,* ed. Tim Ingold and Jo Lee Vergunst (Ashgate, 2008), 1–20.

6 Martin, interview with author, November 15, 2024.

7 Martin, clarification following interview with author, June 12, 2025.

8 Martin, clarification following interview with author, June 12, 2025.

9 Redaksjonen, "Største ombrukssentral i Europa," *Arkitektur,* June 13, 2022, https://www.arkitektur.no/aktuelt/miljoe/stoerste-ombrukssentral-i-europa/.

10 Strategic partners supporting Ombygg's development include Statsbygg, Oslobygg, Entra, OBOS, and Mustad Eiendom, who also make regular use of the facility's services. Ombygg's parent company, Resirqel, receives investment from Franzefoss, as part of a broader network of stakeholders. This information was provided by Martin, clarification following interview, June 12, 2025.

Franzefoss is a family-owned Norwegian company founded in 1919 with origins in limestone and dolomite extraction. It has since expanded into sectors including mineral-based materials processing, aggregate production, industrial waste recycling, and environmental resource management. See "Om oss," *Franzefoss,* accessed June 21, 2025, https://www.franzefoss.no/om-oss.

11 Stewart Brand's concept of *Shearing Layers* offers one way to distinguish the "archetypical" technical and material categories of architecture: site, structure, skin, services, space plan, and stuff. Interestingly, a copy of Brand's book was on display

in the office of Ombygg's sister company, Resirqel. Stewart Brand, *How Buildings Learn: What Happens After They're Built* (Viking, 1994), 12–23.

[12] Bruno Latour and Émilie Hermant, *Paris: Invisible City* (Les Empêcheurs de penser en rond, 1996), 1–4 and 27–30.

[13] Lionel Devlieger, "Reverse Architecture—The Virtues of Unbuilding and Reassembling," in *Rewriting Architecture: 10+1 Actions—Tabula Scripta*, ed. Floris Alkemade, Michiel van Iersel, Jarrik Ouburg, and Mark Minkjan (Valiz, 2020), 149–50.

[14] Christophe Bonneuil and Jean-Baptiste Fressoz, *The Shock of the Anthropocene: The Earth, History, and Us* (Verso, 2017), 216.

[15] Bonneuil and Fressoz, *The Shock of the Anthropocene*, 215–221.

[16] Tom Schoonjans and Michaël Ghyoot, "Break the Cycle," *The Architectural Review*, no. 1521 (May 2025): 6–12.

[17] Several recent European initiatives have advanced material reuse at scale through pilot projects, policy tools, and data infrastructures. A five-year report by Interreg North-West Europe highlights methods for circulating reclaimed building materials and showcases the work of Rotor (Belgium), Bellastock (France), and Salvo (UK). *HouseEurope!* is a civil campaign and funding mechanism promoting adaptive reuse over demolition, while platforms like Madaster use "material passports" to register the origin, composition, and reuse potential of building components.

Michaël Ghyoot, Hugo Topalov, Léa Bottani-Dechaud, and Esther Rejai, Facilitating the Circulation of Reclaimed Building Elements: A Review of 5 Years of Methods and Experiments in North-West Europe (Interreg North-West Europe FCRBE, 2023), https://vb.nweurope.eu/media/21554/fcrbe_final-report_ve.pdf. HouseEurope!, "Our Goal," accessed May 29, 2025, https://www.houseeurope.eu/157-goal. Madaster Foundation, "Material Passport," accessed June 3, 2025, https://madaster.com/material-passport/.

[18] Edwin Heathcote, "V&A East Storehouse Is a Genuinely Radical New Museum," *Financial Times*, May 29, 2025, https://www.ft.com/content/20dec093-63a0-45f4-a394-9f769e322065.

[19] Timothy Morton, "Architecture Without Nature," *Tarp*, no. 10 (2012): 20–25.

[20] Ginzburg, "Morelli, Freud and Sherlock Holmes," 6–7.

[21] Ginzburg, "Morelli, Freud and Sherlock Holmes," 7–15.

[22] Carlo Ginzburg and Carlo Poni, "The Name and the Game: Unequal Exchange and the Historiographic Marketplace," in *Microhistory and the Lost People of Europe*, ed. Edward Muir and Guido Ruggiero, trans. Eren Branch (Johns Hopkins University Press, 1991), 4–5.

[23] Ginzburg, "Morelli, Freud and Sherlock Holmes," 21.

[24] Sarah Pink, Yoko Akama, and Shanti Sumartojo, "What Is Uncertainty?," in *Uncertainty and Possibility: New Approaches to Future Making in Design Anthropology* (Bloomsbury Academic, 2019), 36.

[25] Spray-painted in 2004 on the side of the Prince Albert pub on Trafalgar Street in Brighton, Banksy's artwork was removed in 2011 and flown to the US before being sold at auction to an anonymous buyer in Miami in 2014. Press Association, "Banksy's Kissing Coppers—Taken from a Pub Wall in Brighton—Sells for $575,000 in US," *The Guardian*, February 19, 2014, https://www.theguardian.com/artanddesign/2014/feb/19/banksy-mural-kissing-coppers-sells-us.

[26] Sophie Raux, "From Mariette to Joullain: Provenance and Value in Eighteenth-Century French Auction Catalogues," in *Provenance: An Alternate History of Art*, ed. Gail Feigenbaum and Inge Reist (Getty Research Institute, 2012), 93.

[27] Christian Fuhrmeister and Meike Hopp, "Rethinking Provenance Research," *Getty Research Journal*, no. 11 (2019): 222, 224.

[28] For further details about the wrought iron bracket housed in the V&A architecture collection (accession no. CIRC.309–1910), see Victoria and Albert Museum, "Bracket," accessed June 4, 2025, https://collections.vam.ac.uk/item/O374116/bracket-unknown/.

[29] STS refers to Science and Technology Studies. Geoffrey C. Bowker and Susan Leigh Star, *Sorting Things Out: Classification and Its Consequences* (MIT Press, 1999), 5.

[30] Dominique Poulot, "Provenance and Value: The Reception of Ancien Régime Works of Art Under the French Revolution," in *Provenance: An Alternate History of Art*, ed. Gail Feigenbaum and Inge Reist (Getty Research Institute, 2012), 78.

[31] Tone Hansen and Ana María Bresciani, eds., *Looters, Smugglers, and Collectors: Provenance Research and the Market* (Verlag der Buchhandlung Walther König, 2015), 9.

[32] Martin, interview with author, November 15, 2024.

[33] Martin, clarification following interview, June 12, 2025.

[34] Product data is submitted via Materia, a Norwegian-based web platform and app that registers building components through user-submitted data entered into preset fields. Materia is one of Ombygg's formal collaboration partners and the

platform is currently being integrated with Ombygg's internal inventory system in an ongoing process informed by their operational experience. Information was provided by Martin, as clarification following interview, June 12, 2025. See "Hjem," *Materia,* accessed June 22, 2025, https://www.materia.no/.

[35] "The History of Villa Stenersen," *Nasjonalmuseet,* accessed June 22, 2025, https://www.nasjonalmuseet.no/en/visit/locations/villa-stenersen/the-history-of-villa-stenersen/.

[36] Tim Benton, "Arne Korsmo: The Villa Stenersen," in *Villa Stenersen, Architect: Arne Korsmo,* asBUILT Classic 21 (Pax Forlag, 2019), 51.

[37] Benton, "Arne Korsmo," 47.

[38] Benton, 51.

[39] Benton, 47, 48, 57, 71. The smaller 5¾-inch glass blocks are mentioned only briefly in these four instances.

[40] Benton, 236–39; Nasjonalmuseet, NMK.2016.0063.002.059 and NMK.2016.0063.002.060. These refer to the archival catalog numbers for the images reproduced on Benton's pages.

[41] Oslo kommune, Plan- og bygningsetaten (PBE), Planinnsyn, accessed September 2, 2025, https://od2.pbe.oslo.kommune.no/kart/. The database lists eight "byggesaker," or building cases, concerning Villa Stenersen, ranging from the original planning permission and proposal drawings in 1937 to later restoration works. It also includes documentation of its temporary change in status from residential to cultural use in 2012.

[42] Oslo kommune, Plan- og bygningsetaten (PBE), *Melding om mindre byggearbeid etter bygningslovens § 86 A,* October 17, 1995, case file 950062992, journal no. 95/65927; *Rammetillatelse – Svar på søknad om tillatelse for tiltak etter plan- og bygningslovens § 93. Vilkår for igangsetting,* February 27, 2003, case file 200211499-3.

[43] Martin, interview with author, November 15, 2024.

[44] Interview with Jawad, Sales Manager at Ombygg, Oslo, November 15, 2024. Conducted in person by the author. Informed consent was obtained.

[45] I use the term "gaze" in reference to Jonathan Crary's account, whereby vision is produced through institutional conditioning and techniques that privilege certain ways of seeing. Jonathan Crary, *Techniques of the Observer: On Vision and Modernity in the Nineteenth Century* (MIT Press, 1990), 1–24.

[46] Terry Cook, "The Archive(s) Is a Foreign Country: Historians, Archivists, and the Changing Archival Landscape," *The American Archivist* 74, no. 2 (2011): 600–32.

[47] Arjun Appadurai, "Introduction: Commodities and the Politics of Value," in *The Social Life of Things: Commodities in Cultural Perspective* (Cambridge University Press, 1986), 3–63.

[48] Bruno Latour, *An Inquiry into Modes of Existence: An Anthropology of the Moderns* (Harvard University Press, 2013), 1–23.

[49] Andrew Ballantyne, "Architecture as Evidence," in *Rethinking Architectural Historiography,* ed. Dana Arnold, Elvan Altan Ergut, and Belgin Turan Özkaya (Routledge, 2006), 48.

[50] Hélène Frichot, "Wasteocene: The Dirty Architecture of Progress," *The Architectural Review,* October 14, 2021, https://www.architectural-review.com/essays/keynote/wasteocene-the-dirty-architecture-of-progress.

[51] Bruno Latour and Albena Yaneva, "Give Me a Gun and I Will Make All Buildings Move: An ANT's View of Architecture," in *Explorations in Architecture: Teaching, Design, Research,* ed. Reto Geiser and Urs Staub (Birkhäuser, 2008), 80.

Figure 1. Siporex-Ytong Elements. Photo: Atelier Rude, 1973. Courtesy of Oslo Museum.

Nicholas Coates and
Eskil Buskov Selmer

Architect Intervention

Operation Siporex

Designed to Move

Siporex, a brand name for autoclaved aerated concrete, stems from a Swedish patent that revolutionized the building industries in Europe following World War I and World War II.[1] Hailed as a material that could do it all, Siporex's simplicity and versatility, coupled with material shortages of wood and steel, created the conditions for unparalleled growth of the company. The versatile, lightweight material and component-based system allowed for it to be used far from the Scandinavian countries where it was developed. By the 1960s, as decolonization reshaped global markets, Siporex was well positioned to extend its reach beyond Europe. Once independent from French colonization in 1960, Côte d'Ivoire was one such market with a vacuum for new materials. The eager company Siporex took advantage of such moments of instability to market their material globally, presenting Siporex as a miraculous solution to local material scarcity while simultaneously creating the conditions for record profitability and strategic Norwegian diplomacy.[2]

Through studying the provenance of a single material and focusing not only on where the constituent ingredients came from but where the final product went, we present a reading of a little known industrial and architectural history. Siporex, through its distribution from a small town in Norway to the global market, tells the story of a material that was designed to be on the move and in turn defined contexts far beyond the building site.

A Complete System

50kg sand
12kg lime
28kg cement
8kg gypsum
2kg aluminum powder
55L water
Pinch of sugar

1. Mix sand with water and grind until a porridge consistency is formed. Add cement, aluminum powder, and sugar and mix thoroughly.

Future Anterior
Volume XXII, Numbers 1–2
Summer / Winter 2025

Figure 2. "Houses are built fire-safe in Siporex/Ytong elements." From *Byggekunst* 47, no. 7 (1966).

2. Pour the mixture into the molds. Over the course of a few days, the cement and sugar will start a yeasting process. When the mixture has stiffened, the yeasting process is complete and can be cut to the desired dimension.
3. Place the pieces in a special oven with a pressure of 11 atmospheres and a temperature of 180°C.
4. After baking for 8–12 hours, the dried and hardened blocks are ready for use.[3]

The genius of Siporex was the addition of aluminum powder into its ingredient list. The mixture would expand at high temperatures, create small pores within the concrete, and result in a material with all the positive properties of concrete, like being fire resistant, but at one-fifth the weight. The low density meant that Siporex elements were insulative and could be used for the entire construction, unlike rival materials that required additional insulation.

Siporex marketed itself as a total prefabricated system wherein any building project could be constructed by using only products and tools found in the Siporex catalog. Siporex took many forms: building blocks, floor slabs, wall panels, interior walls, insulation panels, and roofs, in both reinforced and unreinforced variations. Each element interlocked, making assembly both quick and effortless. In addition to this rolodex of products, custom Siporex tools in their bright-yellow color, such as lifting-clips, lifting-angles, cranes, and distribution wagons, streamlined both assembly and brand image. One did not need anything else. Siporex had engineers, a dedicated telephone line for advice, glue to secure the panels, and, of course, the tools. The company created an ecosystem around the product. Customers could come to Siporex for any building need; they would do the job faster and cheaper than any of their competition.

A Promise

Advertisements throughout the 1950s and 1960s highlighted the speed of new Siporex constructions. The company boasted that structures were completed in record time, as exemplified by headlines such as "new building record of six months" and "a villa blocked, under roof, and plastered in seven days."[4] However, marketing tactics went far beyond advertisements in trade magazines and newspapers. Similar sentiments were reproduced on vinyl records in Germany through a collaboration with comedian Jürgen von Manger. On the back cover of the album, it explained that in addition to records, Siporex also supplied panels for roofs, ceilings, and walls.[5] On track one of two, von Manger, who plays the role of a builder, laments the speed of Siporex construction: He did not even have time to wire the construction office or use the bathroom before the building was completed.

As a company, Siporex manufactured a product and a promise. Siporex embodied modernist ideals of efficiency, rationality, and progress stemming from industry. Through bold advertising campaigns, the marketing of the company constructed a world in which Siporex was more than just a building system of concrete and aluminum powder: It was a new way forward.

The popular meandering of the brand took unexpected turns. In 1966, Aalborg Zoo in Denmark welcomed its first elephant calf and christened it Siporex. The calf was born to parents Frank and Lene, who had been captured in India and brought to Denmark a decade earlier. The birth of the new calf was a celebration locally, nationally, and internationally. Newspapers donned headlines such as "Lene gave birth to a 150 kilo baby yesterday, given the name 'Siporex.'"[6] For such a momentous occasion, the elephant received an equally important name. Siporex lived in Aalborg Zoo for seven years before being sold to Hannover Zoo. In Germany, far from the industry that inspired its peculiar name, many visitors encountered Siporex for the first time. Only, it wasn't a construction material they came to see, but a ten-foot-tall elephant.

Figure 3. Young Siporex, Aalborg Zoo. Unknown photographer, 1966.

Lene fikk 150 kilos baby i går, får navnet „Siporex"

Elefanten Lene i den zoologiske hage i Alborg nedkom i går kveld med en unge av hannkjønn på 150 kilo, den første elefant-fødsel i Danmark på femti år.

Fødselen har vært ventet med spenning i lengre tid. Lene var gravid i 658 dager, og fødselen ble satt i gang med innsprøyting da elefanten hadde gått omtrent en måned over tiden.

Ved 21.30-tiden var veene så sterke at Lene i fortvilelse slo støttennene mot jerngitteret i sitt bur. Ti centimenter av den ene tann brakk under Lenes strabaser.

Selve fødselen tok til kl. 22.00. Direktøren for den zoologiske hag,e Rich. Stenild, som også er dyrlege, tok imot elefantungen som skal få navnet «Siporex».

De første minutter etter fødselen kretset Lene nervøst omkring «den lille» og kom endog til å tråkke på den flere ganger uten at den tok noe men av det. «Siporex» var på beina et kvarter etter å ha sett dagens lys.

*

Figure 4. "Lene gave birth to a 150-kilo baby yesterday, given the name 'Siporex.'" *Bergens Arbeiderblad,* June 22, 1966.

Signing a Deal

In the years following World War II, Siporex exploded on the Norwegian market. Due to a timber shortage and the massive need to rebuild and expand the housing stock, Siporex filled an enormous void. In 1953, a local newspaper reported that a second Siporex factory had opened in Hokksund, a small village southwest of Oslo. Established seven years after the first, the factory would employ a hundred people and produce enough blocks to meet 10 percent of the country's building needs.[7] The ability for a single material to be used for floors, walls, and roofs, coupled with its revolutionary speed of assembly, meant that Siporex was the perfect replacement for timber which had dominated the building industry up to this point. By the mid-1960s, however, the housing crisis had begun to ease, and the market was becoming saturated with competing materials. As competition intensified and the postwar building boom slowed, Siporex quickly lost its raison d'être.

In June 1969, a delegation from Sogefiha, the recently formed government housing corporation in the newly independent Côte d'Ivoire, traveled to Oslo to broker a deal with the

Figure 5. The minister of trade to Côte d'Ivoire and the director of Selmer, signing the first export contract to Abidjan. From Øyvind Steen, *I første rekke: Ingeniør F. Selmer A/S 1906–1981* (Oslo, 1981), 126.

Norwegian Siporex factory for a large-scale housing project in the then capital Abidjan. The initial deal, funded by the newly formed Norwegian development aid program NORAD, proposed the construction of two thousand homes.[8] The Norwegian development company Ingeniør F. Selmer AS joined Siporex to realize the project with the magical material that could meet every need of Côte d'Ivoire. The deal secured the stability of the company through an immediate production increase of nearly 20 percent.[9]

In order for the magic of Siporex to work, deals had to be made, meetings needed to take place, and contracts had to be signed; an entire apparatus invisible to the construction site was necessary in order to capitalize on opportunities and build diplomatic relations.

From Siporex to Abidjan

On October 20, 1969, a day with light precipitation, small waves, and moderate temperatures,[10] fifteen hundred cubic meters of Siporex set sail from the factory in Gullaug to Abidjan.[11] Over the next five years, a total of seventy thousand cubic meters of Siporex traveled from the small town in Norway to the former capital of Côte d'Ivoire.[12]

The factory in Gullaug contained its own port: Siporex Brygge. Throughout the 1960s and 1970s, the local Drammen newspaper *Fremtiden* contained a weekly column about the imports and exports of the various ports in the region. Week after week, entries on the Siporex port describe the distribution of the material—the raw ingredients coming in and the finished blocks going out:

> M/S Faxborg unloads 250 tons of lime from Faxe (February 24, 1971)
> M/S Dorit Lea is loaded with 1200 tons of Siporex for The Bahamas (April 13, 1971)
> M/S Leon Sif is loaded with 1230 tons of Siporex for Abidjan (June 18, 1973)

FØRST MED DET SISTE

Travel aktivitet ved Siporex-kaia i går da «Leon Sif» av København lastet bygnings-elementer for Elfenbenkysten. I forgrunnen ekspedisjonsleder Kjell Svennevig.

Fra Siporex til Abidjan

Ny skipslast med lettbetong-elementer ekspedert i går

En ny skipslast med lettbetong-elementer, den 11. i rekken, ble i går lastet ombord i «Leon Sif» av København ved Siporex-kaia i Lier. I går kveld stevnet skipet ut Dramsfjorden med 1.800 kubikkmeter elementer, som skal nyttes i forbindelse med en storstilet statlig boligutbygging på Elfenbenkysten.

Første skipslast gikk fra Siporex i november 1969 og foreløpig er det tale om å levere i alt 25.000 kubikkmeter Men ekspedisjonsleder Kjell Svennevig opplyser til Fremtiden at forhandlinger pågår om en større leveranse i tillegg til den som nå blir effektuert. I så fall vil det være meget velkomment for de Siporex-ansatte, ettersom planene går ut på at produksjonen i Lier gradvis skal trappes ned, og overføres til Hokksund. Dette kan bety en velkommen utsettelse for de mange som setter pris på sin arbeidsplass ved Siporex i Lier.

Det var i februar 1969 at Edelbetong A/S som ivaretar eksportsalget for Siporex-Ytong inngikk rammeavale med Elfenbenkystens regjering, og en snau måned senere var det første kontraktforholdet til 20 millioner kroner brakt i orden. Senere ble inngått avtale om ytterligere to leveranser, hver på ca. 20 millioner kroner.

Ut fra den motivering at bygningsmaterialene skulle være sikret riktig behandling gikk Siporex-Ytong fra første stund inn for at boligene skulle oppføres i norsk regi. Det ble derfor inngått avtale om at A/S Ing. Selmer skulle forestå utbyggingen.

Leilighetene som oppføres i hovedstaden Abidjan, varierer noe i størrelse — fra ett til fem værelser. Hustypen som ble valgt er i det vesentlige enetasjes atrium i rekker. Da boligfeltet blant annet mangler vei, er det ingen hittil som har flyttet inn i husene. Men arbeidet går ufortrødent videre. For tiden har A/S Ing. Selmer 11 norske ingeniører og arbeidsledere i sving, og dertil er hjelpearbeidere fra stedet engasjert.

Siporex-Ytongs engasjement omfatter også leveranse av pussmaterialer, maling, dører, vinduer, takplater osv. På en måte kan en derfor si at bedriften opptrer som en slags hovedentreprenør overfor oppdragsgiveren.

Figure 6. "From Siporex to Abidjan." *Fremtiden*, January 29, 1971.

M/S Ullgard unloads 900 tons of slag from Caen (November 10, 1973)
M/S Eyvind Sif is loaded with 1250 tons of Siporex for Bahrain (May 19, 1976)

Through these recordings, raw materials can be traced from Denmark, the United Kingdom, and France, with shipments going out to Germany, Liberia, Libya, and Côte d'Ivoire, to name a few.

Staking a Claim

The Siporex project in Abidjan was both elemental and urban. Atrium houses and larger apartment blocks were constructed according to an urban plan drawn by the Selmer engineers. The materials, the building plans, and the urban structure

Figures 7 & 8. Siporex housing project in Abidjan. From Øyvind Steen, *I første rekke: Ingeniør F. Selmer A/S 1906–1981* (Oslo, 1981), 129–30.

were all developed in Norway. The climate of Côte d'Ivoire was well suited for the material properties of Siporex.[13] Its insulative nature kept the heat out during the day while releasing stored heat at night, a complete reversal to its thermodynamic use in Norway. Additionally, termites, a major problem in the typical wooden houses in Abidjan, did not find Siporex especially appealing.

The larger apartment blocks were made of cast-in-place concrete; Siporex was used for exterior walls, insulation, and partition walls. The one-story atrium house created a courtyard free from the city streets, surrounded by interior rooms. Concrete slabs were cast directly on the ground with Siporex wall panels enclosing the space. Openings for windows and doors were based on the modules of the Siporex elements. Doors and windows were manufactured locally in a small factory, also operated by Selmer. To protect the Siporex from moisture and rot, it was clad in a cement-based plaster called Serponit, which is mentioned in a newspaper article, "Hønnefoss man is also part of operation Siporex."[14]

In 1974, Selmer established a local factory under the name Siporex Ivoire SA. Fifteen to twenty-five employees and their families from Norway were stationed in the former capital to run the operations that employed around two thousand people from Abidjan and its surroundings.[15]

The pragmatism of the material, combined with its simple recipe and the bureaucratic apparatus surrounding it—agreements, signed forms, and sanctions—enabled the construction of 12,500 homes. This led to the creation of three entire neighborhoods in Abidjan, a satellite city in Dimbokro (a rural textile-producing area), and generated a revenue of six hundred million Norwegian Kroner.[16] After ten years and with a considerable profit, Selmer left Côte d'Ivoire in search of new opportunities, in places such as Dakar, Senegal; Abu Dhabi, United Arab Emirates; and Mangalore, India.[17]

One in Eight

The rhetoric in Norwegian newspapers was that Norway, through its position as a wealthy European country, could use development aid to help save underdeveloped countries from poverty. Simultaneously, an attorney for NORAD went on record saying that "no one believes or expects Norwegian business to operate in developing countries, or anywhere else, if they are not making money."[18] Sources referred to the operation in Abidjan as the Norwegian colony or Selmer colony, underscoring the foothold of the Norwegians that were operating within a context that was only recently independent from France.[19] These same newspapers wrote about how exotic life was in Africa for the Norwegians living there, including an interview with one family telling of their pet crocodile that they had in a pool in their garden.[20] Headlines such as "Norwegians Sanitizing the Slums" or image captions such as "Slum areas in Abidjan with enormous child mortality rates and such serious crime that not even the police dared to enter have been replaced with atrium houses under Selmer's

Figure 9. Siporex advertisement. *Byggekunst* 48, no. 5 (1966).

direction" highlight the media's propensity to reinforce the narrative that Abidjan was a place to be developed by the Norwegians.[21] However, since these projects utilized Norwegian development aid for financing, it left very little room for the Ivorians to counter the proposals and modernistic vision put forth by Selmer.

From 1969 to 1975, Abidjan had a population increase of around 800,000 (from 400,000 to 1.2 million inhabitants).[22] In the same period, Siporex and Selmer completed homes for approximately 100,000 people, one in eight of the total population increase. Should a European company from thousands of miles away have been responsible for the daily lives of so many? Siporex found opportunity in the disruptions, offering itself as a ready solution in the wake of crisis and transformation. It positioned itself as an entire system that could meet any need; however, once the company left, what was left behind?

Figure 10. Siporex & Selmer, Abidjan, Côte d'Ivoire. Collage by Nicholas Coates and Eskil Buskov Selmer.

Siporex and Selmer

The Siporex factory in Abidjan closed its doors decades ago, but the brand and the names remain. Neighborhoods such as Sogefiha Siporex, Yopougon Siporex, and Yopougon Selmer, together with stores, streets, and schools, keep Siporex present:

> Glacier Siporex (ice cream shop)
> Imprimerie Siporex (print shop)

Skae transport Siporex (transport company)
Boulangerie de Siporex (bakery)
Siporex 1–8 (schools)
Siporex Mosque (place of workshop)
Pôle d'échanges Siporex (transportation company)
Siporex (travel agency)
Intersection Siporex (road intersection)
Epbomi Selmer (place of worship)
Carrefour Marché Selmer (market)
Sicomex Siporex (shopping mall)
Pharmacie Selmer (pharmacy)
Chez DEDE Selmer (restaurant)
La Grace Selmer (medical center)
Selmer Port Bouet (bus stop)

These instances, removed from the industrial history of the material, shine a light on the impact of the operation in Abidjan. The transmission of Siporex and Selmer into the local vocabulary in Abidjan parallels place names in Norway, Sweden, Finland, and Mexico. This was brought about by the material's widespread appeal, its marketing strength, and the invisible yet complex apparatus that facilitated its movement. These names make visible a hidden material: one deriving from a Swedish patent, produced in Norway, shipped by a Danish vessel, assembled by Ivorians, and plastered by a man from Hønefoss, Norway.

Biographies

Nicholas Coates is an assistant professor at the Oslo School of Architecture and Design (AHO) and holds a B.Arch from Virginia Tech and a M.Arch from AHO. His teaching focuses on preservation, transformation, and reuse, with courses that primarily concentrate on buildings and infrastructure from the 1950s onward. Coates is also a practicing architect who runs his own studio and has a particular interest in materials and tectonics, with projects encompassing a range of scales and mediums.

Eskil Buskov Selmer is an M.Arch student at the Oslo School of Architecture and Design. He has worked in the architectural offices of Arkitekt Espen Surnevik and Lie Øyen Arkitekter, and is currently an intern at Kastler Skjeseth Architects. He is interested in the transformation of existing buildings, the relevance of history and theory, and the incorporation of new buildings into specific contexts and local building traditions and climates.

Notes

1 In the article, the author describes the rapid development and expansion of AAC driven by exceptionally favorable material properties and how this coincided with an extreme shortage of building materials in Europe following World War II. Jos Cox, "100 Years of Autoclaved Aerated Concrete," *Cement Wapno Beton* 29, no. 2 (2004): 84–92. https://doi.org/10.32047/CWB.2024.29.2.1

2 Øyvind Steen, *I første rekke: Ingeniør F. Selmer A/S 1906–1981* (Oslo, 1981), 125–26.

3 Recipe based on articles printed in the local newspapers about the newly formed factory. *Drammens Tidende,* August 10, 1946, and March 8, 1947, *Fremtiden,* August 2, 1947, *Buskerud Blad,* April 10, 1948.

4 *Byggekunst,* vol. 48, no. 6 (1966): XIV; and *Bonytt: tidsskrift for hjeminnredning og brukskunst* 16, no. 1 (1956): XI.

5 Jürgen von Manger, "Über Siporex," year unknown. Translation of back cover of record (original German text: "Wir liefern Ihnen außer Schallplatten auch Platten für Dach + Decke + Wand").

[6] "Lene fikk 150 kilos baby i går, får navnet 'Siporex,'" *Bergens Arbeiderblad,* June 22, 1966, 5.
[7] "Storproduksjon av bygge-materialer i lett-betong," *Haugesunds Avis,* April 4, 1953, 5.
[8] Steen, *I første rekke: Ingeniør F. Selmer,* 125–26.
[9] "Lettbetong-elementer fra Lier blir boliger i Vest-Afrika," *Fremtiden,* October 18, 1969, 1.
[10] Norwegian Centre for Climate Services, Weather Statistics for October 20, 1969. seklima.met.no
[11] "Første del av ordre på 20 mill. fra Siporex til Elfenbenkysten," *Drammens Tidene og Buskeruds Blad,* October 18, 1969, 1.
[12] Steen, "Selmer-Abidjan," *F. Selmer Nytt,* April 11, 1975, 18.
[13] Frithjof Gartmann, "Dalen først med lettbetong," in *Sement i Norge 100 år* (Oslo: Norcem A.S, 1990), 205.
[14] "Også Hønefoss-mann er med i 'operasjon Siporex,'" *Drammens Tidende og Buskerud Blad,* March 22, 1973, 10.
[15] Steen, *I første rekke,* 126.
[16] "Norcem skal være med å bygge ett tusen hus," *Fremtiden,* December 2, 1975, 11; and Steen, *I første rekke,* 126.
[17] Steen, 126–27.
[18] "Et eksempel på praktisk utviklingshjelp," *Arbeiderbladet,* February 22, 1975, 3.
[19] "Et eksempel på praktisk utviklingshjelp"; and Steen, "Selmer-Abidjan," *F. Selmer Nytt,* April 11, 1975, cover.
[20] Ole Jacob Bjønness-Jacobsen, "Med Krokodille i hagen," *Stavanger Aftenblad,* February 22, 1975, 9.
[21] Bjønness-Jacobsen, "Nordmenn sanerer slummen i Abidjan," *Stavanger Aftenblad,* February 18, 1975, 1.
[22] "Tusenvis av norske boliger," *Norges Handels og Sjøfartstidende,* April 11, 1978, 5.

Lake Verea

Artist Intervention

One to One: Palace of Fine Arts, Mexico City

The vertigo caused by the monumental nature of the Palacio de Bellas Artes in Mexico City prevents us from grasping its elements at detail. The times and styles that blend are contrasting, intriguing, and tell the story of the construction of modern Mexico. The building was planned under Porfirio Díaz's dictatorial regime, which saw Italy and France as models of high culture and avant-garde. Its construction was interrupted for nearly twenty years with the outbreak of the Mexican Revolution, which lasted from 1910 to 1921. The arrested ruin, left halfway through its construction, awoke from its slumber in a postrevolutionary Mexico that had broken away from the country for which it had been originally designed. The building, originally conceived in the early 1900s as a National Theatre, designed by Italian architect Adamo Boari, built with Carrara marble followed the art nouveau style and standards of European capitals. Finished in 1934 by Mexican architect Nicolás Mariscal, the Palace resumed in an art deco style, with black and red, locally sourced marble interiors—in a new country that shaped the construction of its postrevolutionary identity by returning to pre-Hispanic roots. When finished, the Palace housed the National Theatre, National Museum of Art, and Folk Art Collections.

One to One / Bellas Artes highlights fragments from both periods of construction. The quest is to photograph fragments and use them as words with which we build a discourse that addresses—in a physical confrontation—the idea of monumentality, fragility, and time. We aim to favor a close, intimate gaze that controls the vertigo, brings the inaccessible closer, and portrays details of what we cannot see without the help of cameras and zoom lenses. The selection of these fragments follows our personal impulse in the search for details that captivate us. We understand the Palace as a living entity, with cracks, dust, objects, and elements that come from various places around the world. We pay homage to the countless minds and hands that shaped and built the place throughout its history.

Photography allows us to play with perspective, perception, and interpretation. The portrayed objects are right there in plain view; however, it is difficult to focus on them. The context limits the interpretation we seek to shape, so we decontextualize the fragments and let them shine on their own. We frame and measure each detail, and then carefully print them in their exact size. Between the physical object and our portrait,

Future Anterior
Volume XXII, Numbers 1–2
Summer / Winter 2025

the difference lies in its materiality and volume; its Cartesian coordinates—height and width—are analogous to reality. Every portrait is accompanied by a personal interpretation and a tracking of provenance-related data such as origin, author, and materials. We engage in a conceptual and artistic game in which we take on the role of archaeologists of modernism. We dig into the notion of provenance—of the materials, manufacture, and the inspiration behind the designs. We examine the fragments and reinterpret them in a personal and poetic way, as a crosscutting notion of time and space.

Figure 1. Lake Verea, *One to One, Measure the Column,* 2019, 400 × 240 cm, Lake Verea Collection.

Provenance Data

Walton Goody and Cripps, *One to One, Measure the Column*, Veined marble, Terrace of the west façade of the Palace of Fine Arts, Italy, 1907–1911.

Interpretation

Between 1907 and 1911, Walton Goody and Cripps provided the following works: twenty-three columns and two pilasters, 5.7 meters tall, built in two pieces for the three porticos; twenty-seven columns, 7 meters tall, built in three pieces for the terraces of the side façades; and two monolithic columns for the entrance portico on the main façade, all made from Carrara white veined marble. One to one, we measured and measured ourselves with this column. Together, we sought to understand its dimension, color, smell, and temperature.

Figure 2. Lake Verea, *Crystal Volcano,* 2019, 202 × 180 cm, Lake Verea Collection.

Provenance Data

Tiffany Studios, *Crystal Volcano*, Steel frame, opalescent Favrile glass mosaics, zinc background, bronze structures. Main Hall of the Theatre of the Palace of Fine Arts. New York, United States, 1911.

Interpretation

The theater curtain, made by Tiffany Studio in New York, was transported in 1911 aboard the steamship Monterrey to Mexico. Made with thousands of opalescent Favrile glass pieces, each one has a different shape and color, framed in a bronze structure that simulates a large window, and creates a panoramic view of the Valley of Mexico. Italian architect Adamo Boari designed a double-walled steel frame for the theater curtain. The side facing the stage is covered with corrugated sheets, while the side facing the hall is covered by an opalescent glass mosaic masterpiece carefully manufactured by Tiffany House in New York City from an anonymous design sent from Mexico. The structure also serves as rigid wall that rises like a hatch to protect spectators in case of a fire. We capture the fragment that portrays the summit of the Popocatépetl volcano at sunset. The variety and quantity of shapes and colors in the opalescent glass offer an hyperrealistic vision of a moment frozen in time. The fragment depicts the imposing volcano, almost volumetric—the ideal view from an imaginary perspective.

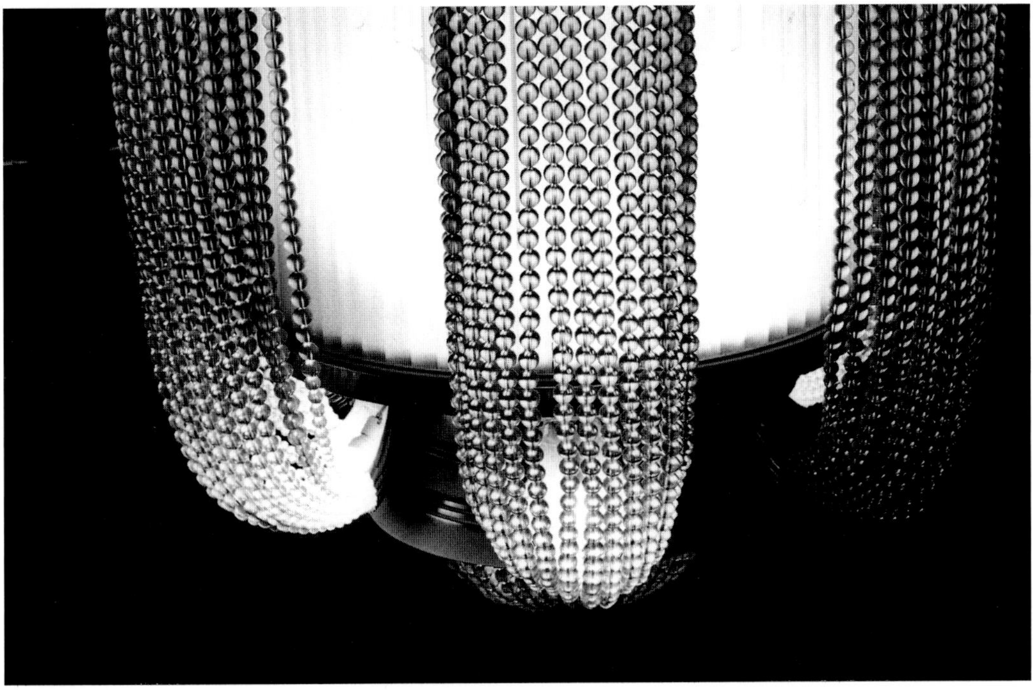

Figure 3. Lake Verea, *Crystal Chandelier*, 2019. 150 × 222 cm. Lake Verea Collection.

Provenance Data

Edgar Brandt House, *Crystal Chandelier*, Crystal, metal, and electrical installation, National Hall of the Palace of Fine Arts, Paris, France, 1933.

Interpretation

The three chandeliers in the National Hall are in the art deco style, a style proposed by architect Federico Mariscal for all the interior details of the Palace. Following a decree issued by President Álvaro Obregón, areas and halls initially intended to host parties would instead be used as a museum, library, and conference hall. The chandelier depicted in this image was built and designed in Paris by the Edgar Brandt House. Since the change in use of the hall, the chandelier was forgotten and hidden behind museum walls. Once a marvel of modernity, its electric light is no longer seen as such. Today, its light is considered harmful to the preservation of works of art. Its mission as a source of illumination and witness to the galas has been lost, and now it is a beautiful, forgotten, hidden, and obsolete object.

Figure 4. Lake Verea, *Two Tlálocs in Metal,* 2019, 120 × 175 cm, MoMA NY Collection.

Provenance Data

Edgar Brandt House, *Two Tlálocs in Metal*, Zinc and Bronze. Main entrance door to the Main Hall of the Palace of Fine Arts, Paris, France, 1933.

Interpretation

For their integration into the door, the representation of Tláloc was redesigned and adapted to the art deco style, as it is possible to identify differences in its qualities compared to the Mesoamerican expressions of the Classic period. Thus, the final details included a strong incorporation of Mexican elements, even though the work was carried out by Edgar Brant House in Paris. What fascinates us about this fragment are the marks of use. Through them, we can understand the many years in which this door has been opened and closed. When the door is closed, the motif of the two golden Tlálocs on the silver background gives it an appearance of pre-Hispanic-modern fortress, worthy of a science fiction movie. Tláloc was redesigned and adapted to the art deco style, which marked the end of the Palace's construction, symbolizing the highest stylistic avant-garde of the time.

Two Tlálocs in 1930s fashion!

Figure 5. Lake Verea, *Empty Pedestal*, 2019, 95 × 142.5 cm, Lake Verea Collection.

Provenance Data

Unidentified, *Empty Pedestal*, Carrara Veined Marble, n.d., West side terrace of the Palace of Fine Arts.

Interpretation

This fragment portrays the enigma of emptiness. If a pedestal lacks a sculpture, does it remain a pedestal, or does it transform into minimalist sculpture?

Figure 6. Lake Verea, *Metal Leaves, 2019*, 249 × 163.42 cm, MoMA NY, Lake Verea Collection.

Provenance Data

Luis Romero, *Metal Leaves*, Iron, Side terrace grilles of the Palace of Fine Arts, Mexico City, 1932.

Interpretation

While the Palace was on halt, in 1920 the Mexican Luis Romero won a competition to create fourteen grilles. The fragment we have recovered is of modest size and could easily go unnoticed due to the naturalism of its craftsmanship and its visible simplicity. The grille is an iconic example of the European art nouveau in a Mexican version. The door is composed of two parts, which we assume as a single piece, just like us.

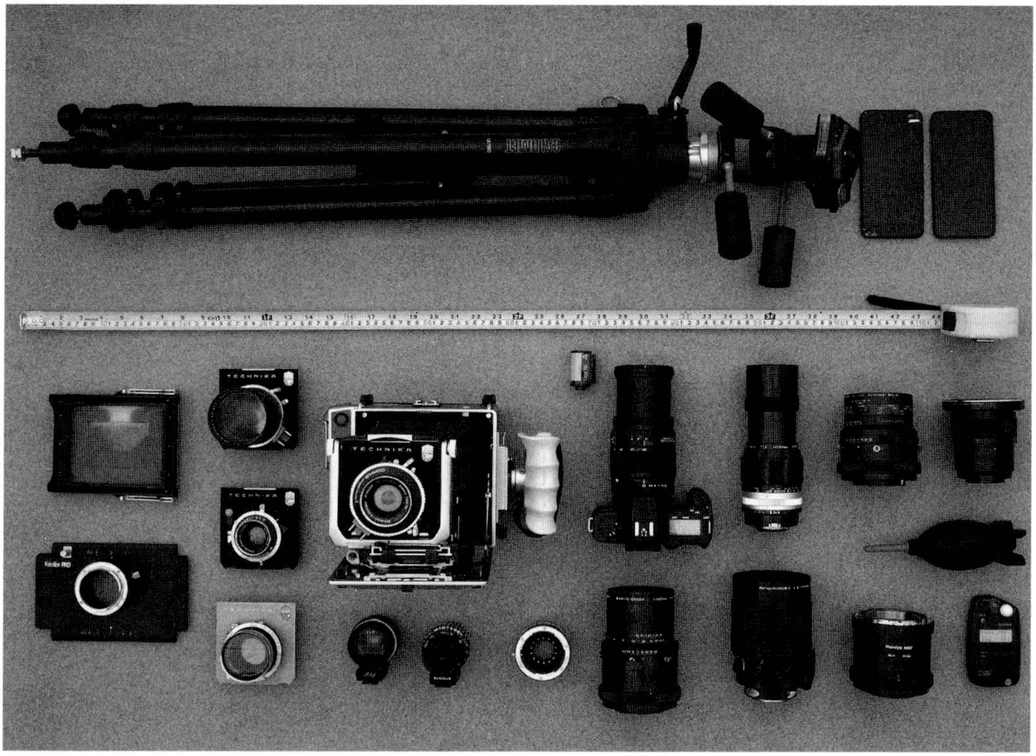

Figure 7. Lake Verea, *Work Tools, 2019,* 93 × 125 cm, Lake Verea Collection.

Interpretation

This is the portrait of the objects we used to create the series: Technica V Linhof, Germany with Schneider lenses 270 mm, 180 mm, 135 mm. Sony A7RIII digital camera, Sony remote shutter, Sony memory cards 2018. Analog-digital adapters. Mamiya RZ67 lenses, Contax Carl Zeiss lens, Nikon 500 mm, Sekonic light meter, Japan 2010; 5 meter measuring tape, Mexico 2018; Manfrotto tripod, Italy 2010; Rocket-shaped dust blower, China 2018; Two iPhone 7s.

Meet our allies in the adventures of exploration and portraiture of the fragments. The sum and combination of the equipment resulted in the ability to bring a close-up view that surpasses what the human eye can see.

Biography

Lake Verea is a queer artist duo formed in 2005 by Francisca Rivero-Lake Cortina and Carla Verea Hernández from Mexico City. Their interdisciplinary practice blends expanded photography with installation, textiles, performance, and video. They explore themes of memory, portraiture, modern architecture, and artists' archives, often questioning authorship and identity. Using both analog and digital cameras, including antique models and iPhones, they create intimate portraits of architecture and objects. Notable projects include *Paparazza Moderna,* which captures iconic modernist houses, and *Uno a Uno Bellas Artes,* focusing on fragments of the Palacio de Bellas Artes. Their work has been exhibited internationally and is part of collections such as MoMA, Museo Jumex, and Museo Tamayo.

Book Review
Håvard Breivik-Khan

Architecture of Migration: The Dadaab Refugee Camps and Humanitarian Settlement

Anooradha Iyer Siddiqi
Duke University Press, 2024

The history of the fraught relationship between space, aid, and control is well documented across the humanities and social sciences. Central to this discourse is the infamous camp, which evokes a global imagery of rows of tents in desolate environments. Criticism of the camp in displacement-oriented theory largely centers on the production of spatial conditions that perpetuate the inhumane treatment of displaced populations—and, by extension, a reproach of the actors providing aid, whether international organizations or state entities. The spatial logic of the refugee camp and its architecture evokes a history of loss, hardship, violence, and a sudden change in human status—or, in the words of Anooradha Iyer Siddiqi, "a stratification of personhood."[1] Yet these spaces frame the daily lives of millions, and the *camp,* Siddiqi writes in *Architecture of Migration: The Dadaab Refugee Camps and Humanitarian Settlement,* is "a prolonged event in a history, marked through architecture,"[2] set in Dadaab camp, a refugee complex established in 1991, when refugees fleeing the civil war in Somalia started to cross the border into Kenya.

The subject of the spatiality of displacement management in scholarly research has, over the past few decades, migrated from the camp—described by anthropologist Michel Agier as "extra-territorial out-places made by humanitarian organizations for a section of the world population who are deemed undesirable and vulnerable"—to the more intangible phenomena of *urban displacement* and other *non-camp settings.*[3] Nevertheless, the critique of the camp also extends to environments beyond the physical boundaries of confined spaces and rigid mandates tied to a linear temporal axis encompassing gradations of humanitarian response and development interventions. As human geographer Cathrine Brun notes, "the international refugee regime has not come up with an alternative to camps that includes social and legal protection: even forced migrants in a non-camp solution cannot escape the camp-logic of care and control, temporary lives and exclusion."[4]

Attached to the scholarly critique of displacement management is the "prominent silence"—as phrased by geographer Romola Sanyal—in urban studies on the question of refugees: "refugee spaces are emerging as quintessential geographies of the modern, yet their intimate and everyday spatialities remain underexplored."[5] Architect and historian Andrew Herscher—a longtime collaborator of Siddiqi—points out that refugees are conspicuously missing from the literature on displacement and architecture, though recent scholarship on the architecture of refugees in camps and cities has begun the important work of historicizing the refugee as architect.[6] Siddiqi makes a solid contribution to the writing of this history.

On the other hand, urban theory is not overly concerned with the experiences of spatial professionals involved in creating these so-called extraterritorial everyday spaces. The displacement management discourse is primarily oriented toward system-level critique of global mechanisms and mandates, and thus, implicitly, also toward the individuals working within these organizations. Generally speaking, theorists within displacement management critique are neither spatial designers nor planners, nor are they aid workers. The object of their criticism, nevertheless, frequently concerns the spatial output of displacement management—that is, camps, but also emergency shelters, which are typically described as objects contextually detached from their surroundings.[7] Together, *the camp* and *the shelter* constitute a prominent symbol of the international community's shortcomings in preventing and responding to displacement. There is, however, a cyclical history of emerging and fading interactions between the two domains of architecture and displacement management—an evolution that Siddiqi traces through an eclectic account of architectural contributions to displacement management, marked by equally varied architectural ambitions.

Siddiqi's *Architecture of Migration* is indeed a critique of the planned refugee camp, the emergency shelter, and the mechanisms that produce these living and life conditions. This, however, is not the central takeaway of her thorough study of the Dadaab camp, presented here as the result of research spanning more than a decade, including multiple stays and various professional affiliations. The camp, as a concept, but more importantly in this book as a built typology, is used to offer a perspective grounded in the lived experiences of both refugees and aid workers. Phrased as questions Siddiqi sets out to explore how a refugee camp reveals insights into displacement, survival, and human resilience, and how the architecture of migration generates knowledge and awareness that extend beyond the camp itself. She invites the reader to dwell on displacement terminology. Her mission is to generate both a new language with cues from poetics rather than bureaucratic terms, and new ways of speaking about Dadaab, and by extension, other worlds belonging to migrants.[8]

Siddiqi's conversations with inhabitants and aid workers in the Dadaab camp are used to illustrate that camps and other displacement settlements are not ahistorical places without architecture; they also reveal the connections between space and power. "The experiences of these refugees underlie the making of this significant environment," Siddiqi explains, stating that she sees refugees as architects, and their work as an architecture of migration.[9] A central question is therefore what architecture is and what it does—for better or worse—but also who gets to be called an architect: "If the term *architecture* implies an aesthetic approach that misunderstands or disregards political and humanitarian exigency, then this book begins with an argument for a different urgency, in which aesthetics and politics are inextricably entangled."[10]

Siddiqi's treatment of the elusive qualities of architecture—the ever-present but often unspoken concept of *aesthetics*—is particularly interesting in displacement contexts, and a particularly compelling aspect of this book. Not because the term itself is undertheorized in scholarly literature, but because it is a powerful tool, always present in the relationship between architecture and politics, perhaps even more so in displacement contexts. From this perspective, questions about the spatial and social expertise of the relatively small group of professionals with significant impact on people's lives globally, the humanitarian site planner and shelter architect, remain undertheorized. More importantly, however, these discussions are largely absent from the built environment components of displacement management policy and practice. Siddiqi provides a strong contribution to this discourse.

Built structures in displacement settlements are closely tied to the internal governance of these spaces in ways that are both immediate and traceable. A 2011 conversation between Siddiqi and Isnina Ali Rage, an inhabitant of Dadaab since 1991 and later Chairlady of the Ifo section, illustrates this point. Rage recounts how the election process for her political position was shaped by the camp's spatial layout, with rounds of voting organized according to its divisions into blocks and sections. Humanitarian site planners have long followed global templates for camp design, such as those in the *UNHCR Emergency Handbook,* first published in 1982. Architect and scholar Manuel Herz argues that most of the several hundred UNHCR-run camps worldwide can be traced back to the twenty-page chapter "Site Selection, Planning and Shelter."[11] As Siddiqi reflects, "As we conversed, it became difficult to distinguish story from setting; the twists in the Chairlady's narrative mapped directly onto the planned blocks and sections where they took place."[12]

In the local and regional context of Dadaab, Siddiqi draws parallels between the spatial principles of humanitarian settlement—or the camp—and colonial approaches to land use and tenure in East Africa, which favored the sedentarization of nomadic and pastoral forms of living.[13] Through images and richly detailed textual descriptions, Siddiqi recounts the spatial clashes between the mobile architecture of the East African *tuqul*—a dome made of bent wood and textiles—and the visual modernity of the refugee camp, which includes satellite dishes, aeronautic fleets, tarmac, aluminum and polyvinyl chloride water storage towers, and hydraulic extraction machinery, though not modernist in the stylistic sense.[14] The refugee camp—and more specifically its alleged placelessness—has indeed been compared to critiques of modernist architecture and urban planning within spatial displacement theory.[15] The intertwining of aesthetics and politics in the humanitarian archive is recounted by Siddiqi in the context of Dadaab as a curious entanglement of military models and town planning, shaped by modernist approaches to standardization and flexibility implemented in both European and African cities. She further writes, "While humanitarian spatiality at Dadaab has prolonged the existence of a political space evacuated of civic belonging, producing permanent ephemerality, more momentous than the political crisis is the array of aesthetic workings that brought this form of settlement into being in the first place."[16]

Siddiqi claims that the paradoxes of sedentarization, emergency, and land also manifest architecturally, at the scale of the building unit.[17] The construction and the social and cultural significance of the aforementioned tuqul is highlighted by Siddiqi as notable for many reasons, including its connection to gender identity. The tuqul was, and continues to be, designed and built by women. This typology has occasionally housed aid workers alongside refugees, is used by urban refugees from other parts of Africa, and, according to Siddiqi, has become the architectural symbol of the Dadaab refugee camps.[18]

Siddiqi contrasts these types of domestic structures with the shelter, which she claims is the endgame of intervention in emergency relief by professional spatial practitioners, and she questions whether these practitioners have an awareness of domesticity. Siddiqi asserts that professional spatial practitioners involved in camp-making often treat privacy, interiority, and comfort as luxuries that refugees neither need nor deserve. Yet displaced people continue to create domestic spaces that nurture emotional, social, and physical life. Based on these observations, Siddiqi turns to the term *domesticity* as it "offers a theory that moves beyond consigning displacement to the domain of lack."[19] Domesticity is an affective, poetic, and existential form of expertise that, she argues, informs competence on shelter, including professional competence.[20] The concept of domesticity introduced here is a key term for recognizing the architectural contributions of refugees, framing domesticity as a form of knowledge. A theory of domesticity is needed to understand the architecture of the shelter as well as the camp, as it enacts the deeper practice of inhabitation, she writes.[21]

Furthermore, to connect architectural expertise with homemaking in emergencies, Siddiqi draws on a theory of *insurgent domesticities,* exemplified by the spatial disobedience of Dadaab's inhabitants. She develops this claim through the account of her conversation with Shamso Abdullahi Farah, a resident of the Ifo part of Dadaab, who was also involved with developing "domesticity knowledge" for the Norwegian Refugee Council's (NRC) and its shelter program in Dadaab.[22] Siddiqi attributes Norwegian government funding, the extra time that allowed the NRC to produce "a strange, carefully detailed, and well-made object" that considered Dadaab's extreme environmental factors. As in many other low-income displacement contexts, the, relatively speaking, high shelter standards built by international organizations led to conflicts with the host community members, many of them living in homes of lower material standards, also in the Dadaab context. This aesthetic conflict also extended to other donor organizations, who viewed the high shelter costs as inappropriate. This view excludes domesticity and inhabitation.

Siddiqi accounts for her extensive architectural study of the humanitarian archive, one that "contributes to a complex landscape of historical evidence, consisting of the work of institutionally trained architects and autodidactic designers and builders of the environment together."[23] Her focus is on "the conventional practice of seeing through visual materials" that, she rightfully points out, have not before been presented as a coherent archival corpus.[24] Assembling documents for an architectural study of Dadaab in this way, could be attributed to Siddiqi's training and professional experience as an architect, which is not a common background from scholars in displacement-oriented theory.

The archival studies also include a historical overview of how the camp developed through the years and explain how tensions between emergency relief and development shaped the early phases of humanitarian intervention in Dadaab. The shift from a transitional to a protracted condition is highlighted by Siddiqi's recount of internal memos of international organizations. However, the sociospatial complexities of the region, including sedentarized nomadic groups, also contributed to tensions both within the camp and with the host community. The historical account of this region and the question of how spatial planning can accommodate situations in constant flux is increasingly pressing, as climate change triggers mass displacement and shifts migration patterns. Scholarship like Siddiqi's teases this out. How to address this in a future-forward and practical sense, however, remains a question.

Toward the end of the book, Siddiqi focuses on the component architectures of the Dadaab camp by providing a historical account of the global history of displacement design in parallel—ranging from well-known examples such as Le Corbusier, Buckminster Fuller, and Alvar Aalto's design contributions in the inter- and post–world wars, to Shigeru Ban's paper tubes in the 1990s—alongside the shelter expertise built up internally within the humanitarian system, a process that eventually led to the specialization of shelter design and camp planning by certain aid organizations, with the NRC as a leading example. This overview also includes discussions about aid organizations that would not necessarily be seen as shelter actors, but whose operations depend not only on built structures but also on the distribution of "artifacts"—for example, life-saving medical kits; exemplified by Médecins Sans Frontières (MSF), one of the aid organizations labeled as "design as infrastructure," contributing to the "component architecture" of Dadaab and many other camps. Siddiqi highlights, among many other camp components, the recognizable *tarp*—extensively used in displacement contexts—to express a concern "with the placement of systematically manufactured emergency objects within a regime of signature practices."[25] This concern can be read into a broader discussion Siddiqi brings up, on the complicated balancing act that comes with building in crises, here elegantly summarized in two sentences: "The aesthetic burden on these architectures [shelters in Dadaab] was to communicate ephemerality, to act as signifiers of impermanence. Architectural signs of permanence threatened societies and governments, complicating the activity of relief donors and aid organizations, irritating host communities, and reifying the displacement of people from home."[26]

At a theoretical level, Siddiqi's findings are undeniably significant. The alternation between more accessible sections, such as conversations and descriptions of spatial conditions, and longer theoretical passages filled with scholarly references allows readers to engage with the book on multiple levels and in various ways. This structure, however, also has its limitations. The 433-page volume with its rich and at times dense language creates the impression that skipping even a sentence might mean missing crucial information. While demonstrating the author's vast knowledge, it may affect the book's accessibility to practitioners in both displacement management and the built environment who would otherwise benefit greatly from Siddiqi's work. Nevertheless, these potential limitations must be accepted in light of the value of firsthand insights that seek to explain the complexities of the architecture of migration.

This book is the result of many years of research, in the so-called field, in humanitarian parlance, and in archival studies. Siddiqi's ambition to replace bureaucratic terms with a language drawn from poetry does not necessarily make the book more accessible. What it does accomplish, however, is to elevate the lived experiences and contributions of the people of Dadaab, rethink conventional displacement language, and fulfill the aim of honoring those whose lives and work have situated them within the humanitarian system as refugees or laborers.

Biography
Håvard Breivik-Khan is an architect, researcher, and expert in international emergency planning and response. As a member of the Norwegian Refugee Council's (NRC) emergency capacity NORCAP, he has been deployed to government ministries in Moldova and Romania, and United Nations agencies in Haiti, Nepal, North Macedonia, Hungary, and at UN Headquarters in New York. He is the co-creator of the *In Transit Studio* (2016–2023) at the Oslo School of Architecture and Design, established in collaboration with NORCAP, which bridges the fields of architecture, urbanism, and global displacement. He is currently an adjunct assistant professor at Columbia University's Graduate School of Architecture, Planning and Preservation (GSAPP).

Notes

[1] Anooradha Iyer Siddiqi, *Architecture of Migration: The Dadaab Refugee Camps and Humanitarian Settlement* (Duke University Press, 2024), 52.
[2] Siddiqi, *Architecture of Migration,* 1.
[3] Michel Agier, *Managing the Undesirables: Refugee Camps and Humanitarian Government* (Polity Press, 2011), 4.
[4] Cathrine Brun, "The Place of the Camp in Protracted Displacement," in *The Routledge Handbook of Place,* ed. T. Edensor, T, A. Kalandides, and U. Kothari (Routledge), 8.
[5] Romola Sanyal, "Urbanizing Refuge: Interrogating Spaces of Displacement: Urbanizing Refugee Spaces," *International Journal of Urban and Regional Research* 38, no. 2 (March 2014): 5, 10. https://doi.org/10.1111/1468-2427.12020.
[6] Andrew Herscher, *Displacements: Architecture and Refugee* (Sternberg Press, 2017), 5, 10.
[7] Håvard Breivik-Khan, "The Concept of Place in Displacement Management," *Nordic Journal of Architectural Research* 34, no. 1 (2022): 119–45.
[8] Siddiqi, *Architecture of Migration,* xvi.
[9] Siddiqi, 2.
[10] Siddiqi, 4.
[11] Manuel Herz, ed., *From Camp to City: Refugee Camps of the Western Sahara* (Lars Müller, 2013).
[12] Siddiqi, *Architecture of Migration,* 6.
[13] Siddiqi, 48, 100.
[14] Siddiqi, 99.
[15] See for example political scientist Lionel Beehner's article, written some five years after the Syrian war broke out, which draws on his qualitative research from the Za'atari refugee camp in Jordan, and on how middle-class Syrians spatially rebel against uniformity of the "modernist" camp. Lionel Beehner, "Are Syrians Do-It-Yourself Refugees Outliers or Examples of a New Norm?" *Journal of International Affairs* 68, no. 2 (Spring 2015): 157–75. https://search.proquest.com/docview/1679734106?accountid=26310.
[16] Siddiqi, *Architecture of Migration,* 200.
[17] Siddiqi, 130.
[18] Siddiqi, 135.
[19] Siddiqi, 146.
[20] Siddiqi, 146.
[21] Siddiqi, 172.
[22] For full transparency: I have been a roster member of NORCAP, part of the Norwegian Refugee Council (NRC) since 2010, and, as a site planning expert, been deployed to many of the United Nations agencies mentioned in Siddiqi's book. I have not, however, worked as a site planner in East Africa or directly with the NRC Shelter team.
[23] Siddiqi, *Architecture of Migration,* 188.
[24] Siddiqi, 210.
[25] Siddiqi, 268.
[26] Siddiqi, 258.

Things That Move: A Hinterland in Architectural History

Tim Anstey
MIT Press, 2024

Traditional accounts of architectural history rooted in monumentality, stability, and individual authorship are increasingly under revision. A growing body of scholarship is reimagining the field through frameworks that unsettle canonical narratives and foreground movement, mediation, and material flows. This historiographical shift has taken many forms. Accounts of portable or mobile structures, narrated through colonial, military, humanitarian, or technological histories, have redirected attention from monumental to transient aspects of architecture and urbanism.[1] Significant contributions have emerged from studies of architecture's circulation through various media: from professional journals to plaster casts.[2] In other cases, portability has been examined as a tool for both the preservation and destruction of monuments, closely tied to the formation of heritage regimes.[3] Finally, building materials histories foregrounded cities' resource and energy hinterlands, tracing how extractive flows and labor shape architectural form and spatial politics.[4] Collectively, these diverse strands point to an expanding historiographical project: one that decentres permanence and fixity, emphasizing instead the fluid, temporal, and logistic qualities of the built environment.

Tim Anstey's book *Things That Move: A Hinterland in Architectural History* not only engages fluently with these existing currents but also pushes their implications further, tracing architecture's moving parts (both literally and conceptually) across time, geography, and disciplinary terrain. Rather than presenting a straightforward history of portable structures or mobile typologies, Anstey advances a more expansive argument: that both architecture and the architectural profession have always been in motion, and that writing their history requires grappling with their unstable, mediated, and often overlooked supports. Defined through the notion of a "hinterland," this capacious yet neglected archive of architectural acts and objects encompasses, among other examples, treatises on naval architecture, elaborate engineering systems for transporting obelisks and domes, illustrated newspaper supplements, and even the itinerant library book-retrieval system. Anstey demonstrates that this hinterland is not simply a repository of marginal practices or sources but a broader epistemology in which mobility is as fundamental as stasis. Divided into three parts, "Cargoes 1530–1910," "Dispatches 1450–1590," and

"Vehicles 1890–1960," the book weaves together maritime, imperial, and modern historical episodes and themes. In doing so, architecture emerges as a discipline that is closely linked to the technologies of construction, movement, and representation, stretching far beyond the drawing board or the catalog of a designer's completed projects.

In the introduction and part II (specifically in chapters 4, "Dealing with Decorum," and 5, "Domenico Fontana and the Vatican Obelisk"), Anstey scrutinizes the disciplinary boundaries of architecture by engaging with varied definitions of the architectural profession as articulated by Late Roman Republic and Renaissance authors. He begins by recalling Vitruvius's tripartite categorization of architectural practice: *aedificatio,* the art of assembling and stabilizing materials into enduring structures; *gnomicae* (from *gnomon,* the vertical element of a sundial), the translation of celestial movements into terrestrial orientation and temporal order; and *machinatio,* the design and deployment of mechanical systems for construction, transport, or hydraulics. Anstey then highlights how later treatises, notably Leon Battista Alberti's *De re aedificatoria* (1452), privileged aedificatio, associated more with structures in the state of relative permanence, marginalizing the other two domains. It was around then, the author suggests, that the notion of architectural fixity became dominant in the European historiographical tradition, eclipsing a broader, more dynamic conception of architectural labor. This shift is particularly visible in the sidelining of machinatio as an architectural concern. Anstey seeks to recover this forgotten genealogy, positioning logistic ingenuity as integral to architectural history. He does so through the analysis of Domenico Fontana's treatise *Della transportatione dell'obelisco Vaticano e delle fabriche di Sisto V* (1590) on re-erecting the Vatican obelisk in a new location in Rome. Anstey emphasizes that Fontana did not design a new structure in this case; he orchestrated the movement of an existing one, for which he received much praise. Therefore, the architectural value of this work, the book highlights, lay not in authorship of form but in the successful organization of logistics, labor, and technology. These challenge prevailing paradigms of creativity and authorship by suggesting that architecture may be less (or not exclusively) about designing buildings than about conjuring movement of objects and matter in space. The implications for contemporary architectural thinking are profound, especially in an era shaped by logistics and the pursuit of more sustainable modes of material procurement. In advancing these fields, as *Things That Move* hints, architecture may no longer be defined by what stands still.

To further denaturalize certain stereotypes about architectural work, chapter 4 historicizes the evolving notion of "decorum," which has long been perceived as one of the central concerns for architects to grapple with. Anstey's historiographical rereading of the term, drawing on Cicero and the oratory tradition, reminds us that decorum originally signified more than mere ornamentation or stylistic propriety; rather, it encompassed a broader disciplinary logic that regulated behavior, professionalism, and the scope of legitimacy—the art of "fitting in" or being appropriate. As demonstrated here, the notion of decorum evolved to become a self-reinforcing mechanism through which architects could assert social authority. This tradition, while ostensibly abstract, had real consequences for the historical development of architectural identity. The architectural ideal of decorum, rather than encouraging systemic critique or experimentation, insisted on cultivation of a skill of "fitting" into existing rhetorical and visual conventions.

Part I, "Cargoes," comprises chapters 1 to 3 and focuses on the histories of naval architecture, imperial interiors, and the transportation (and its representation) of historical monuments. These chapters effectively expand architectural historiography into thematic domains traditionally considered peripheral. Chapter 1, "Architecture Aslant," examines the reciprocal influences between naval and terrestrial architectures across the Swedish, French, and British imperial formations. Through a close reading of naval architecture treatises, particularly Fredrik Henrik af Chapman's *Architectura Navalis Mercatoria* (1768), Anstey shows how shipbuilding developed distinct representational systems, with drawings that layered external appearance, internal organization, and intended performance on water into a single projection, offering a more dynamic vision of built form. This is contrasted with contemporaneous terrestrial architectural elevations and plans, which typically separate these dimensions. The book demonstrates that naval and terrestrial built environments were likewise connected via figures such as the painter Charles Le Brun, who moved seamlessly between embellishing ships and imperial palaces. This highlights the symbolic power of naval architecture and the interconnectedness of terrestrial and floating structures in the architecture of empire. But beyond symbolism, vessels also directly served empires' colonial ambitions: they transported goods and people but also styles, technologies, and social hierarchies to far-flung locations.

From the sea back to imperial centers, chapter 2, "Economies of the Interior," traces the emergence of architectural definition of interior among European elites during the early nineteenth century. Anstey argues that these spaces should not be viewed in isolation from but as accumulations of global extraction networks in which their owners actively participated.

"Interior," then, is understood in two ways: as both a physical space within the home and a hinterland forged by imperial trade or outright plunder. Exotic materials and motifs evoking distant times and places, often featured in elite interiors, indexed the colonial origins of wealth. Anstey presents these interiors as both architectural and geopolitical spaces adorned with Persian carpets or rendered in marble became screens through which the wealthy could encounter and aestheticize the imperial periphery. The chapter also raises a broader concern: how architecture functions as a surface for imperial fantasy, mediated through orientalist aesthetics and designed to obscure the violence of extraction.

Chapter 3, "Moving Large Things about in the Nineteenth Century," examines the transportation (and representation thereof) of the ancient Egyptian obelisk known as "Cleopatra's Needle" from Alexandria to London. As Anstey shows, the logistics of moving such monuments became public spectacles and media events, reflecting a broader nineteenth-century fascination with engineering feats. Yet this fascination also shaped cultural imaginaries of permanence and its vulnerability. Newspapers, engravings, and lithographs circulated images of architecture in transit or at risk: flooded monuments, crumbling bridges, relocated obelisks. Anstey foregrounds the notion of "hiatus" to describe these moments of disruption, where a monument or an infrastructural object is suspended between states: displaced, unsettled, or in motion. In the illustrated press, architecture thus appeared not as a static object but as a node within networks of representation, movement, and affect.

Part III ("Vehicles") shifts toward the twentieth century and the subjective experience of architectural and urban spaces. Chapter 6, "The Tenant's Furniture," traces the relocation of the Warburg Institute from Hamburg to various sites in London, focusing on how the migration of books, furniture, and classification systems shaped memory and intellectual experience in each new location. In Anstey's account, the Warburg Library becomes a mobile architecture for knowledge production. Its physical arrangement, with its intricate shelving principles and furniture, he argues, enabled specific readerly gestures and associations, functioning as a mnemonic device that fostered a certain mode of assembling and retrieving information. Architecture here is, therefore, not merely a container of memory but an active producer of it. Chapter 7, "Early Electric," turns to Stockholm's Slussen area and the evolving experience of urban life in an electrified metropolis. Anstey links this to the rise of film and mass entertainment, particularly the role of cinema in changing perceptions of urban space and movement within it. Slussen is interpreted as an urban landscape shaped by spectacle, circulation and consumption. Spaces such as Coney Island and early department stores offered urban dwellers the opportunity to purchase leisure time, combining electricity-powered amusements and architecture. Through this lens, Anstey connects urban design to the formation of modern subjectivity, in which movement through space is increasingly informed by media and consumer infrastructures.

The afterword stands out as a rare moment of autobiographical reflection in architectural scholarship. Anstey shares how *Things That Move* emerged not only from scholarly interest of specific themes but also from personal and professional experiences: family ties to maritime history, inheriting a copy of *The Illustrated London News* featuring Cleopatra's Needle, doctoral research at the Warburg Institute, institutional affiliation with the Oslo School of Architecture and its focus on media, and his residence in Stockholm. This positionality reminds us that historical writing is never a neutral task, but one shaped by context and perspective. The personal and analytical converge in a moving meditation on what drives historical inquiry, while also acknowledging the limits of the single-author monograph.

In this regard, *Things That Move* raises vital questions about the scope and method of architectural history. Its archival, chronological and thematic breadth is impressive, yet the book remains grounded in familiar tools of architectural analysis: interpretation of drawings, classical treatises, building plans, and legacies of historically privileged institutions. This creates a productive tension. On one hand, the book opens the discipline to broader concerns: labor, material flows, and imperial networks. On the other, its methodology remains confined by art historical tradition. Ships are treated as design objects and representations rather than as workplaces structured by labor; extraction and inequality appear but remain peripheral in the overall narrative. This invites a broader methodological reflection: What kinds of knowledge are needed to write a history of architecture in motion? As Anstey notes, the topic demands insights from naval engineering, social history, material science, and media studies—fields no single scholar can fully master. Yet this very impossibility opens new directions. Architectural historians might collaborate more actively with historians of science and empire, library and information specialists, or experts in construction and economic history, adopting new methods and expanding their source base—and, by extension, the range of voices included—to trace how architecture moves. *Things That Move* offers no final answers but reorients the field toward more expansive questions, asking not only what architecture is but what architectural history might become.

Biography

Ksenia Litvinenko is a historian of the built environment whose current research explores the role of portable structures and fly-in fly-out urbanism in the history of fossil fuel extraction. She received her PhD in architecture from the University of Manchester in 2023 and is currently a Walter Benjamin Postdoctoral Fellow at the Leibniz Institute for Research on Society and Space in Erkner, Germany. She is also a 2025 research fellow at the Canadian Centre for Architecture in Montreal.

Notes

[1] For example, Matthias Ludwig, *Mobile Architektur* (Deutsche Verlags-Anstalt, 1998); Irit Katz, *The Common Camp: Architecture of Power and Resistance in Israel–Palestine* (University of Minnesota Press, 2022); Robert H. Kronenburg, *Houses in Motion: The Genesis, History and Development of the Portable Building* (Academy Press, 2002); Peter Šenk, *Capsules: Typology of Other Architecture* (Routledge, 2017); Robert Jan van Pelt, *The Barrack, 1572–1914: Chapters in the History of Emergency Architecture* (Park Books, 2024).

[2] For example, Thordis Arrhenius et al., ed., *Place and Displacement Exhibiting Architecture* (Lars Müller Publishers, 2014); Mari Lending, *Plaster Monuments: Architecture and the Power of Reproduction* (Princeton University Press, 2014); Mari Hvattum and Anne Hultzsch, *The Printed and the Built: Architecture, Print Culture and Public Debate in the Nineteenth Century* (Bloomsbury, 2018); Véronique Patteeuw and Léa-Catherine Szacka, eds., *Mediated Messages: Periodicals, Exhibitions and the Shaping of Postmodern Architecture* (Bloomsbury, 2020); Eva Maria Froschauer, *'An die Leser!': Baukunst darstellen und vermitteln—Berliner Architekturzeitschriften um 1900* (Wasmuth Verlag GmbH, 2010); Matteo Burioni, *Weltgeschichten Der Architektur: Ursprünge, Narrative, Bilder 1700–2016* (Dietmar Klinger Verlag, 2016); André Tavares, *The Anatomy of the Architectural Book* (Lars Müller Publishers, 2025).

[3] For example, Fred Kaspar, *Bauten In Bewegung* (Zabern, 2007); Lucia Allais, *Designs of Destruction: The Making of Monuments in the Twentieth Century* (University of Chicago Press, 2018).

[4] For example, Jane Mah Hutton, *Reciprocal Landscapes: Stories of Material Movements* (Routledge, 2020); Barnabas Calder, *Architecture: From Prehistory to Climate Emergency* (Pelican, 2021); William Cronon, *Nature's Metropolis: Chicago and the Great West* (W. W. Norton & Company, 1992); Kiel Moe, *Empire, State & Building* (Actar, 2017).

Submission Guidelines

Future Anterior is a peer-reviewed (refereed) journal that approaches the field of historic preservation from a position of critical inquiry. A comparatively recent field of professional study, preservation often escapes direct academic challenges of its motives, goals, forms of practice and results. *Future Anterior* seeks contributions that ask these difficult questions from philosophical, theoretical, and critical perspectives.

Formatting Requirements: Articles should be no more than 4,000 words (excluding endnotes) with up to seven illustrations. Text and citations must be formatted in accordance with *The Chicago Manual of Style*, 18th Edition. Citations must be formatted as endnotes. All articles must be submitted in English, and spelling should follow American convention. A brief abstract (200 words) and author biography (around 100 words) must accompany the submission, but in a separate file to preserve the double-blind peer review process. References to the identity of the author must be removed from the manuscript before submission. All text files must be saved as Microsoft Word or RTF format.

Illustration/Image Requirements: Figures should be numbered clearly in the text, after the paragraph in which they are referenced. Image captions and credits must be included with submissions. It is the responsibility of the author to secure permissions for image use and pay any reproduction fees. Images must be sent as TIFF files with a resolution of at least 300 dpi at 8″ by 9″ print size. Acceptance or rejection of submissions is at the discretion of the Editorial Staff. Please do not send original materials, as submissions will not be returned.

Checklist of documents required for submission:

__ Abstract (200 words)
__ Manuscript (4,000 words, excluding endnotes)
__ Illustrations/Images (maximum of 7)
__ Captions for Illustrations/Images
__ Illustration/Image Copyright information
__ Author biography (100 words)

All submissions and questions about the submission process must be submitted to future.anterior.journal@gmail.com.

https://www.arch.columbia.edu/future-anterior

Become a *Future Anterior* Sponsor

Future Anterior is funded by grants and distributed in the spirit of making knowledge available to everyone. Donations are critical to helping us accomplish this mission. If you would like to become a sponsor, please fill out this page and mail it, with a check payable to Columbia University, to:

Future Anterior
Graduate School of Architecture, Planning, and Preservation
400 Avery Hall
1172 Amsterdam Avenue
Columbia University
New York, NY 10027

Or contribute by credit card online at:
https://arch.givenow.columbia.edu/#

All sponsors will be recognized in each issue of *Future Anterior* and receive a one-year subscription to the journal.

Please check the appropriate sponsorship level:

Individual Sponsor: ❑ begins at $100/year
Institutional Sponsor: ❑ begins at $500/year
Patron: ❑ begins at $1,000/year

Name*: ______________________________

Address: ______________________________

____

City: ______________________________

State: ______________ Zip: ______________

Country: ______________________________

Institution/Office: ______________________________

Email: ______________________________

*Please provide your name exactly as you would like it to appear in print.